IMAGES
of America

SAGINAW COUNTY
MICHIGAN

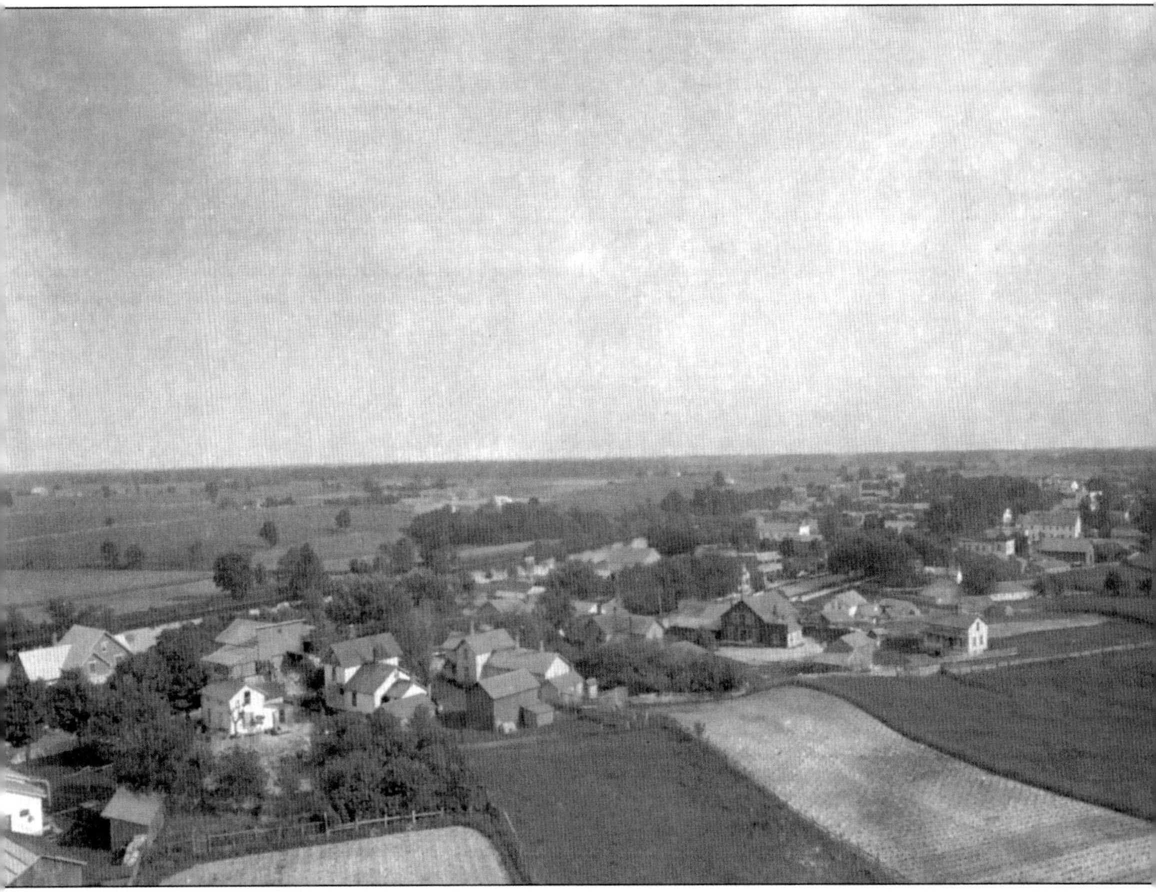

Sauk Indians established their villages along the many rivers in the beautiful Saugenah Valley. Later, several villages emerged along the same rivers during Saginaw County's lumber era. This picturesque Frankenmuth community, nestled between well-kept farm fields and the banks of the placid Cass River, was viewed in 1910 from the south steeple of St. John's Lutheran Church.

Front Cover Illustration: Drained by the Bad River, Beaver Creek, and Swan Creek, Swan Creek Township was organized in 1860. After its lumber era, it developed into an agricultural and coal mining area. The children from grades one through eight in Swan Creek School have gathered in front of their two-room school in the 1920s. School was held in this building until it burned in January 1967.

IMAGES
of America

SAGINAW COUNTY
MICHIGAN

Roselynn Ederer

ARCADIA
PUBLISHING

ISBN 978-0-7385-3161-8

Published by Arcadia Publishing
Charleston, South Carolina

Printed in the United States of America

Library of Congress Catalog Card Number: 2003107214

For all general information contact Arcadia Publishing at:
Telephone 843-853-2070
Fax 843-853-0044
E-mail sales@arcadiapublishing.com
For customer service and orders:
Toll-Free 1-888-313-2665

Visit us on the Internet at www.arcadiapublishing.com

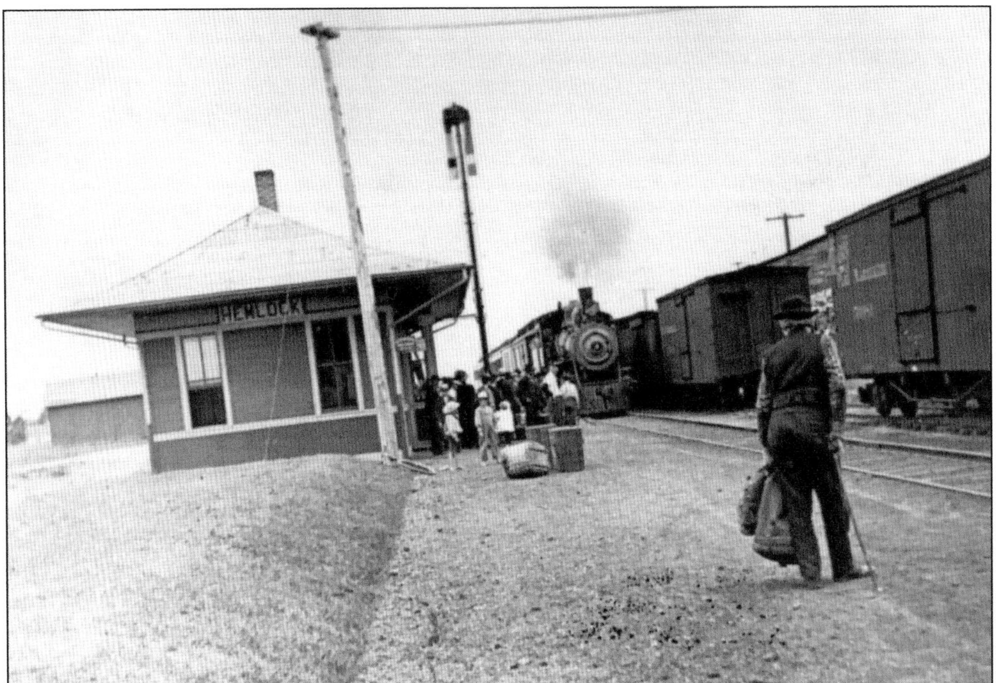

Railroads built in the 1800s throughout Saginaw County provided necessary transportation to Saginaw and other cities. This Pere Marquette depot, built in Hemlock in 1907 and painted coach green with maroon trim, was always a busy place with several departures and arrivals daily. In 1983, this depot was moved to Saginaw and restored as a railroad museum.

Contents

ACKNOWLEDGMENTS

A debt of gratitude goes to Ann Laundra for her time and assistance in scanning and preparing all the photos collected for this book.

Special thanks are extended to all the following individuals and historical societies who have given their time, photographs, histories, and moral support for this publication: Birch Run Historical Society, Jerry Boyd, and James Brasseur; Bridgeport Historical Society, Katrina Brugge; Chesaning Area Historical Society, Judy Corne, and Sheila C. DiBerardino; Frankenmuth Historical Association, Dale Greve; Hemlock Historical Society, Marie Jarema, David J. Kern, Franklin L. Kern, Irving Kime, Harold Madler, Mary Nuechterlein, Ralph Roberts, Alice Shindorf, and Michael Slasinski; St. Charles Historical Society, Swan Creek Township, Howard Vasold, and Marie Walter.

This book is dedicated to all past, present, and future Saginaw County residents.

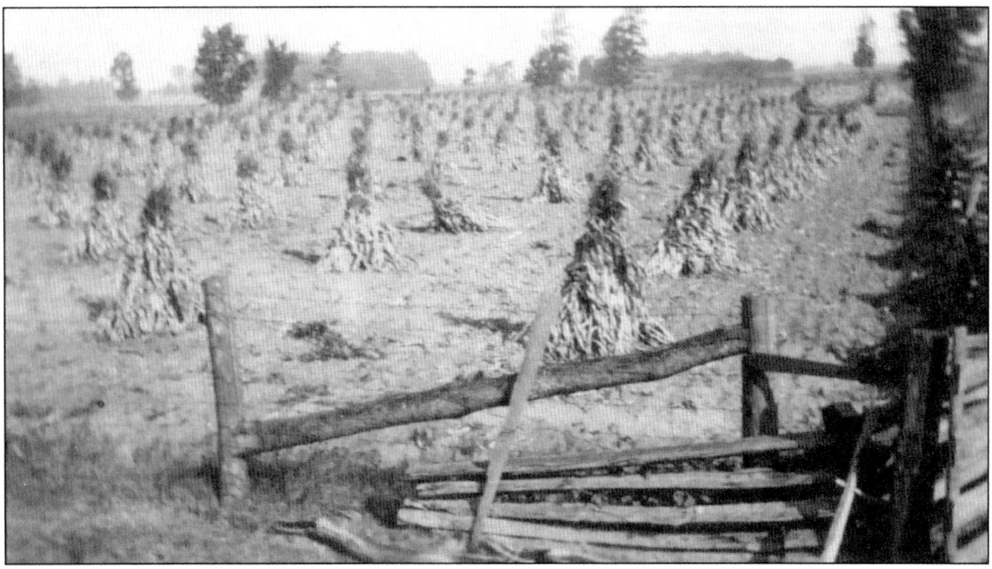

Like the Sauks and Chippewas before them, farmers also found their cleared land conducive to growing corn. This corn-shocked field on South Dehmel Road in Birch Run was a scene repeated many times throughout the county during fall harvest time.

INTRODUCTION

For centuries the Sauk Indians had inhabited the beautiful Saugenah Valley. There was an abundance of wild game, fish, fruits, and nuts. The land along the many rivers was ideal for raising corn. In the 1600s, the Chippewa and Ottawa nations took over the Saugenah Valley and moved into the vacant Sauk villages along the many rivers.

The French Canadian voyageurs and the fur traders were the first white men in the Saugenah wilderness. Louis Campau came in 1816 and established a trading post on the Saugenah River. The Treaty of 1819 deeded Indian Territory to the United States Government. The Third United States Infantry arrived in 1822 and built a military reservation on the Saugenah River. They left permanently in 1823 because of the harsh winter, spring floods, and mosquitoes. Some pioneers from New York, Canada, Scotland, and Ireland were beginning to settle along the Valley's many rivers.

Under the 1830 Territorial Government, Saginaw County's courthouse would be located in Saginaw City. Saginaw Township was organized on March 2, 1831. It was comprised of 36 Congressional townships, attached to Oakland County, including all of Saginaw County, part of Midland County, Bay County, Genesee County, and Saginaw Bay. Saginaw County was officially organized on January 28, 1835 and its governing body was then elected. Michigan became a state of the Union on January 26, 1837.

Townships were organized gradually as settlement increased. Traveling to Saginaw County was difficult. From Detroit, travelers proceeded by train to Pontiac, then by horse and wagon to Flint. The trip to Saginaw was on horseback or foot. Being closer to Flint, the eastern county was settled first. As the dense forest was cleared for its timber, more land was homesteaded. Western county townships were organized. Altogether, 27 separate townships and Saginaw City and East Saginaw were organized by 1879.

Birch Run Township, surveyed in 1822 but organized in 1853, was named after the creek that flowed through its center. The old Military Road ran from Flint to Saginaw and helped greatly in the settlement of Birch Run and Saginaw. James H. Trumble settled in 1841. Jesse Hoyt's sawmill was established to build the Plank Road from East Saginaw to Flint in 1852. This Saginaw Turnpike became the Dixie Highway. It brought mail from Flint and settlers from the east coast, Canada, England, Ireland, Scotland, and Germany.

James McCormick settled near the Flint River in 1832. Faymouth Township was organized in 1842. Scottish settlers changed the name to Taymouth, after the River Tay in Scotland. Verne, Blackmar, Morseville, and Fosters emerged alongside the Pewonogowink Indian Village. When lumberman Wellington R. Burt built the Cincinnati, Saginaw & Mackinaw Railroad in 1888, the village of Burt emerged.

Ariel Campau settled near the Cass River, naming it "Cass Bend" in 1819. The first bridge was named "Cass Bridge." Charles A. Lull built the first tavern, the "Bridgeport Center House." Settlers arrived. The township was organized in 1848 and both it and the village were named Bridgeport. Michigan's best cork pine was cut on the Cass River and sawed in Bridgeport. This cork pine was the material that began Saginaw's lumber industry in 1847.

Fifteen Bavarian Lutherans from Franconia, Germany, arrived on the banks of the Cass River in August 1845, led by Reverend August Craemer. Named Frankenmuth, meaning "Courage of the Franconians," the Indian missionary colony established St. Lorenz Lutheran Church and Christianized the Chippewas. In 1854, Frankenmuth Township was organized and separated from Bridgeport Township.

Tittabawassee Township, including Midland and Gratiot Counties, was organized in 1841. Joseph Busby purchased land there in 1833. Mammy Freeland ran a tavern and hotel on the Tittabawassee River for the lumbermen. The Flint & Pere Marquette Railroad ran nearby. Its station was called Freelands' Depot. The village was also later named Freeland.

In 1855, Thomastown Township was organized west of the Tittabawassee River. Lemuel Cone had settled further west in 1857. Richland Township organized and separated from Thomastown in 1862. Because of its heavy timber tracts, the village was named Hemlock City. Edward Jones had settled even further west in 1857, in the township organized as Jonesfield in 1873. Lumberman N.W. Merrill looked after the village's interests, and it was named Merrill in his honor. Lumberman W.F. Glasby built Plank Road, now known as M-46, so that the lumber from Hemlock and Merrill could be brought to Saginaw.

Because of the dense forest, settlers could arrive only by river along the Shiawassee and Bad Rivers. Charles S. Kimberly, a wealthy gentleman of refined culture, opened the first general store. He was nicknamed "Saint Charles" by the rowdy lumbermen. When the township was organized in 1853, and the village organized later, both were named St. Charles. Brant Township was organized in 1858 along the North Branch of the Bad River.

George W. Chapman, Wellington Chapman, and Rufus P. Mason settled in 1841 by the "Big Rock." Northampton Township, named after their former New Hampshire home, was organized in 1847. In 1853 both the township and the village were renamed Chesaning, the Chippewa name for Big Rock. Phillip Mickle had built a tavern further southwest in 1847. Brady Township, named after General Brady of Detroit, was organized in 1856. Oakley was named after a resident's uncle, Judge Oakley of New York. Maple Grove was organized in 1857 and named for its maple sugar groves. The Jackson, Lansing & Saginaw Railroad had been built through St. Charles, Chesaning, and Oakley and served as the most important shipping road in Saginaw County.

Europe's Great Potato Famine in the 1850s brought immigrants from Germany, Ireland, Scotland, England, and Canada as well as Easterners. Immigrants from Poland, Italy, Russia, Hungary, and Yugoslavia came in the 1890s. This diversity of nationalities merged many cultures, religions, and customs, all of which helped Saginaw County develop its prosperous lumber, agricultural, agribusiness, and coal mining industries. The self-sufficient villages were similar yet each had its own individual characteristics. Each emerged with the lumber industry but survived after the lumber became scarce.

One

Exploring the Rivers

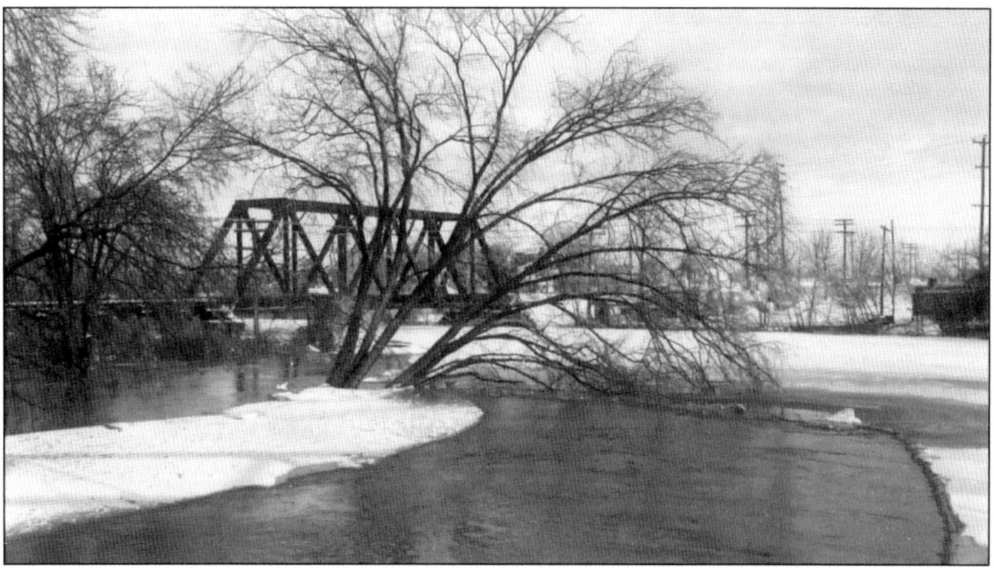

The Flint & Pere Marquette Railroad built this bridge over the Cass River in the mid-1800s. The railroad connected eastern Saginaw County to East Saginaw and Flint and was important for shipping lumber, agricultural products, and other materials. This picturesque scene over the Cass River in Bridgeport was photographed in 1949. The Chesapeake & Ohio Railroad continues to use the bridge today.

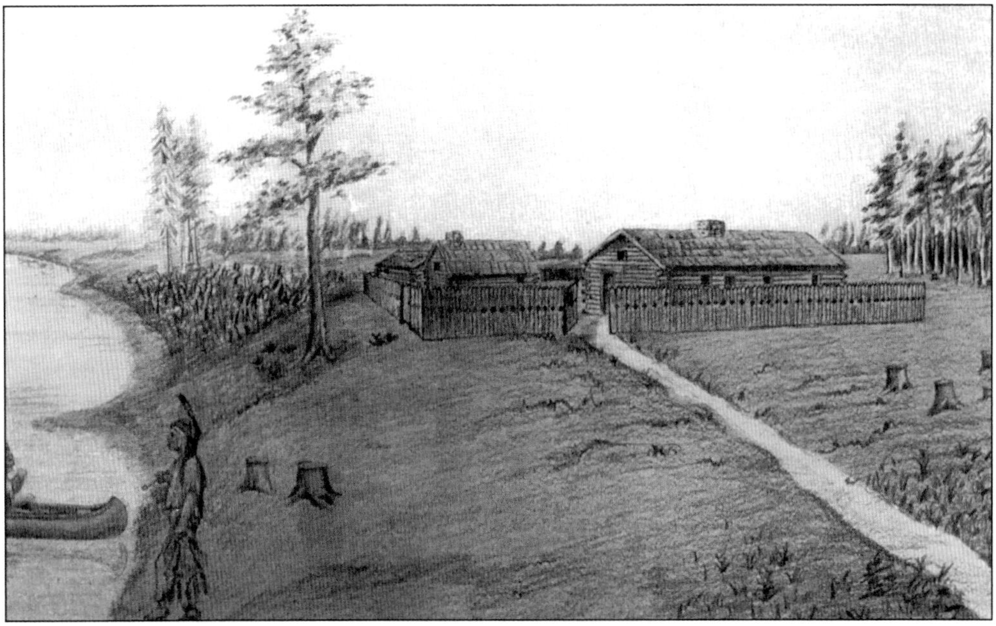

The Third United States Infantry under Major Daniel Baker's command arrived on July 25, 1822 and built this stockade for 150 people on the banks of the Saginaw River, where the Taylor House was later erected. After experiencing the harsh winter, spring floods, mosquitoes, and ague, they left permanently on October 23, 1823.

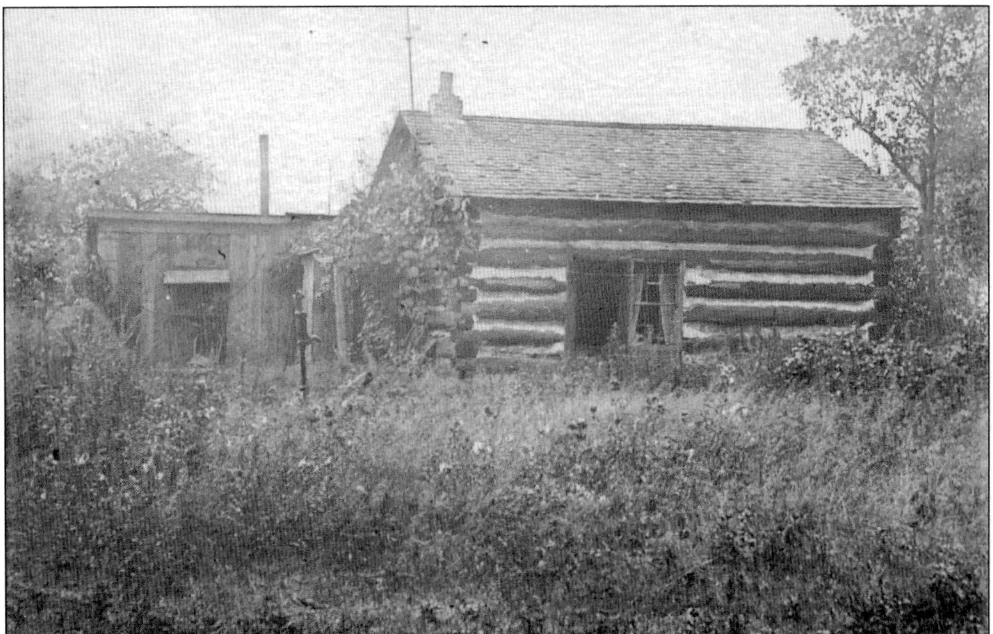

The first settlers built log cabins near the rivers. Their cabins caulked with wood sticks and clay had one door, a window, a dirt floor, two rooms, and a fireplace for cooking and heating. A pan of grease with a coiled rag was used as a candle. Their furniture was crude. Their food was wild game, fish, and rutabagas. This Bell Road Bridgeport cabin was still standing in 1902.

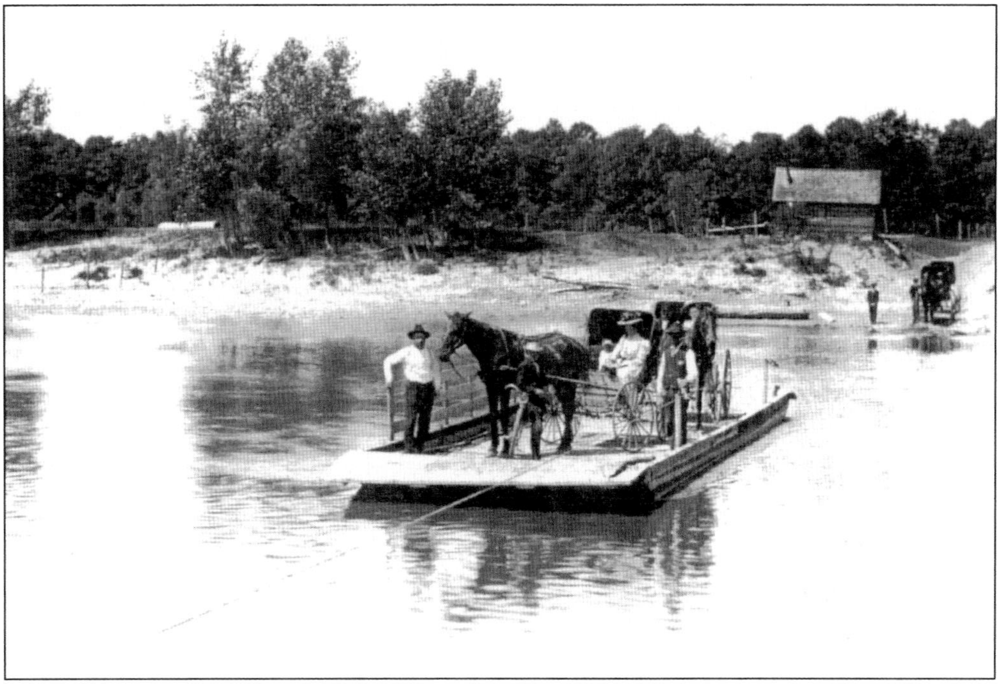

Ferries and scows were used to cross the county's rivers until bridges were built. Martin Kapitan ran this toll-ferry across the Tittabawassee River near Freeland. Seen here in the 1880s, he would pull on the cable attached to each side of the riverbank to bring the barge and passengers to the opposite side. Ferry service was discontinued in 1909.

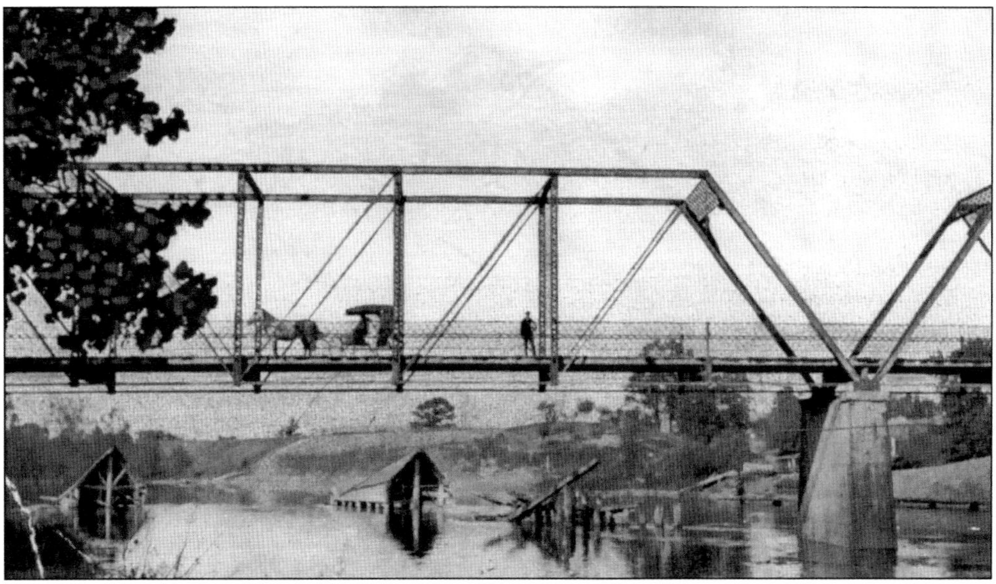

The first Freeland Bridge, built across the Tittabawassee River on March 31, 1870, cost $5,000. It was 286 feet long, 16 feet wide, had a 16-foot truss height, was elevated 24 feet from the water, and had three spans. The second bridge shown here was completed in 1895 at a cost of $10,000. Two icebreaker sheds kept the ice from piling and collapsing the bridge.

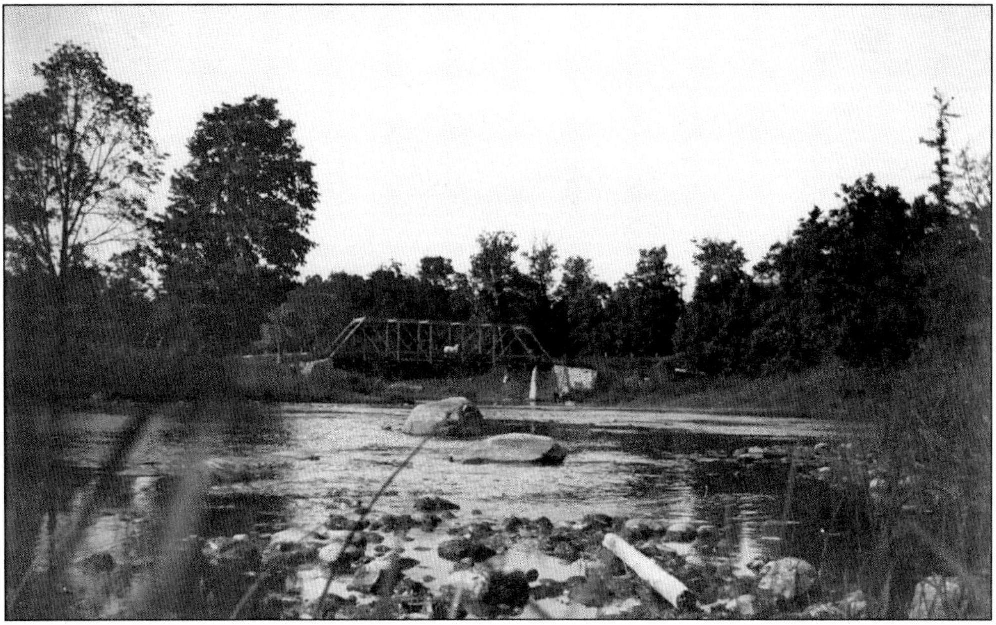

Soon after Israel Parshall built a flourmill on the Shiawassee River in the mid-1800s, a small community with a sawmill, houses, a general store, and a school emerged. An iron bridge was built at Parshallburg in 1887. With the Parshallburg community long since abandoned, the bridge was restored and moved to Chesaning's Cole Park in 1999.

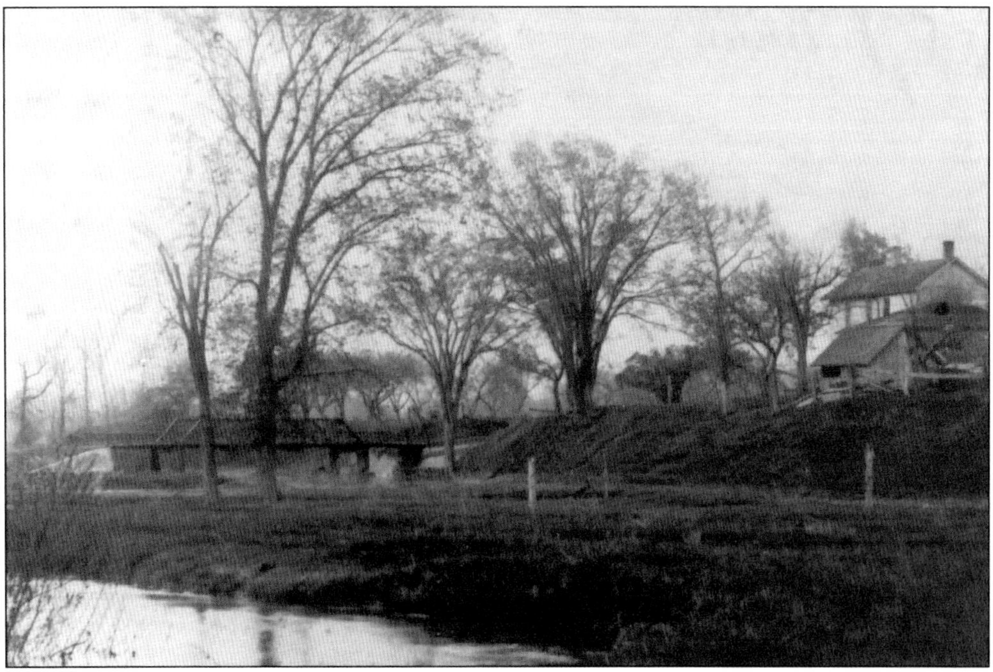

Many small creeks and streams drained the townships in Saginaw County. Smaller bridges were built over these waterways wherever they crossed well-traveled roads or trails. This small bridge was built on the Horseshoe Bend of the Beaver River at Nelson Corners in Fremont Township in the 1800s.

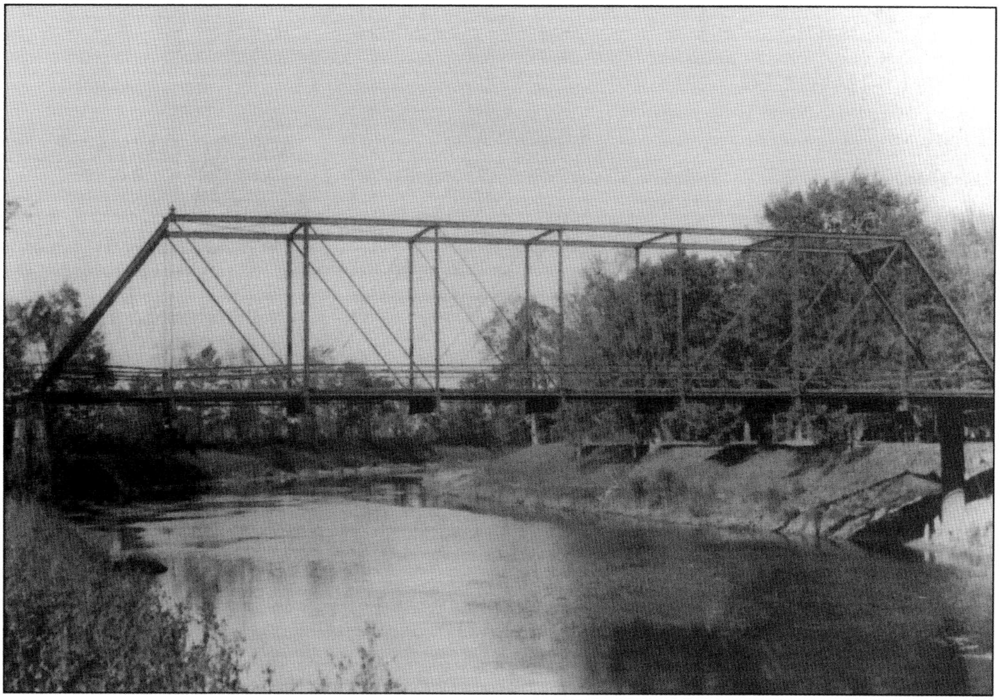

The Smith Bridge Co. of Toledo, Ohio, built this iron bridge at the Horning Bridge site across the Flint River in 1885 at a cost of $3,000. This Flint River Bridge in Taymouth Township has been named a Michigan Historical Site.

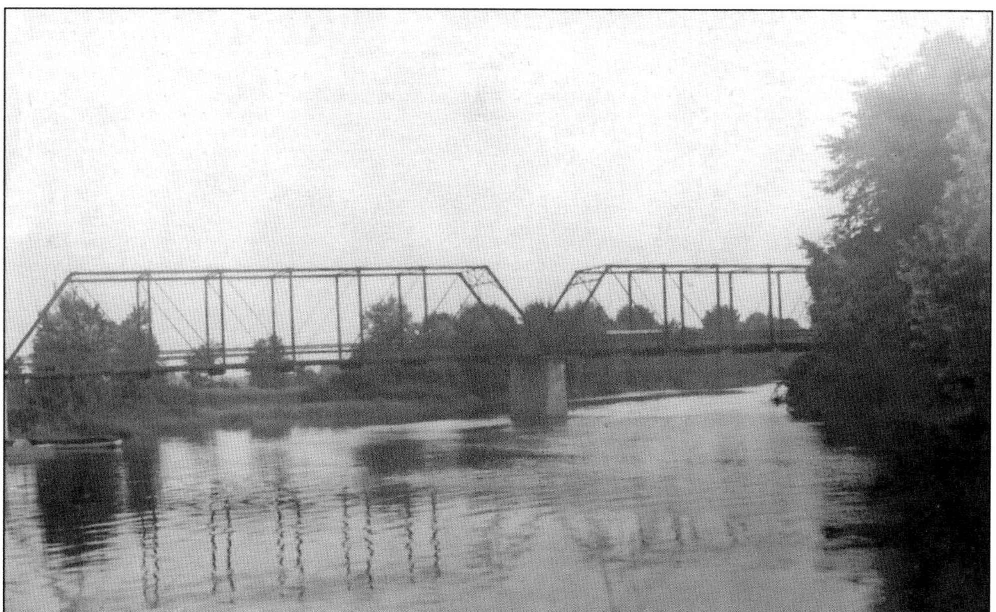

The first "Cass Bridge" was built where the old Military Road crossed the Cass River. Lilly Cook began the Bridgeport Village at this location. The original bridge disappeared. The village moved to State Street. The Fort Road Bridge, above, replaced Cass Bridge in the 1800s. The bridge today has been closed to all vehicular and pedestrian traffic.

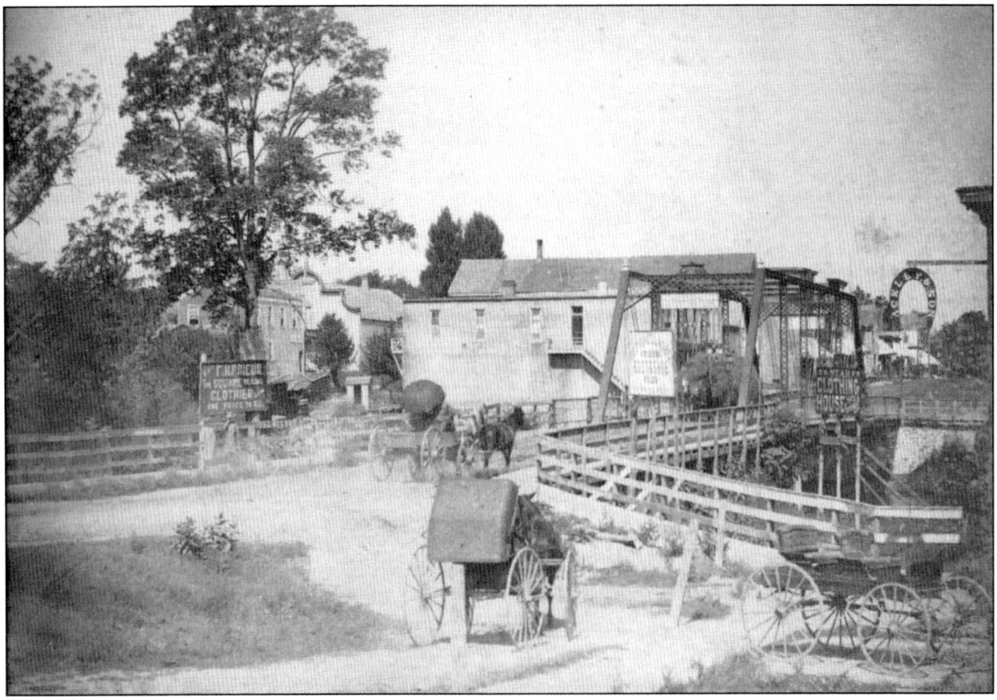

The Shiawassee River runs through Chesaning Village, furnishing its waterpower. Businesses emerged near the river's wooden bridge. This 1890 view of the second iron bridge looks west from the east end of the bridge. At the far right is Ackley & Son Blacksmith. A wagon of logs crosses the bridge. The Chesaning Opera House is at the rear left.

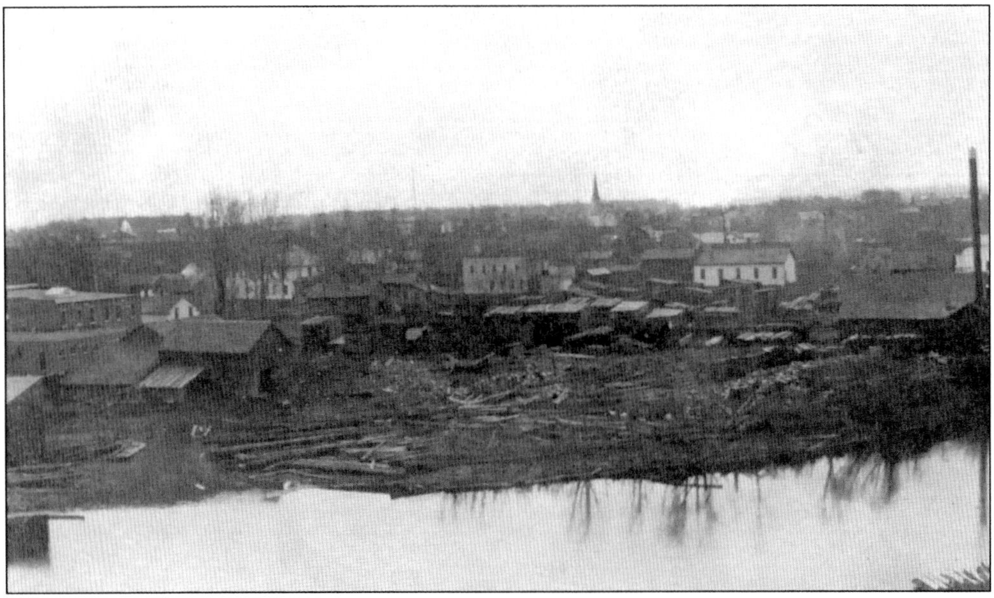

Michigan's best cork pine was found along the Cass River. Logs felled in Frankenmuth were floated to the Cass River's Hubinger Sawmill. Brothers John Mathias and John George Hubinger built Frankenmuth's first industry with their dam, sawmill, and gristmill, in 1847. Township buildings were built with this lumber. Local grain was milled here.

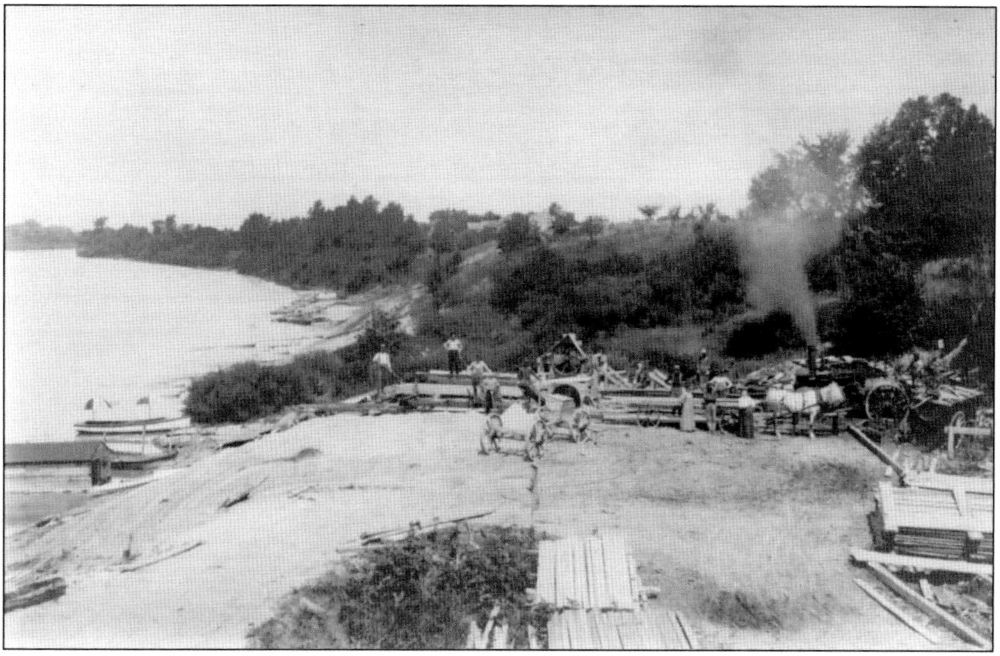

Tittabawassee Township was a bustling scene of lumbering activity throughout the 1800s. Every spring, logs were brought down the Tittabawassee River from central Michigan lumber camps. Timber was also harvested locally in the township. These two late-1800s scenes show a busy sawmill near Freeland on the Tittabawassee River. Horse teams and steam-powered equipment are being used to process the logs locally instead of sending them to the Saginaw River sawmills. The lumber would be used locally in Freeland or sold to nearby communities for building houses, barns, and pine plank roads.

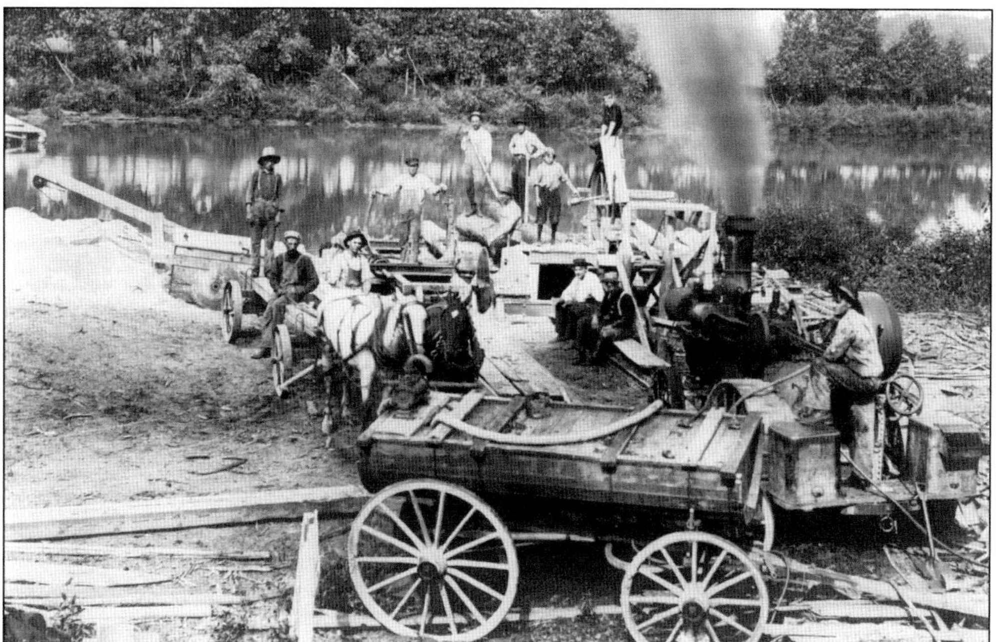

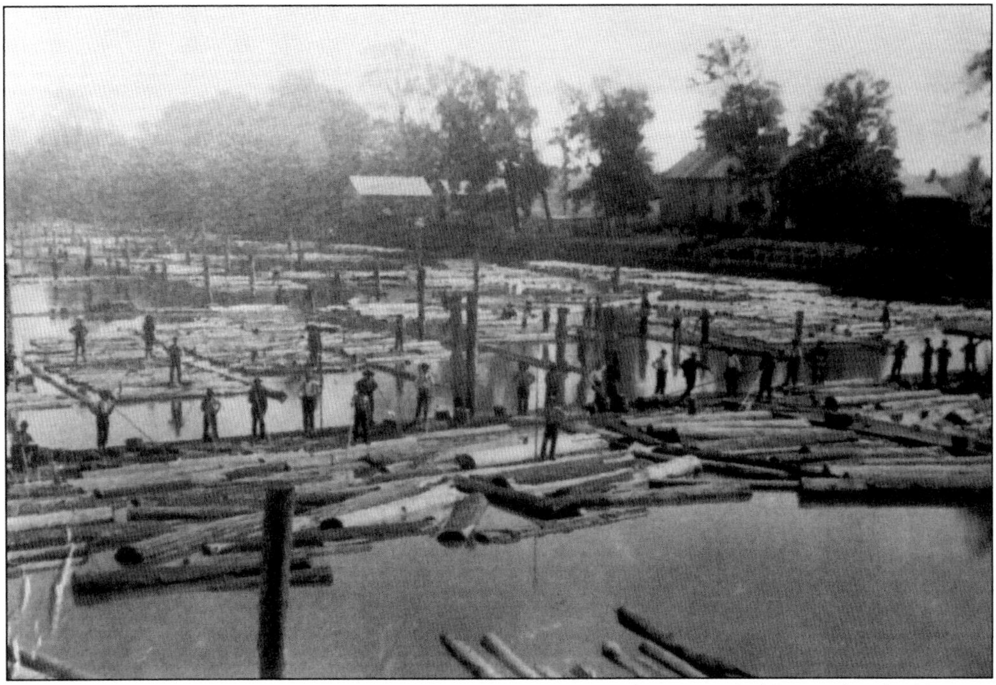

After the logs were brought down the Tittabawassee River, they were held in individual booms at Bryant's Trip, State Road, and Merrill Bridge on the river in Thomastown and Saginaw Townships. Tittabawassee Boom Company's men would then sort, pin, and raft an owner's logs by his individual log mark before towing them downstream to the Saginaw River sawmills.

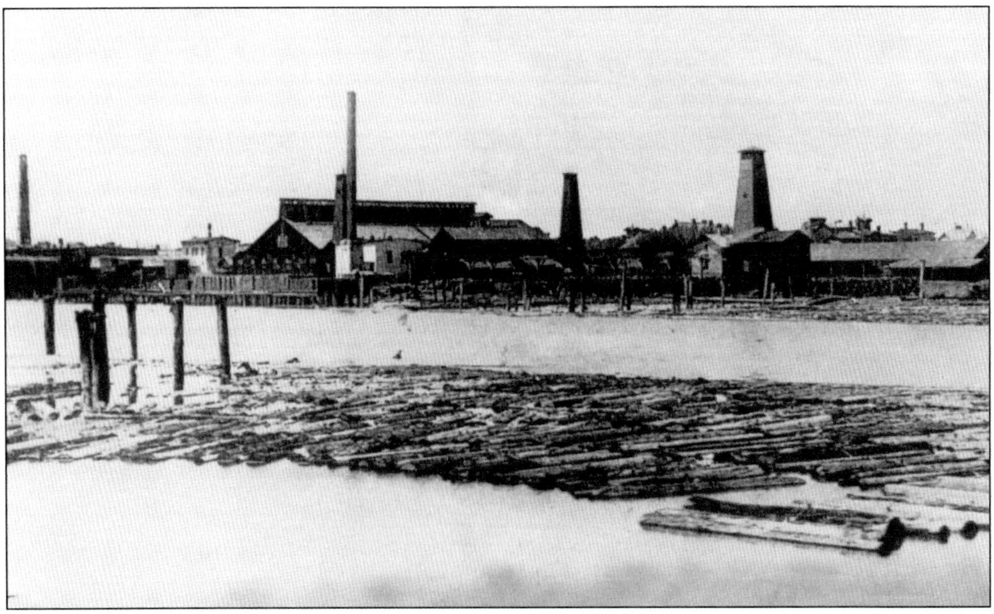

This was a scene repeated often all along the Saginaw River to Saginaw Bay during the lumber era. Rafted logs wait in the mill's holding pond. Steam from its tall smokestack supplies the sawmill. The two towers on the right house the salt-pumping machinery. Brine is pumped from underground, and boiled with lumber refuse into salt crystals.

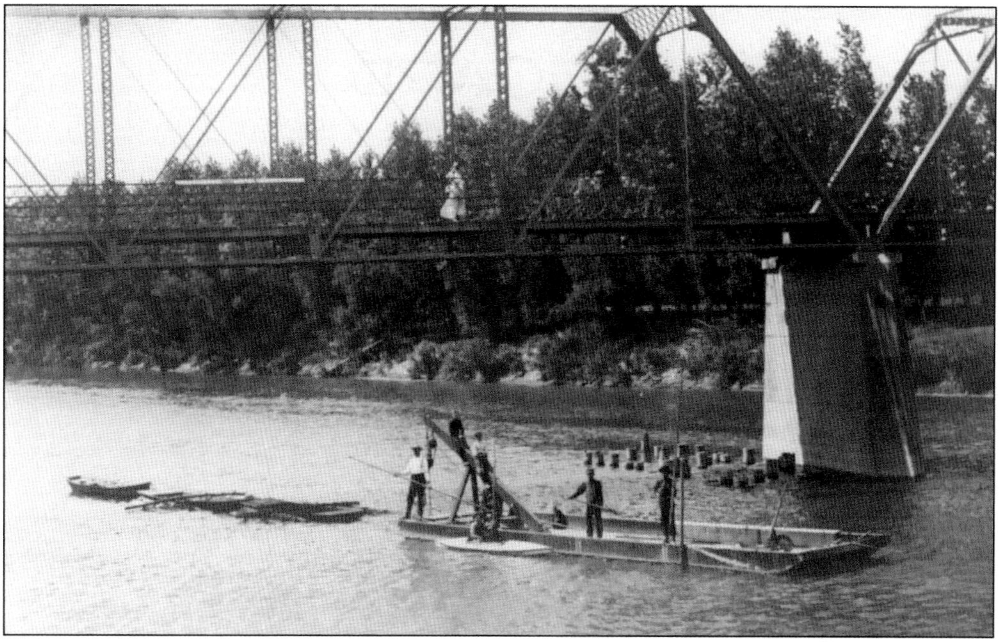

The above photo is the second iron bridge built across the Tittabawassee River at Freeland in 1895 by the Wrought Iron Bridge Company of Canton, Ohio. A barge towing a raft of logs passes underneath the bridge while people walk over the bridge. The bottom photo shows the same bridge during the flood of 1912. All surrounding land is completely underwater, and the water has almost crossed over the bridge. The floodwaters have originated north above Midland along the many tributaries and are raging down the Tittabawassee River that is part of the Saginaw River watershed.

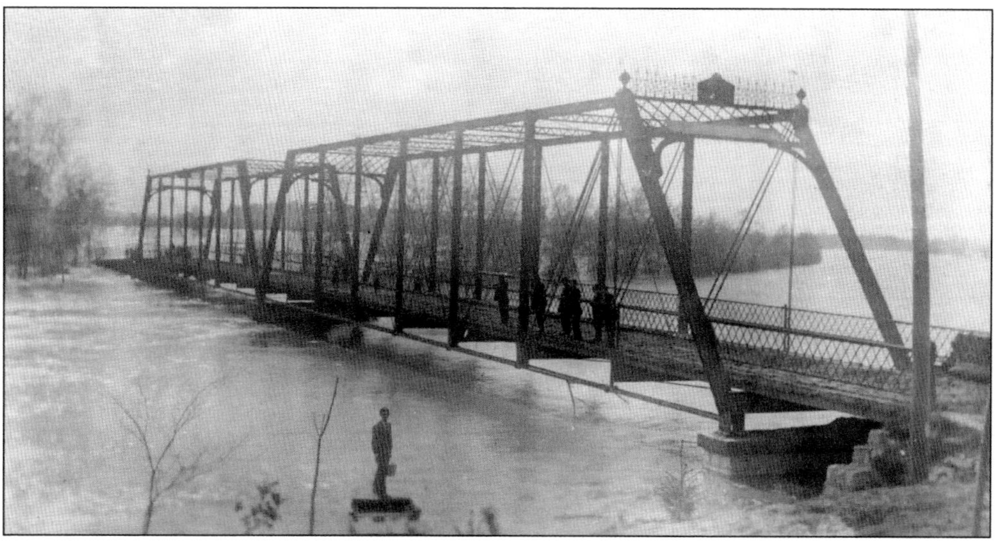

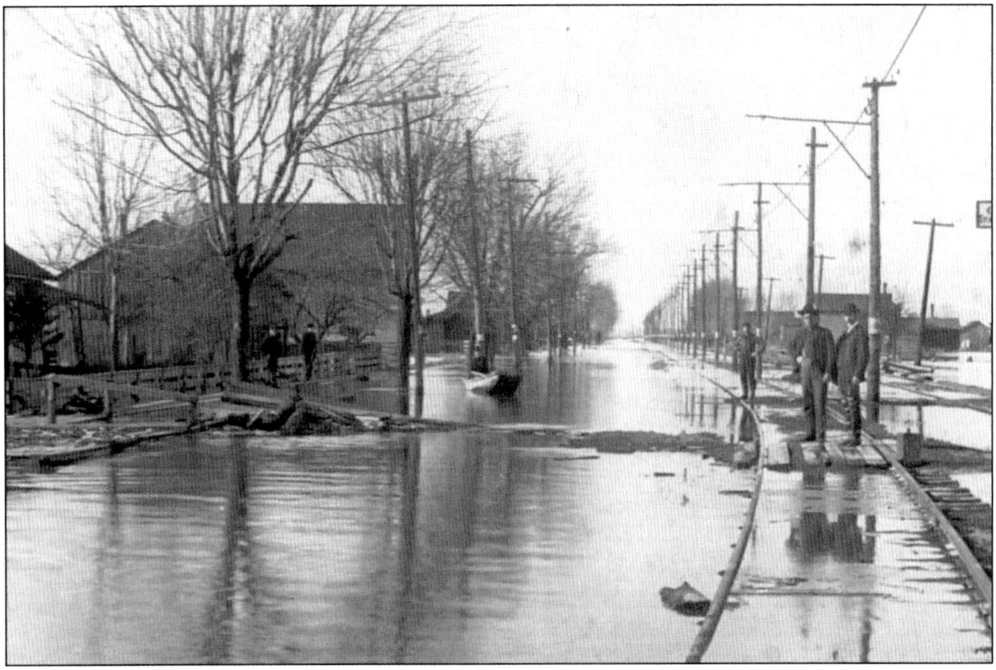

With every major flood, many roads, bridges, and communities throughout the county are inundated with floodwaters. In this image, the Saginaw River has flooded Zilwaukee. A canoe is being used to evacuate residents. Three men are standing on the railroad tracks in this view south of town on Westervelt and Green Streets. St. Matthew's Church is on the left.

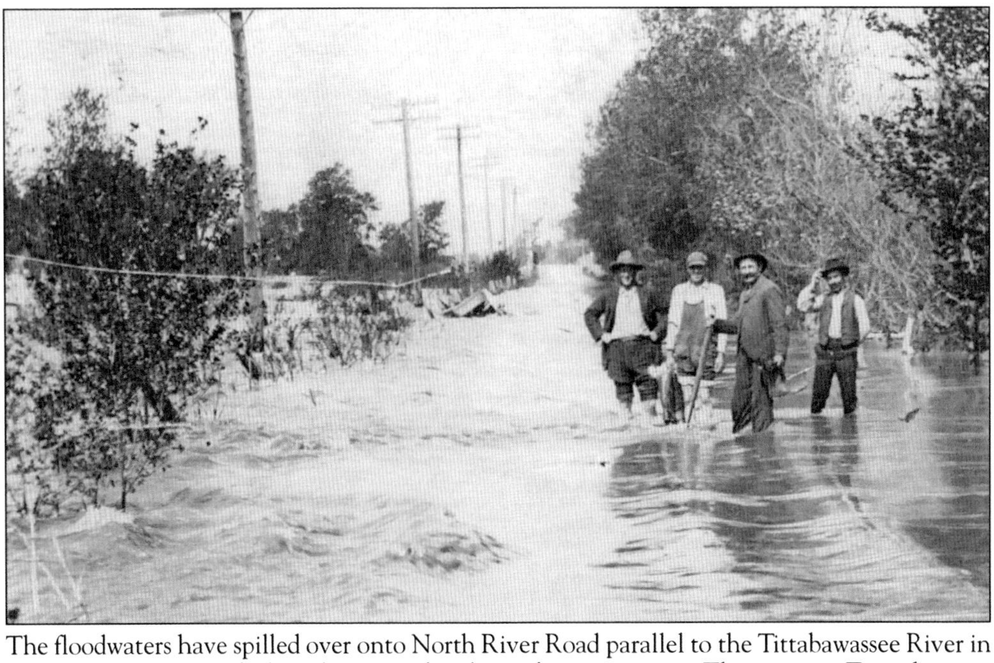

The floodwaters have spilled over onto North River Road parallel to the Tittabawassee River in this 1912 flood. Identified residents standing knee-deep in water in Thomastown Township are, from left, Herman Meyer and Edward Ederer. Mr. Maike's horse drowned when the swift current upset his wagon near the telephone poles. The four men are going to his rescue.

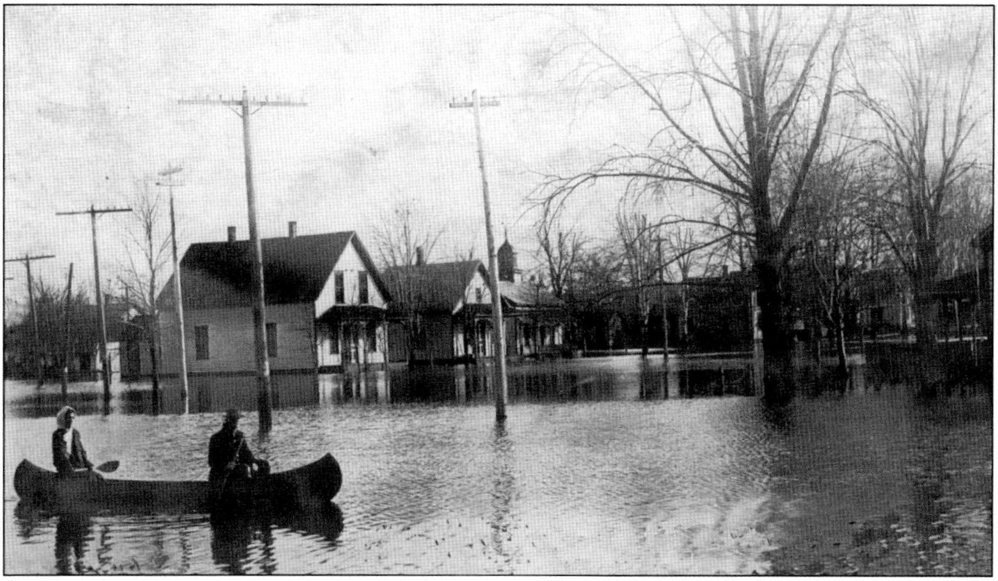

The Bad River overflowed its banks causing havoc in these 1912 St. Charles flood scenes. Residents of several neighborhoods were forced to evacuate their homes, as shown above. As shown below, the main business district is also flooded. Mr. Holst is standing in the doorway of his tailor shop in the first building on the right. Kufahl's Dry Goods is the middle building. The third building is Lyness Bazaar. Lyness' built-up pilings were not high enough to keep the ground floor above water during this flood.

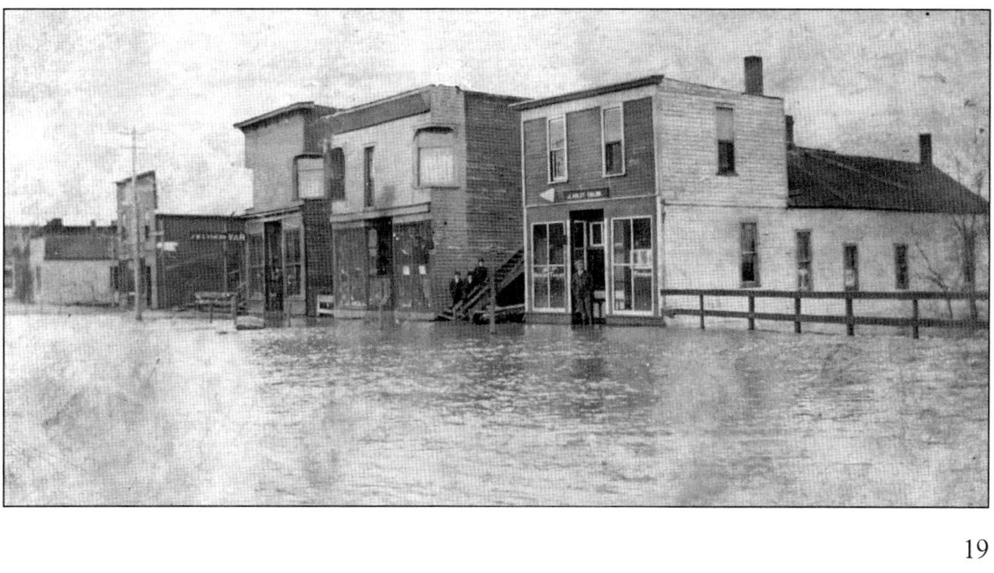

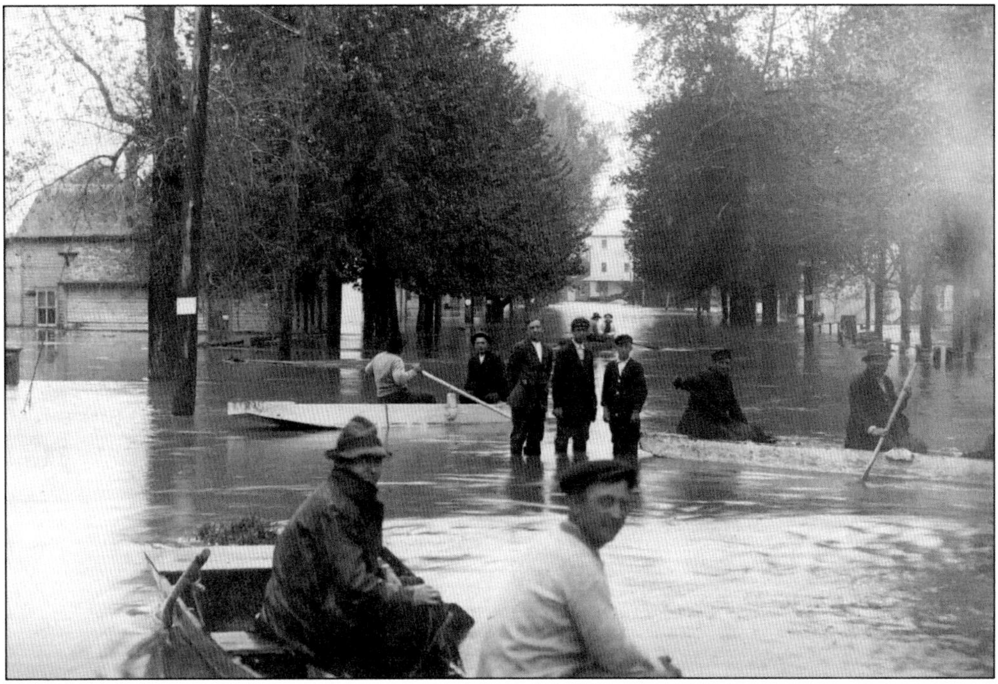

The Cass River flooded Frankenmuth annually until dikes were built in 1949. The town was flooded for three days during the 1912 flood. The Star of the West Mill is at the end of Main Street. Pictured in the front canoe are John Hilbrandt and Herman Honold; standing, from left are Ruben Kern, Oscar Ranke, and Walter Kern; and in the back left canoe are Martin Eischer and Carl Neuchterlein.

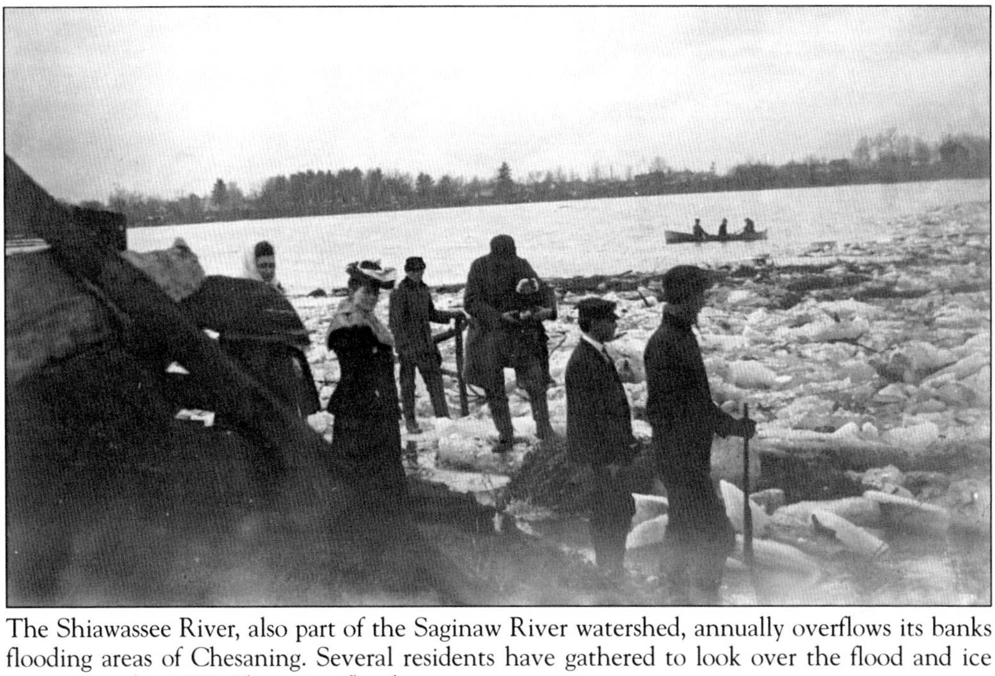

The Shiawassee River, also part of the Saginaw River watershed, annually overflows its banks flooding areas of Chesaning. Several residents have gathered to look over the flood and ice scene after this 1903 Chesaning flood.

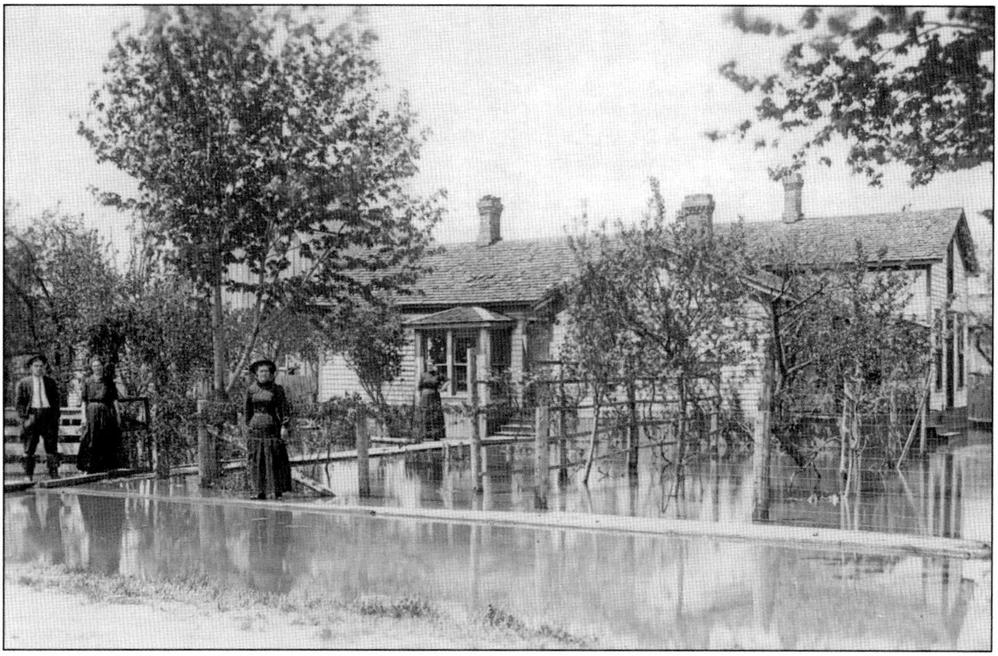

Oliver and Mary Metiva were early Zilwaukee settlers. The Metiva homestead on Adams and Schust Streets stands in water in this 1912 flood scene. The above photo shows a side view of the home. Standing on the wooden plank sidewalks floating on top of the water are, from left to right, Norman Burke, Lucy Rivett, and Delilah Burke. The front of the house is shown below with Elmer Burke in the boat and Norman Burke standing knee-deep in the water. The three ladies found some dry ground.

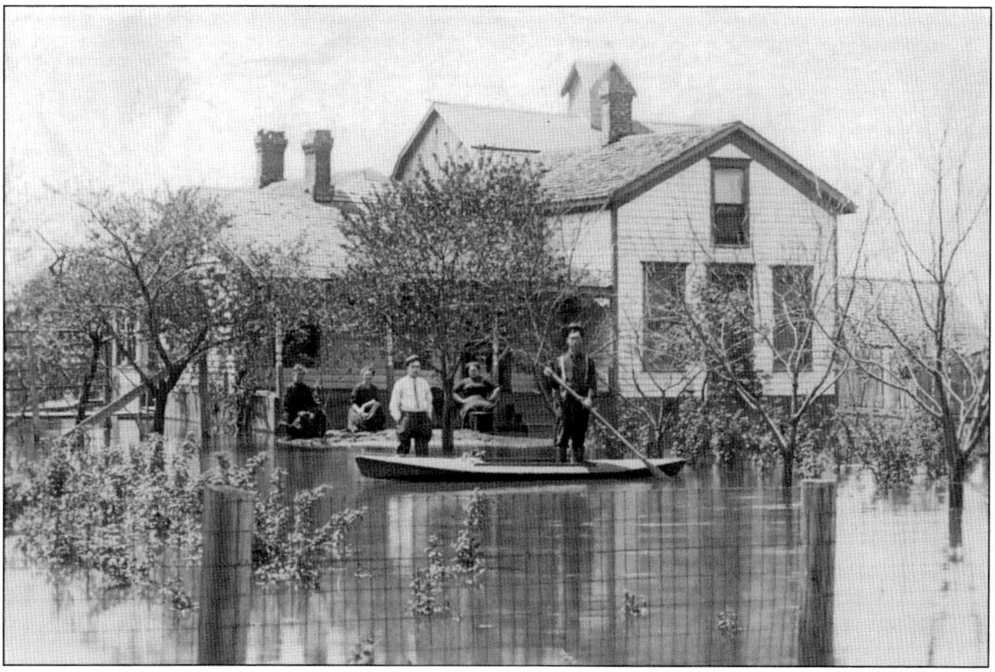

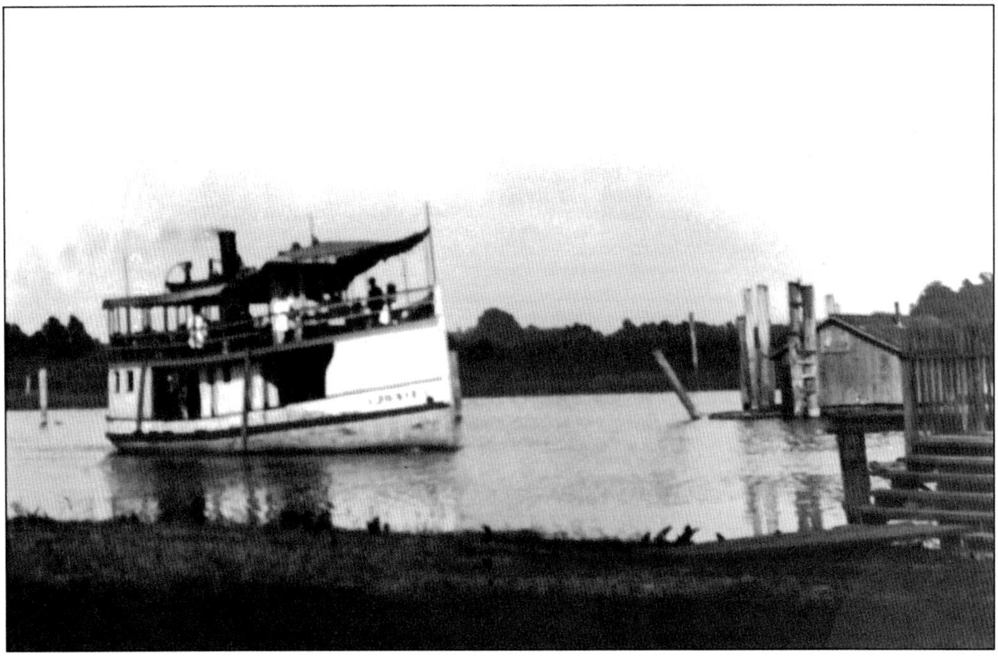

Steamers sailed regularly from the Saginaw River to the Tittabawassee, Shiawassee, and Bad Rivers carrying passengers and cargo during the 1880s and 1890s. Some traveled to Midland. Others went near St. Charles. The *Josie* is docking at Carr's Landing in James Township on the Shiawassee River above. Shown below, the *Josie* ran a scheduled line from Saginaw to Carr's Landing, Green Point, the Saginaw River, Bay City, and Point Lookout. Built as a tugboat in Bay City in 1893, *Josie* was converted to a pleasure boat in 1896. In 1899, *Josie* tried unsuccessfully to come to St. Charles.

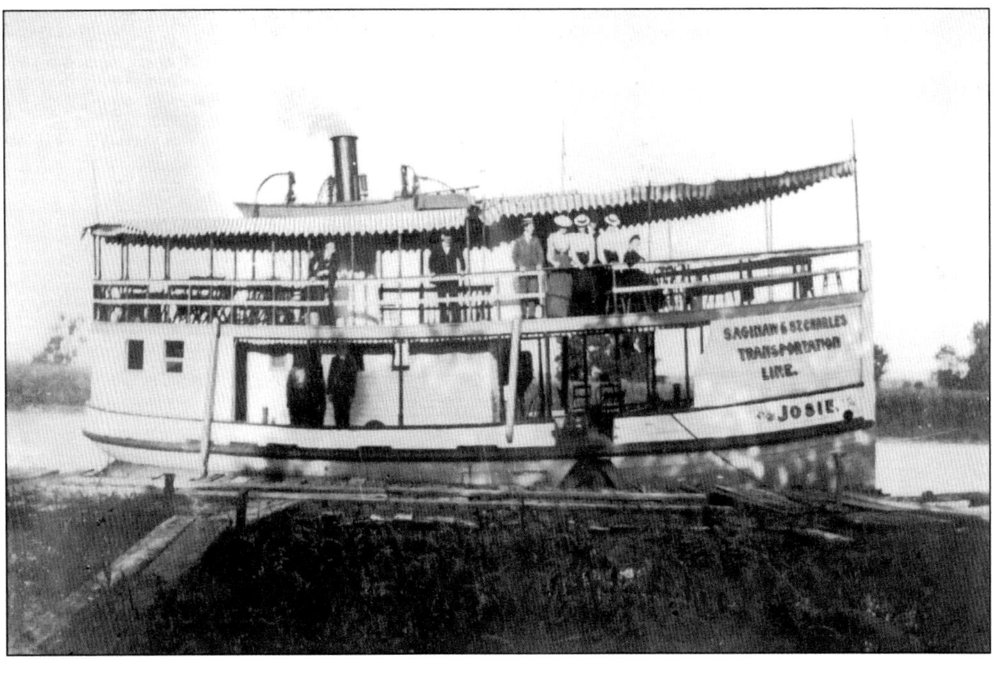

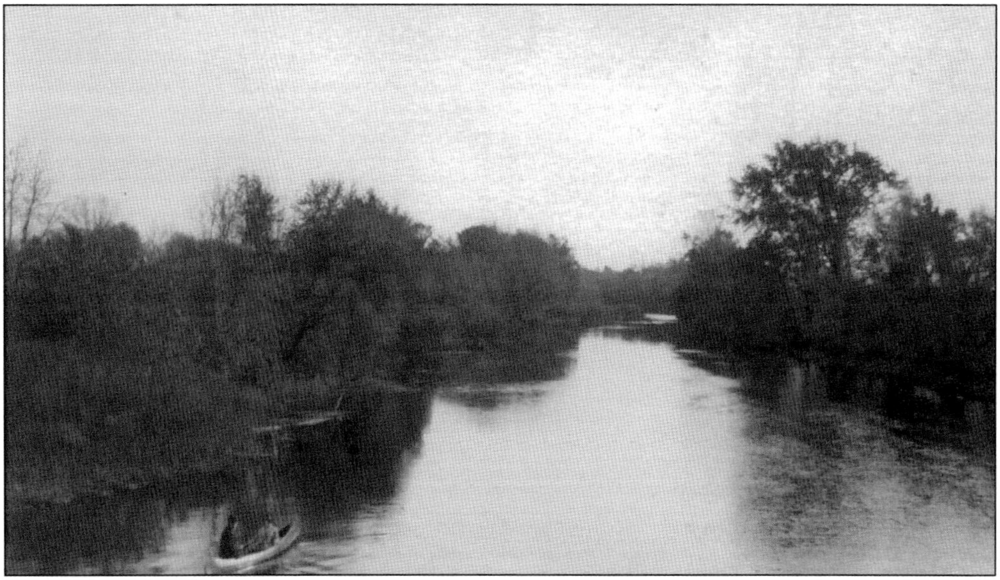

Residents spent pleasurable afternoons boating on the county's many rivers and streams. A pleasure trip is taken on the Cass River near Bridgeport in this early 1900s photo.

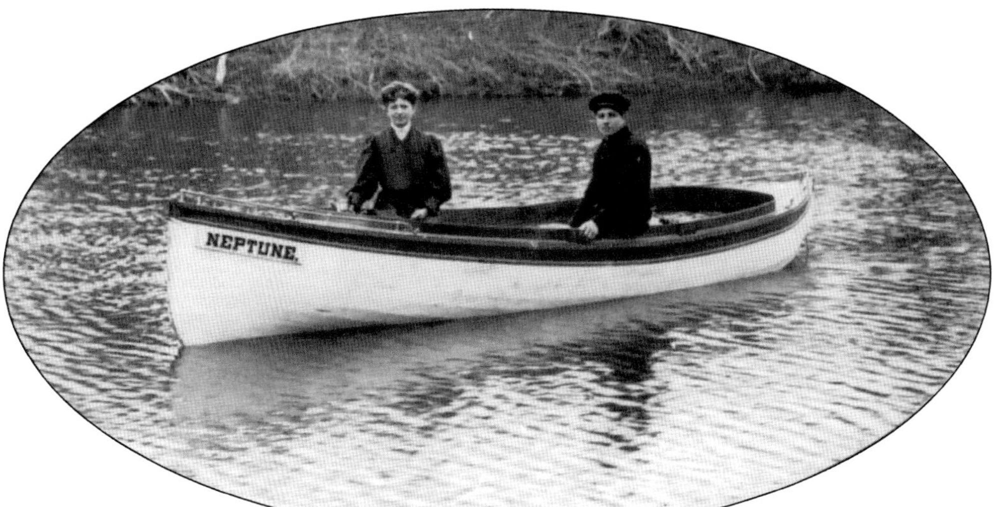

Carl Tausch built and launched the *Neptune* in the 1890s in St. Charles. He built boats with one or two horsepower gas engines. Carl, shown on the right in this 1905 photo, and his sister, Elizabeth Tausch, are taking a pleasurable boating trip down the Bad River in St. Charles.

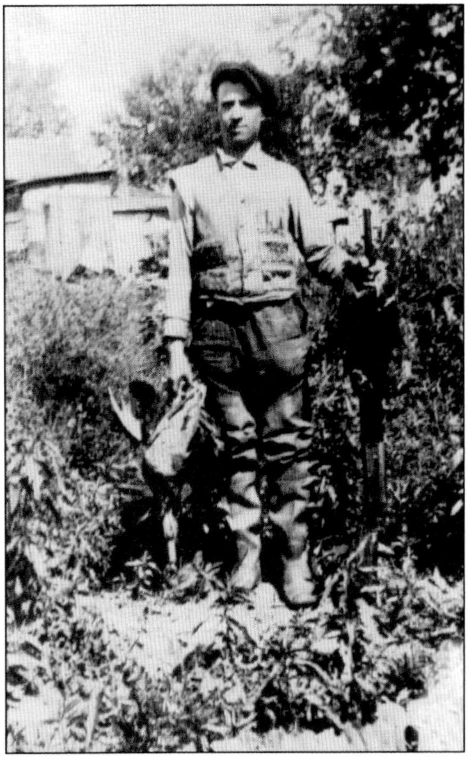

Life-long St. Charles resident Otto Greve has had a most successful day duck hunting with his twelve-gauge Remington automatic shotgun at the Shiawassee River Flats in 1907.

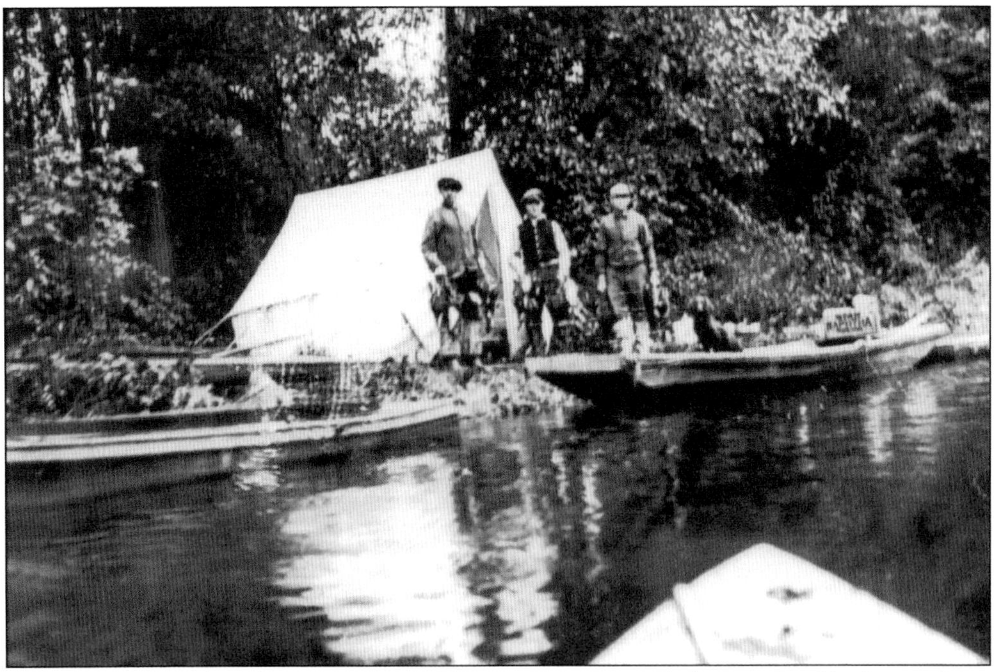

Duck hunting on the Shiawassee River Flats was a sportsman's haven. St. Charles residents (from left to right) Otto Greve, Elzie Spencer, and Lindsay Spencer camped in the Shiawassee woods along Ash Creek in 1923. They then traveled the waterways in their punt boats looking for ducks. This photo was taken from Andrew Maier's boat.

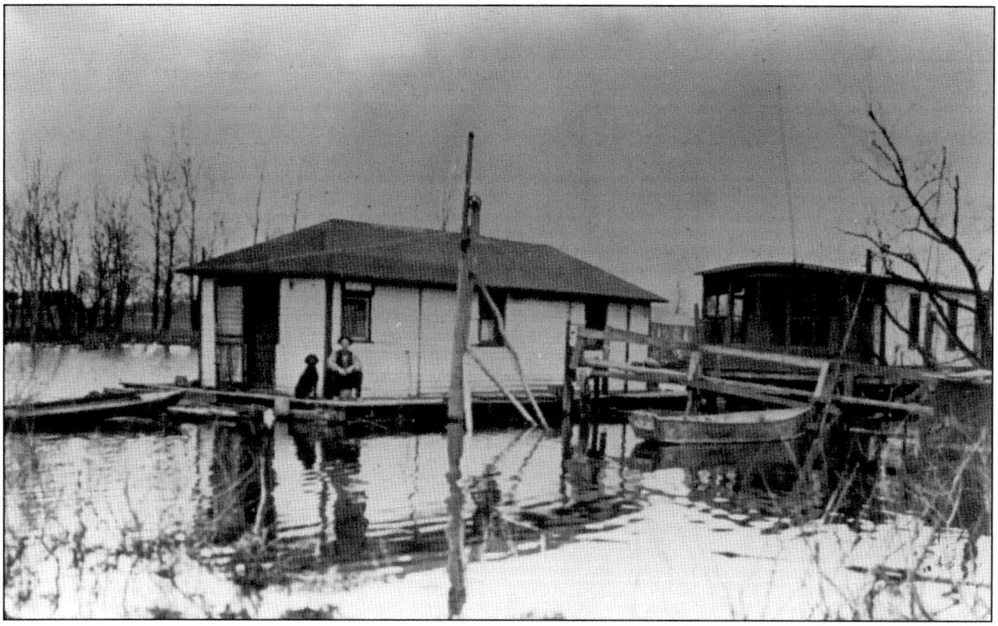

Some St. Charles residents used houseboats for hunting and fishing, steering them with pike poles or securing them for winter ice fishing. Joe Mason and his dog are sitting near his houseboat used for hunting. Mr. Evans lived in his houseboat year-round (at right). This early 1920s Bad River scene was photographed below the railroad bridge near Lumberjack Park.

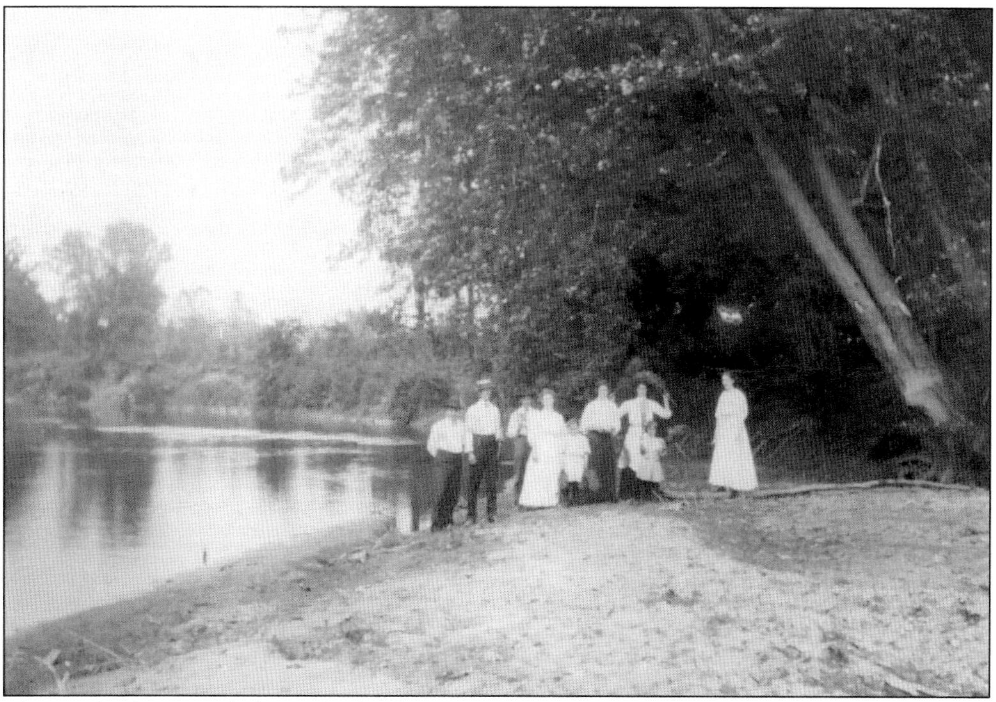

The riverbanks were ideal sites for family picnics and reunions. Picnicking, swimming, and boating could make a pleasurable afternoon's activities. These Chesaning friends are enjoying a picnic on the banks of the Shiawassee River near Gary Road in 1908. Mabel Waldron is on the far right side.

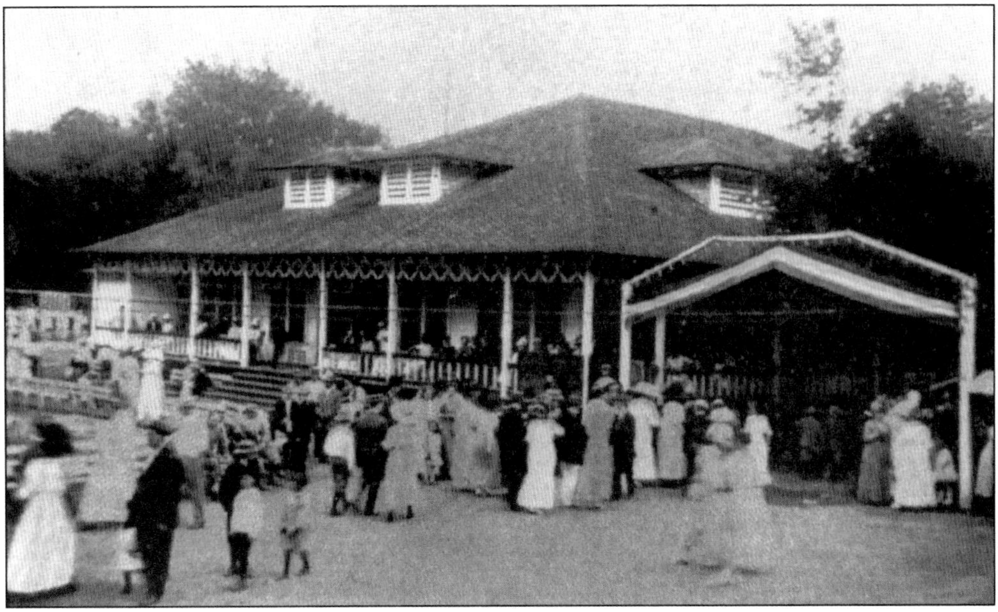

Riverside Park was established as a summer amusement park in 1894 at Green Point where the Tittabawassee, Shiawassee, Bad, and Cass Rivers meet to form the Saginaw River. Everyone stopped at the Casino, shown above, where vaudeville, concerts, and dancing entertained park visitors nightly. Visitors came to the park by Saginaw streetcars or boats.

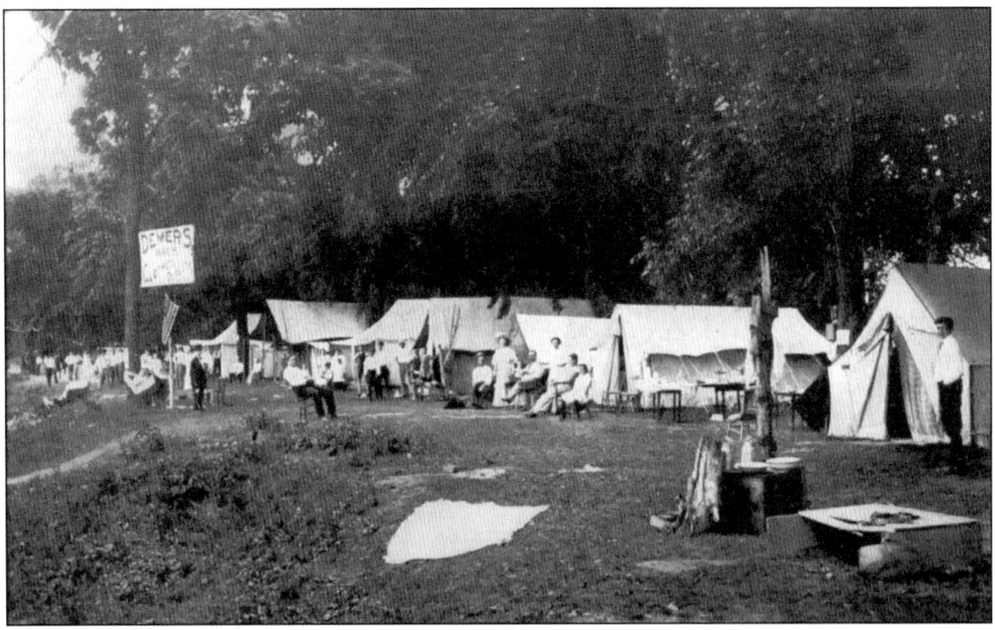

Several resort houseboats were docked opposite Riverside Park throughout the summer. The tent camp, shown above, was also located near the houseboats in the gap known as Demers Landing. Entire families spent their summer camping out in this northern resort at Green Point, enjoying the park rides, restaurants, and the evening entertainment.

Two

TRAVELING THE ROADWAYS

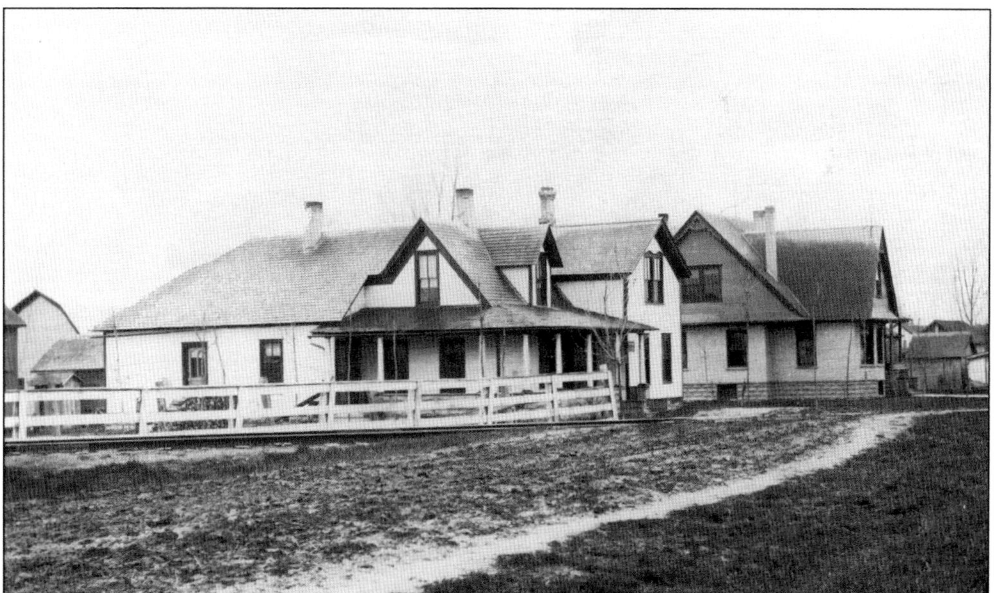

The county's earliest roads followed American Indian trails that were widened as traffic increased. These dirt pathways became mud roads with the spring thaws. The heaviest traveled rural roads were pine planked. Midland Road in Freeland was a narrow, rutted roadway for horse and wagon travel in the early 1900s. Today's Midland Road is a well-traveled paved highway.

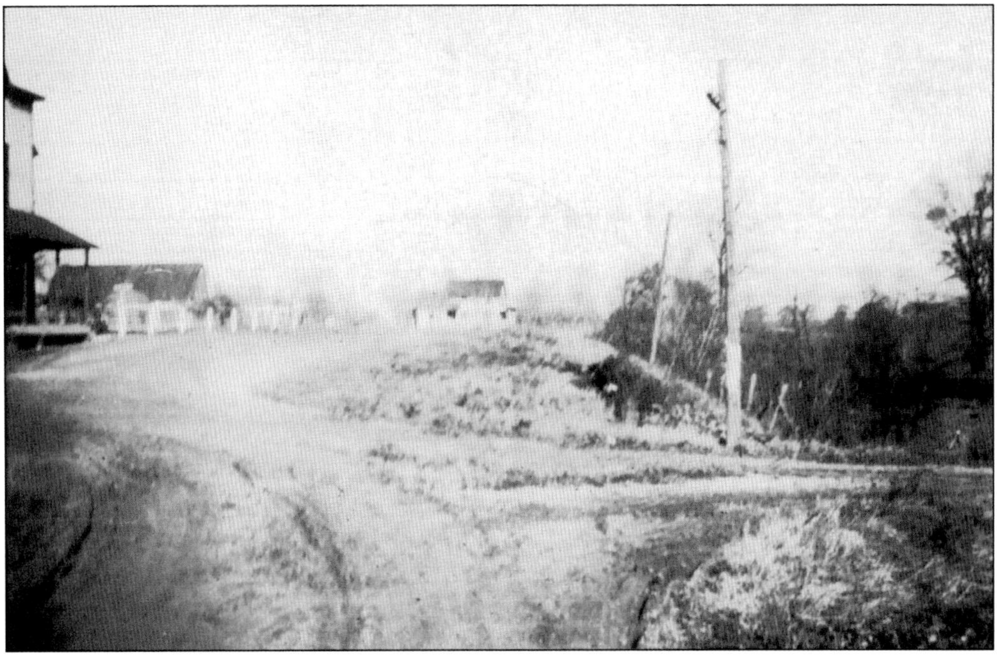

This Frost Corners intersection at Frost and Lone Roads in Thomastown Township in the early 1900s shows a typical rutted rural road. Part of Meade's Hall porch is shown on the left. Neighbors came to Meade's Hall to barter, shop, visit, or dance, and this corner was a busy intersection. The roadway has been built up with a deep ditch on the right.

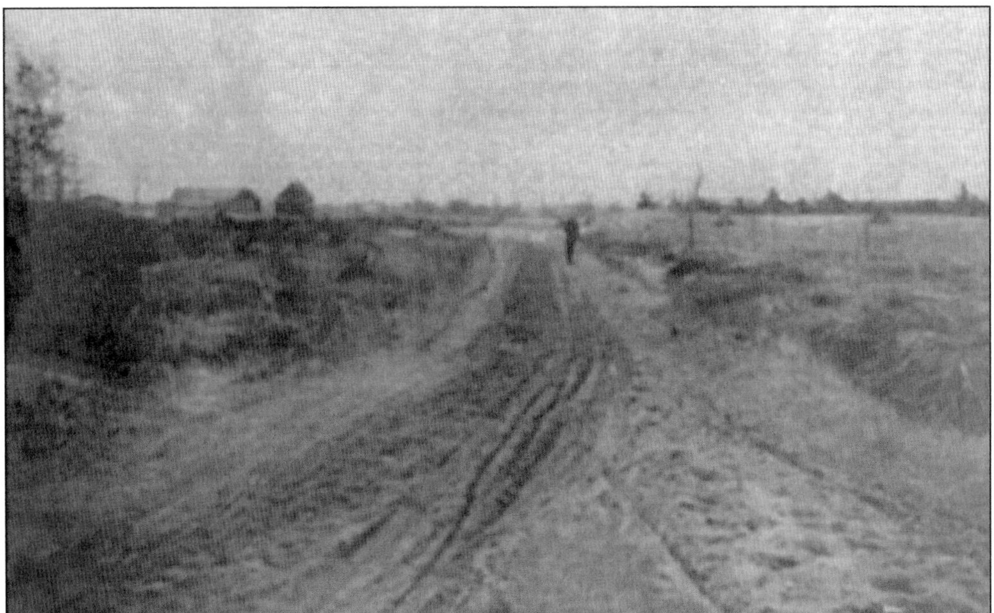

This photo of present day M-52 near the intersection of Swan Creek Road in Swan Creek Township was taken looking south in the early 1900s. The rural highway was the main roadway for travel to St. Charles and beyond. Today's M-52 is a heavily traveled highway for many trucks heading south through St. Charles, Chesaning, and Oakley.

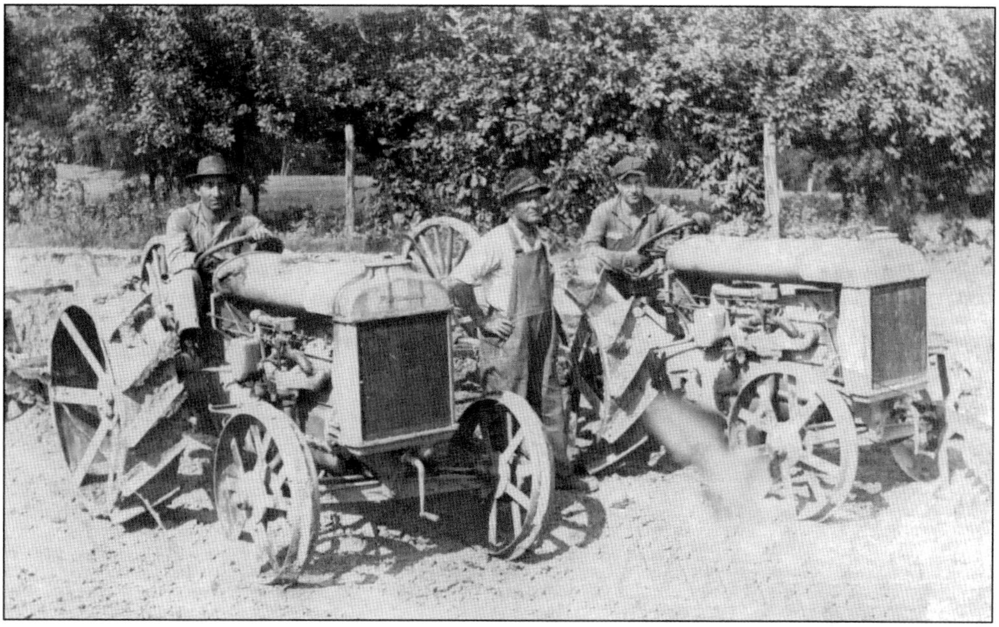

Macadam or stone-paved roads replaced the dirt roads when more automobiles began replacing the horses and wagons. When a road was being improved, the local farmers were required to help. Martin Holubik Sr. and his neighbors were using their own tractors to help build North River Road in Freeland in 1920.

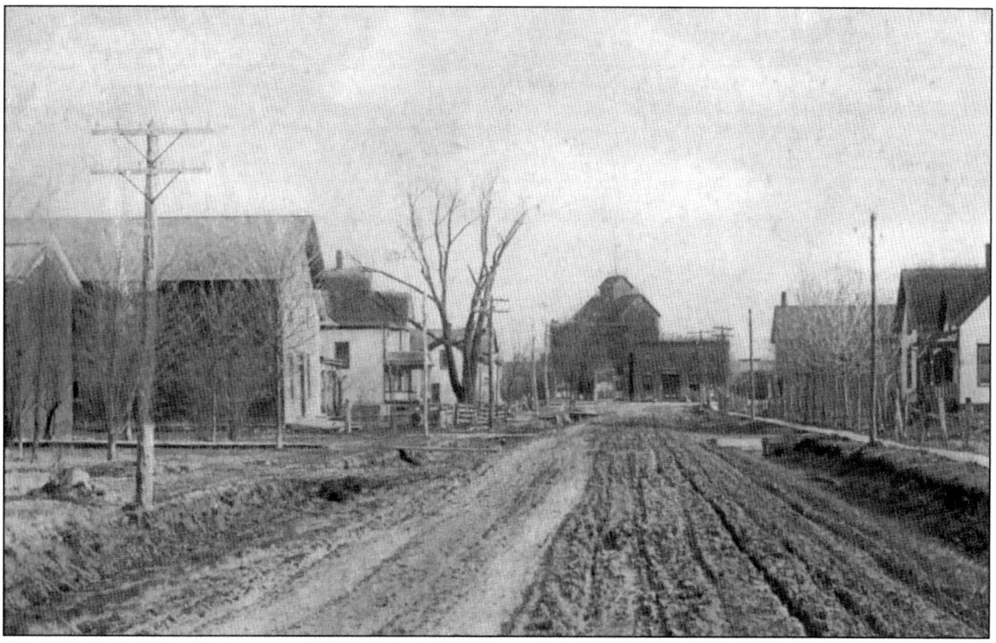

Church Street leading to Wolohan Elevator in Birch Run was a busy thoroughfare in the early 1900s. Even though it still remained a dirt street, it was graded periodically to keep the roadbed level. Pine plank sidewalks parallel Church Street. Every house has its own page wire or pine rail fence to keep stray livestock from entering the yard.

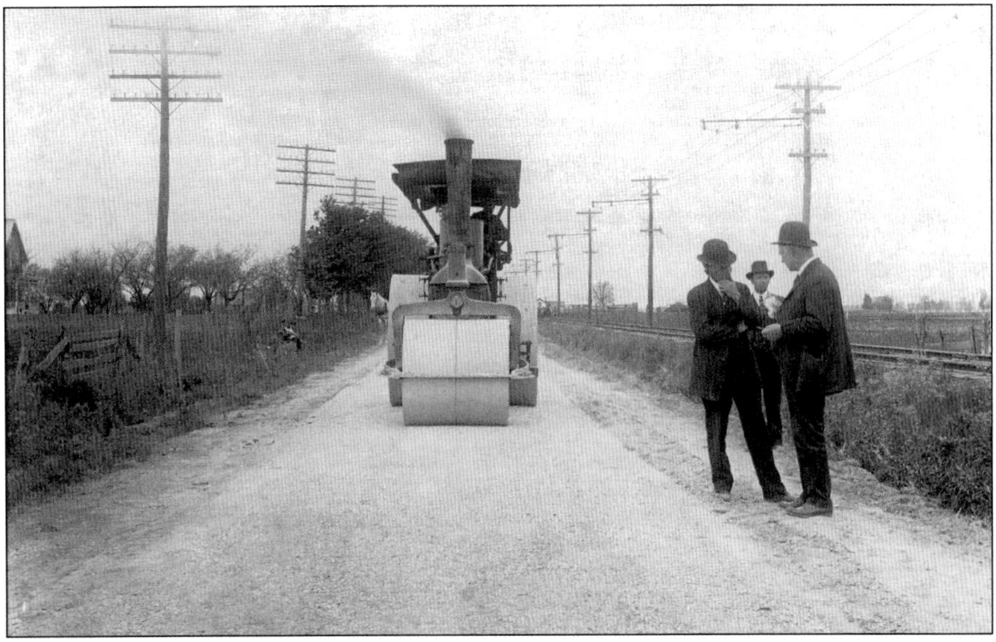

Buena Vista roads were the first county roads to be built after the Good Roads Movement Act of 1898. Stone from Port Austin quarries came by train. Farmers with their horses and wagons hauled the stones from the railroad depot and spread them on the road. A county steamroller pressed the stones into a hard-surface roadway as shown in this 1910 photo.

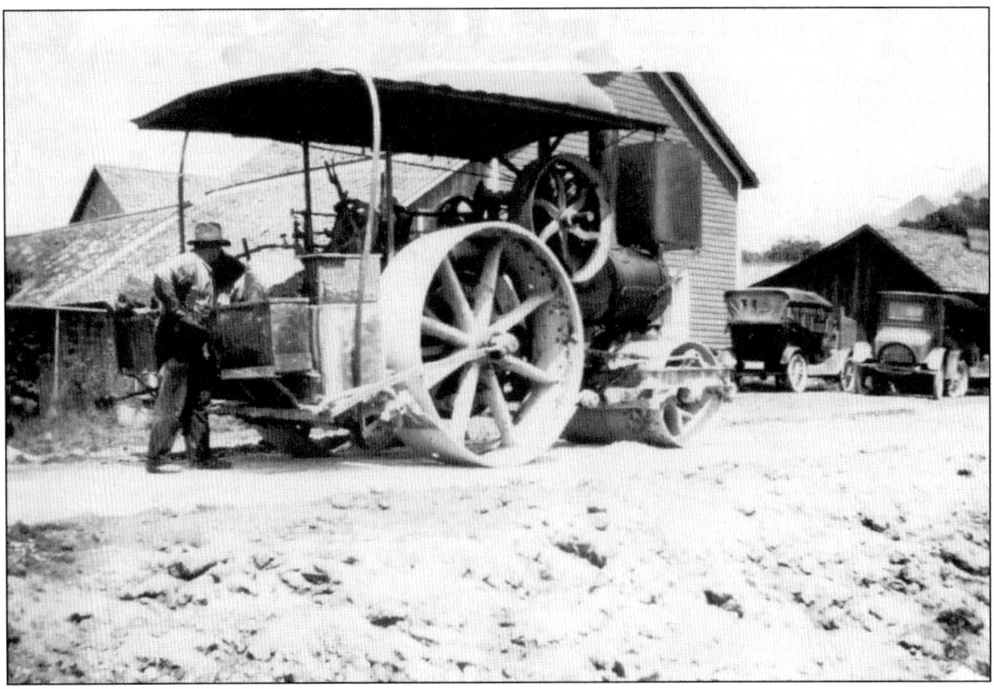

This county road commission's steamroller is pressing the stones into a hard-surface roadbed on Frost Road in Thomastown Township in the 1920s. It was easier for automobiles to travel on these macadam roads since they often became stuck in the muddy, rutted rural roads.

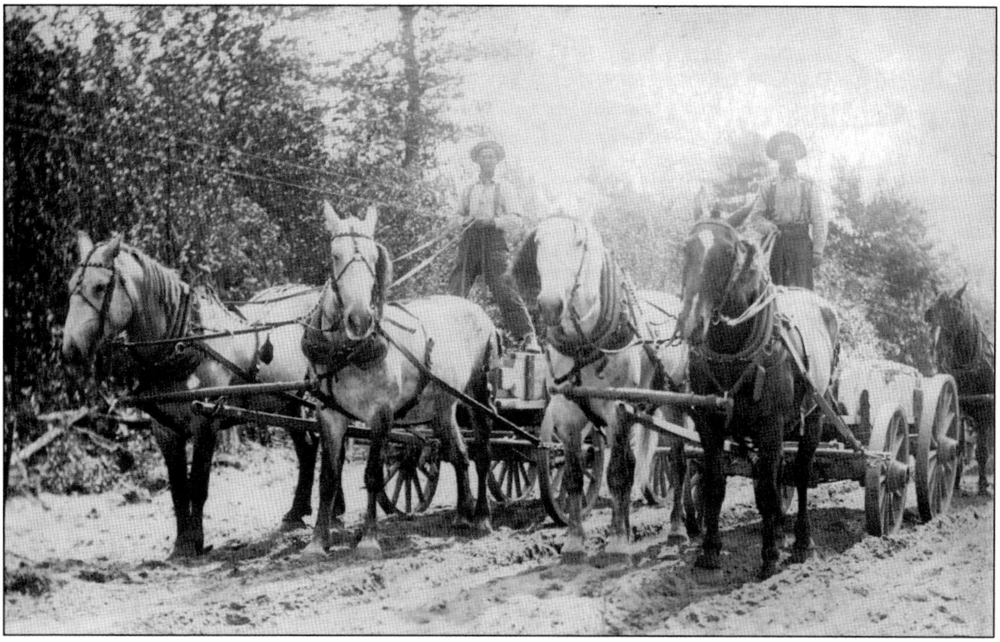

Nelson Corners emerged in Fremont Township at the intersection of Hemlock and Nelson Roads with a church, town hall, and general store. These farmers and their double horse teams are hauling shale to build Hemlock Road near Nelson Corners with a hard-surface roadbed in the late 1910s.

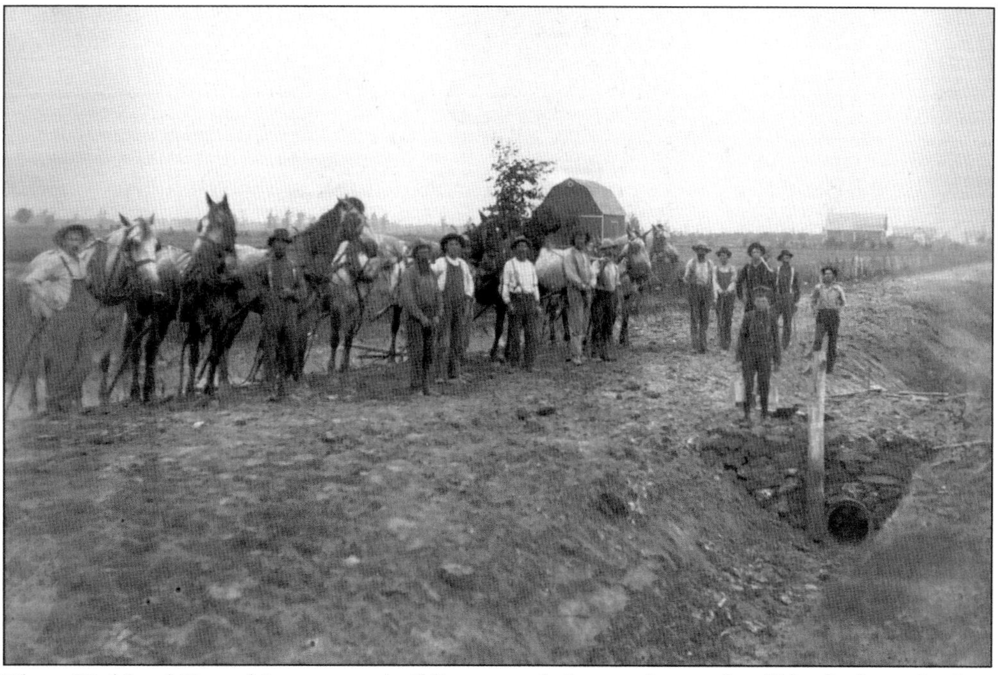

These Richland Township men are building a road three miles south of Hemlock in the late 1910s. Bob Niersal's house and Cleveland School can be seen in the background. All road building was done with manual labor and horse teams. Farmers living along rural roads were expected to help build the roads, using their own horses and equipment.

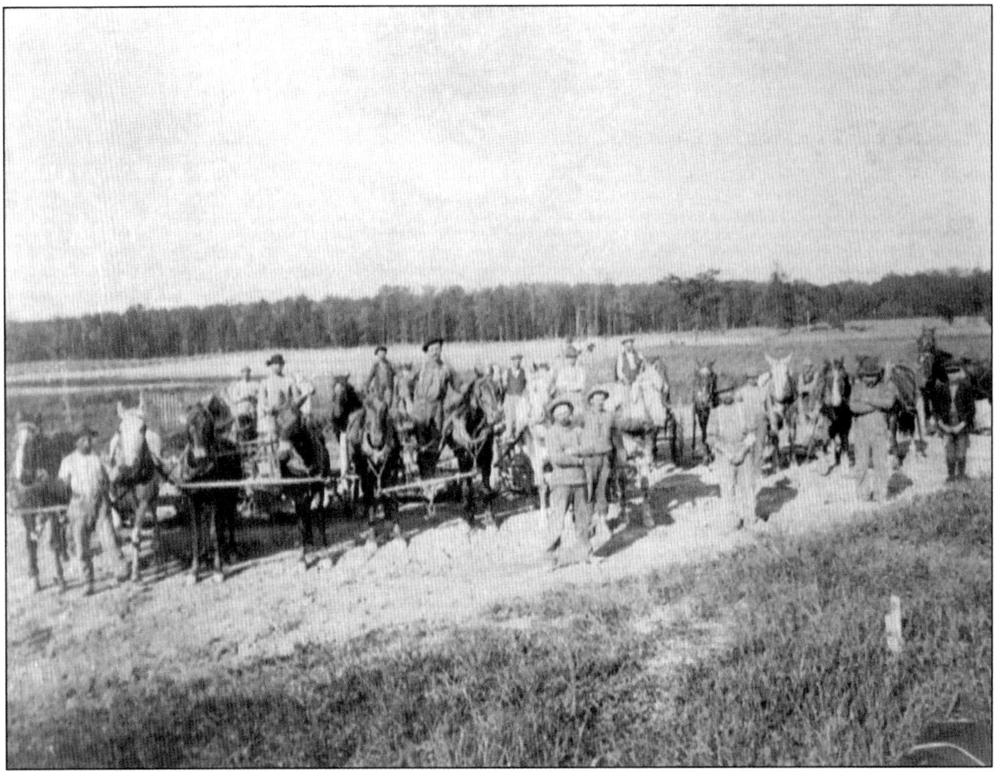

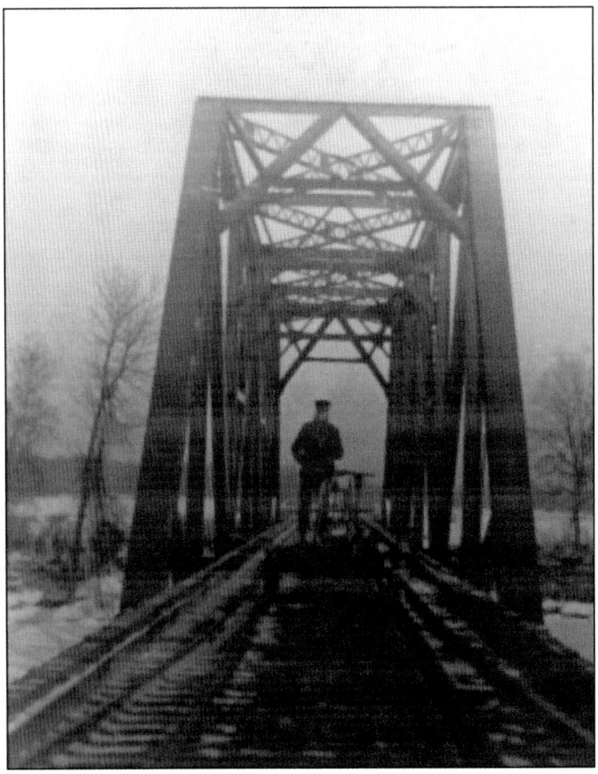

The Cincinnati, Saginaw & Mackinaw Railroad constructed a spur line from the Verne Station to the Verne Coal Mine and roads to Fosters and Burt in 1888. Wellington R. Burt was responsible for getting the road to Burt, which was named in his honor. These local men are building the railroad grade in 1889. The railroad became Grand Trunk Railroad.

This Grand Trunk Railroad bridge trestle crossed the Flint River near Fosters in 1900. Workmen kept the railroad in good condition. A regular train schedule included daily stops for both passenger and freight at Verne, Fosters, and Burt, connecting Taymouth and Albee Townships to Saginaw, Durand, and Flint. The train is still important to the area today.

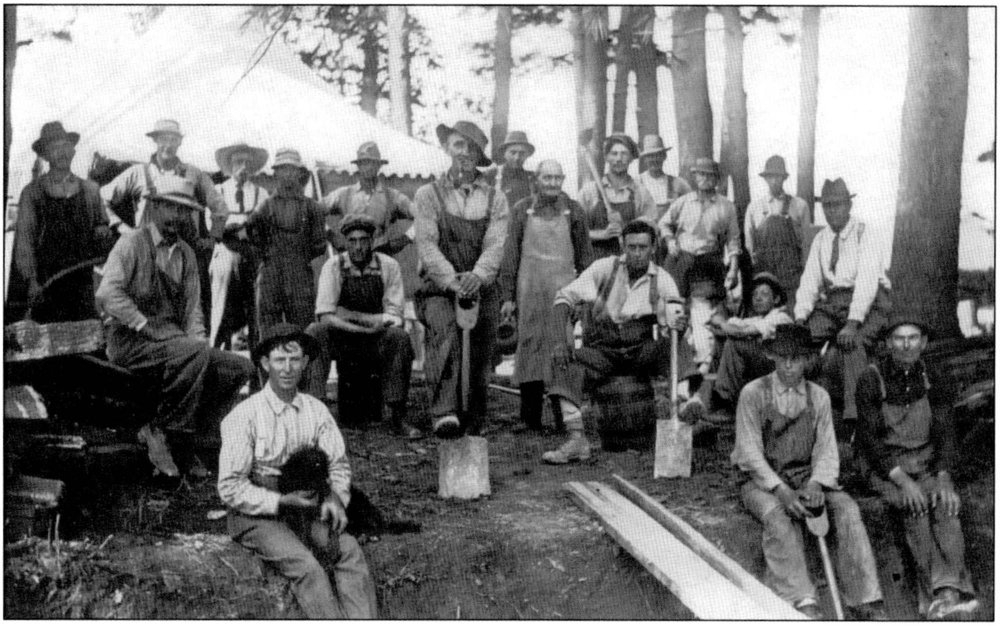

These interurban workers in Bridgeport have paused from their daily work long enough for this photo session in the early 1900s. The interurban was an important link, providing a direct line to East Saginaw and Flint. Many local men were employed to keep the rail lines and the interurban running smoothly.

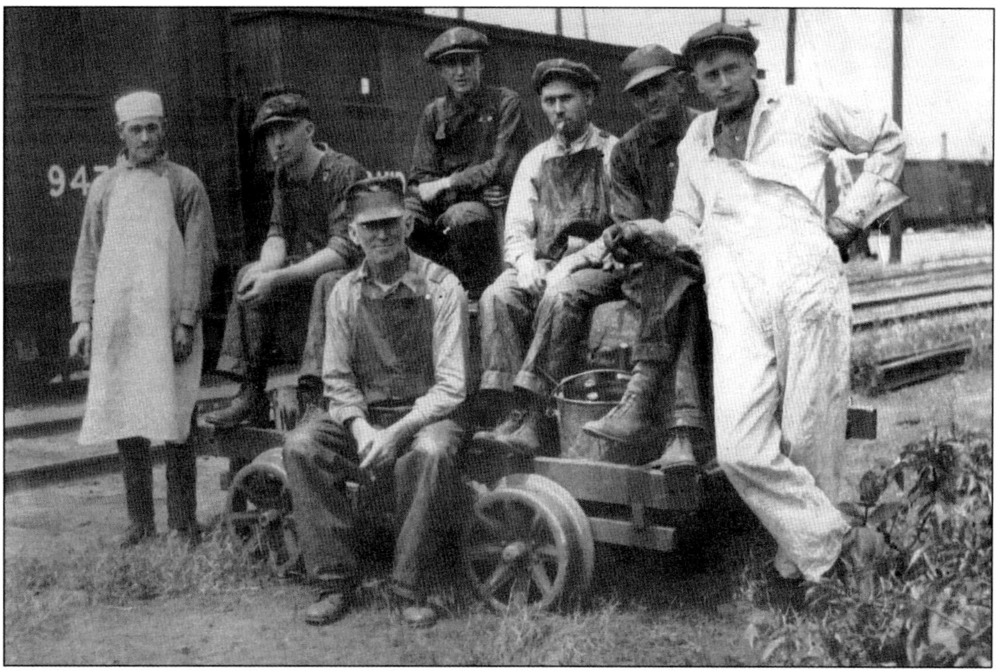

A railroad work crew from Taymouth Township posed for this photo in Grand Rapids. Standing from left to right are Dan Tinkham, Judd Bullard, Lloyd Tuttle, Pearly Green, Harry Tinkham, and Harold Barrett. Mr. Cartwright is sitting. The crew traveled along the railroad wherever they were sent, sleeping in boxcars and the cook's shanty.

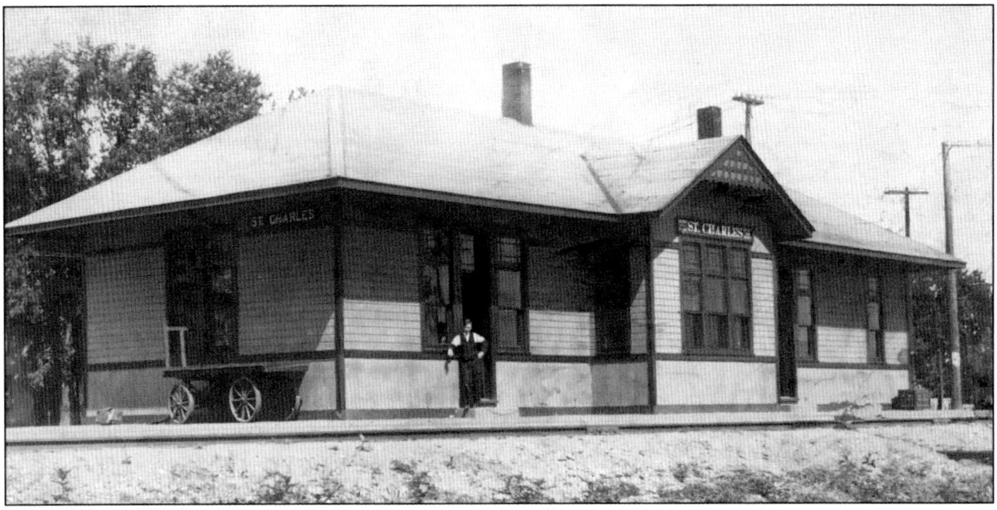

Charles S. Kimberly built the first St. Charles Railroad Depot for the Jackson, Lansing & Saginaw Railroad connecting the small community with Saginaw City and Lansing in 1867. In 1910, Michigan Central Railroad replaced the original depot with this depot which provided important service until it was demolished in the 1960s.

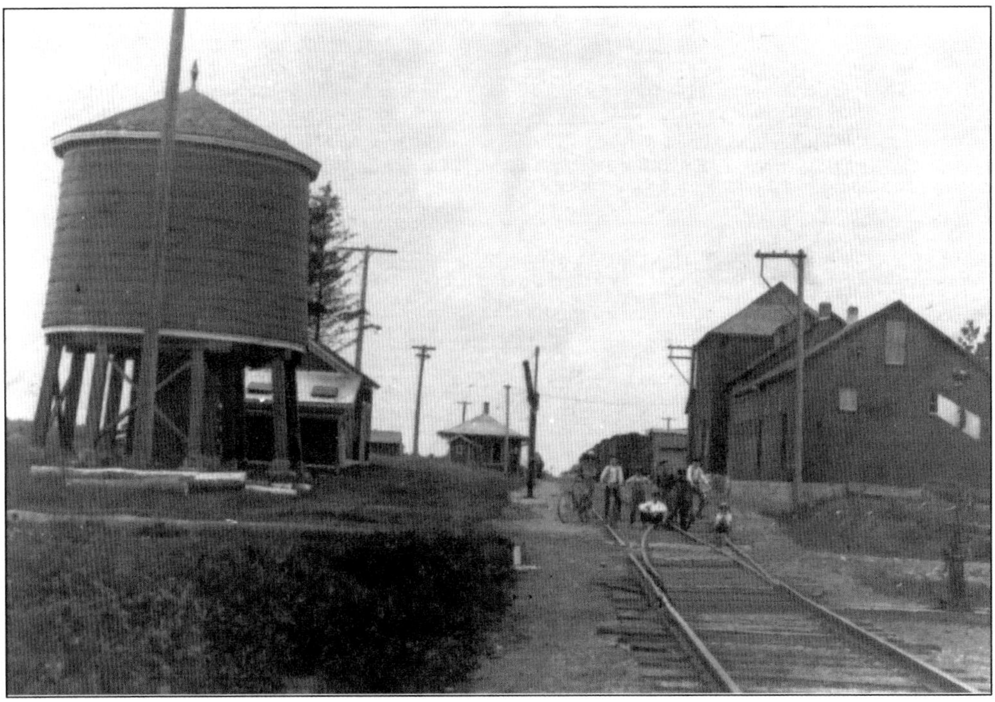

The Hemlock Railroad Depot is seen in the distance. The tracks pass the Hemlock elevators on the right and the large water tower on the left. The Saginaw Valley & St. Louis Railroad came in 1871. It became the Pere Marquette Railroad in 1907 and the Chesapeake & Ohio Railroad in 1947. The depot was moved to Saginaw in 1983 for a railroad museum.

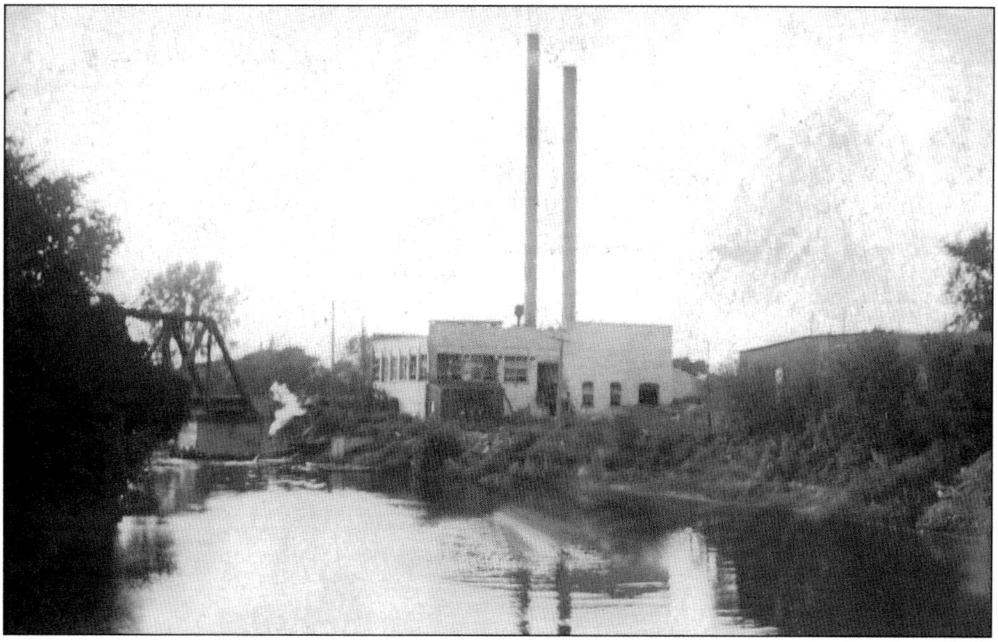

George Silsby organized the Saginaw Suburban Railway Company in 1898, providing interurban service from Bridgeport to Frankenmuth, Birch Run, Clio, Mt. Morris, and Flint. Consolidation with the Saginaw Valley Traction Company expanded direct service to Saginaw and Bay City. This Bridgeport Powerhouse was located at the southwest corner of Williamson Road and the Chesapeake & Ohio Railroad tracks. Shown below, four employees are working inside the Bridgeport Interurban Powerhouse in 1904. The interurban was a major Bridgeport employer.

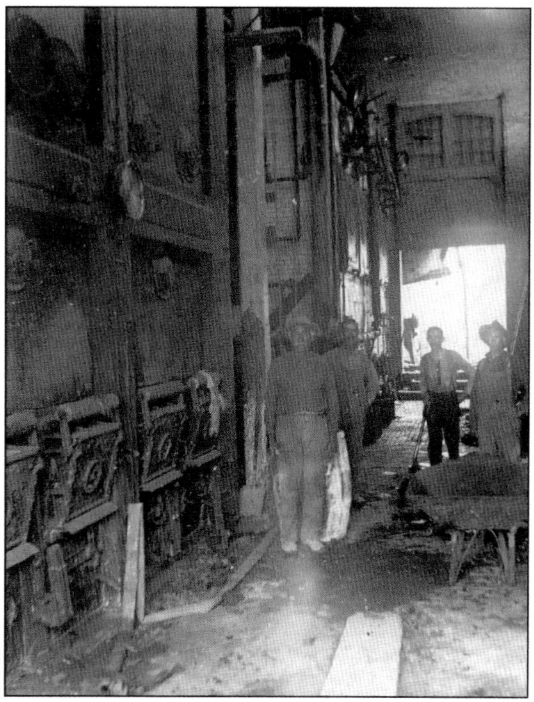

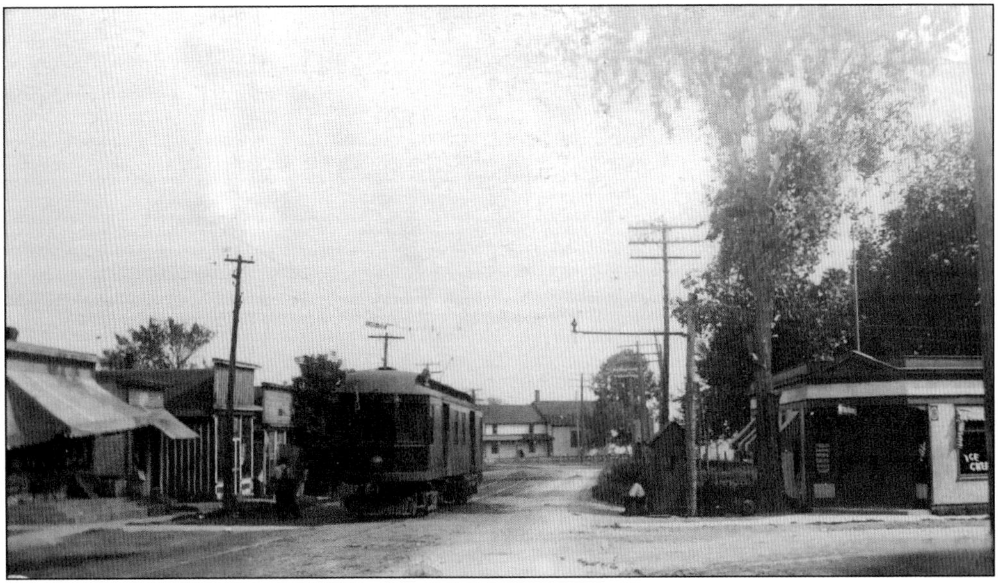

The interurban train stop and waiting room in downtown Bridgeport, south of State Street, are shown in these 1912 photos. The Bridgeport Masonic Lodge is in the distance on the Dixie Highway. On the left side of the above photo are a store, a barbershop, an implement store, and the train stop. The waiting room is on the right. The bottom photo shows a close-up view of the waiting room and ice cream parlor with a phone booth near the curb. Residents enjoyed pleasurable excursions traveling to downtown Saginaw for shopping, performances at the Auditorium, or other activities, and then returning home to Bridgeport the same day.

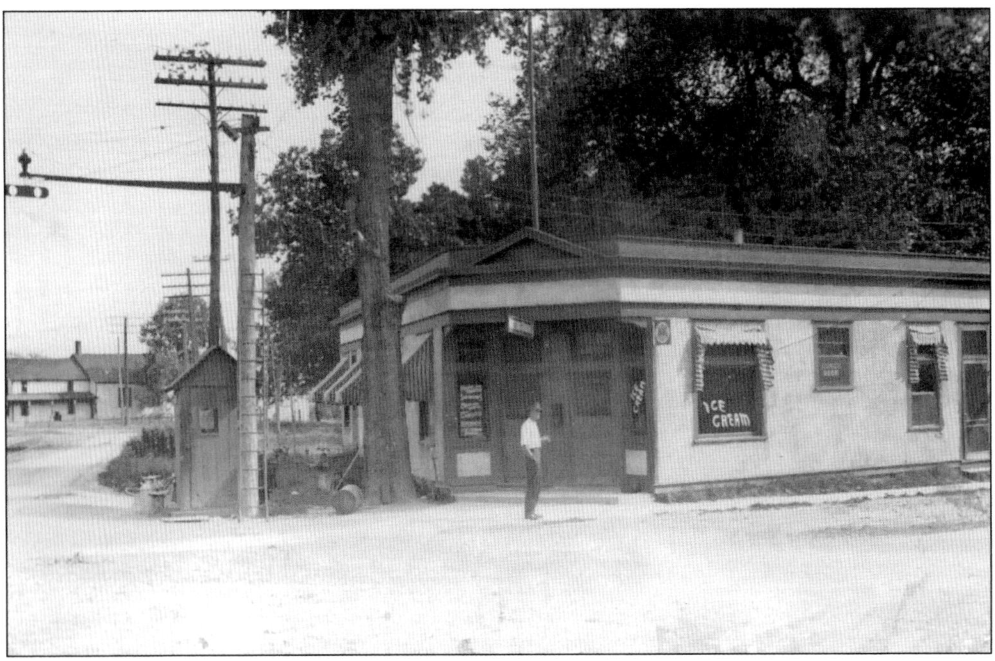

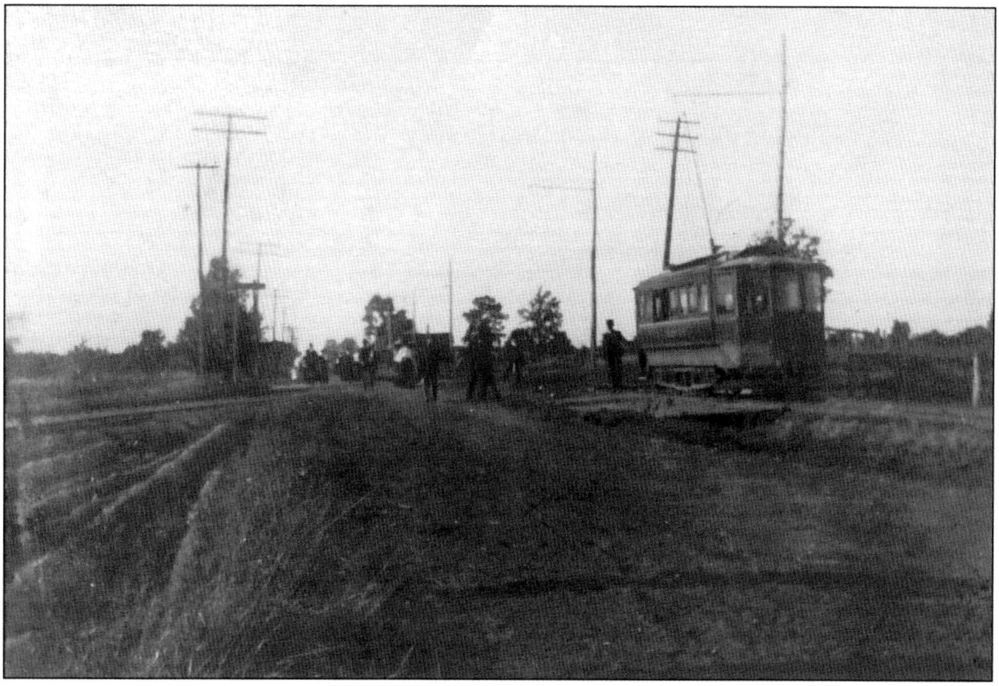

The interurban provided convenient, fast transportation between Saginaw, Bridgeport, Birch Run, and Flint. Fares were 2¢ per mile per passenger. The Birch Run Depot was always a busy place. People traveled back and forth frequently to Flint. This 1904 photo shows the interurban traveling outside Bridgeport.

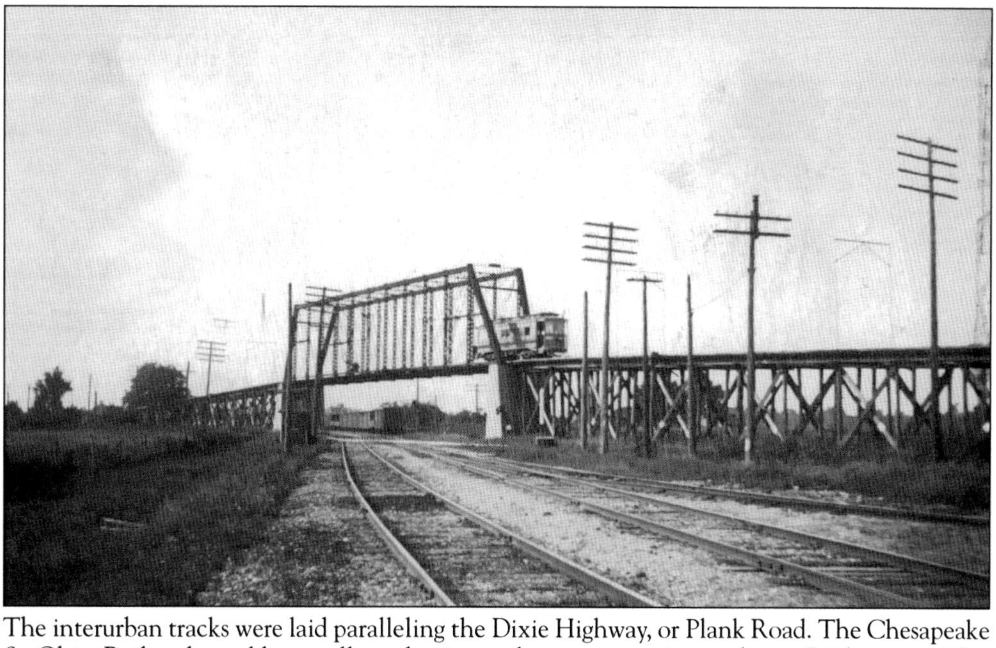

The interurban tracks were laid paralleling the Dixie Highway, or Plank Road. The Chesapeake & Ohio Railroad would not allow the interurban to cross its tracks at Bridgeport. After intervention by the State Railroad Commissioner, a viaduct was built over the railroad tracks, permitting the interurban to cross, as shown in this photo of 1904.

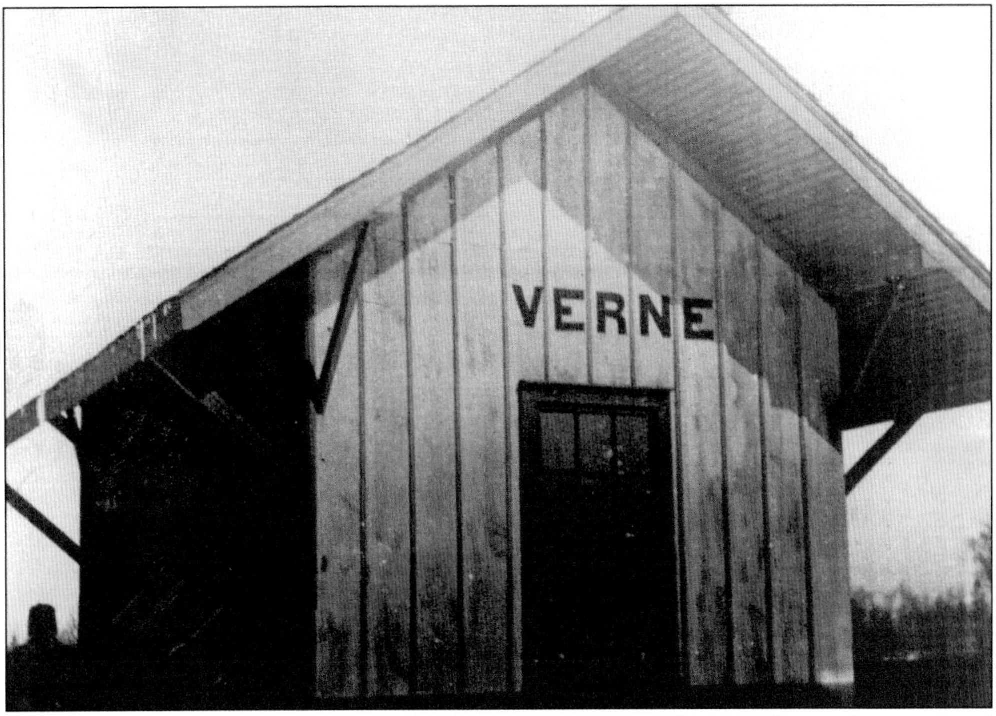

Albee Township's Verne Mine began in 1894 and was Saginaw County's first coal mine. A rail spur line was built from Verne Station to the Verne Mine. A company town with boarding houses, hotel, store, saloon, and blacksmith shop was built for West Virginia coal miners. This Grand Trunk Train Depot remained long after the town was disbanded.

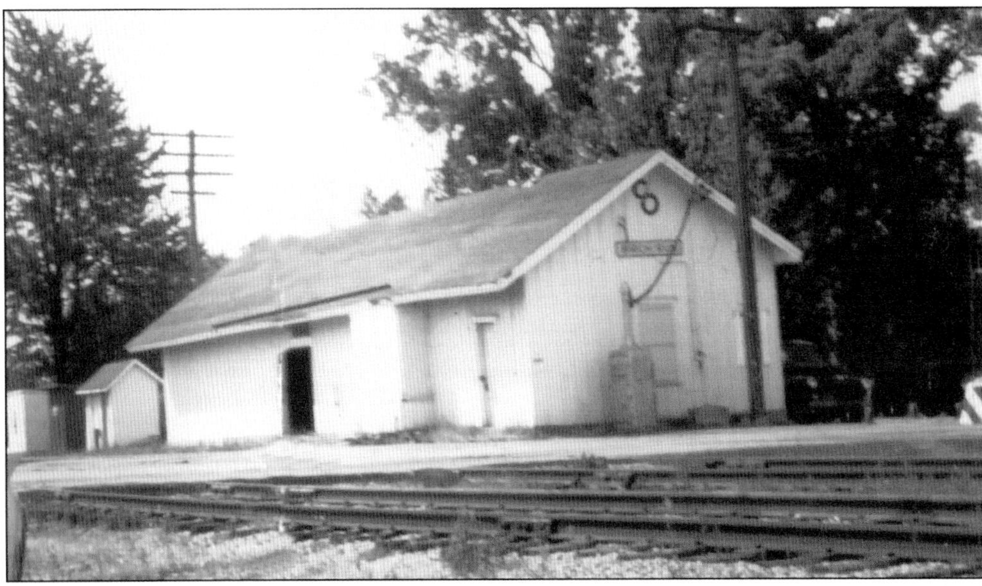

Jacob Tremper's home was used as the first railroad station until this Birch Run Depot was built on Main Street. The first Flint & Pere Marquette Railroad ran from Saginaw to Mt. Morris with a fuel stop at Birch Run in 1862. Birch Run's timber supply provided a steady fuel source for each train stop. The railroad helped in Birch Run's growth.

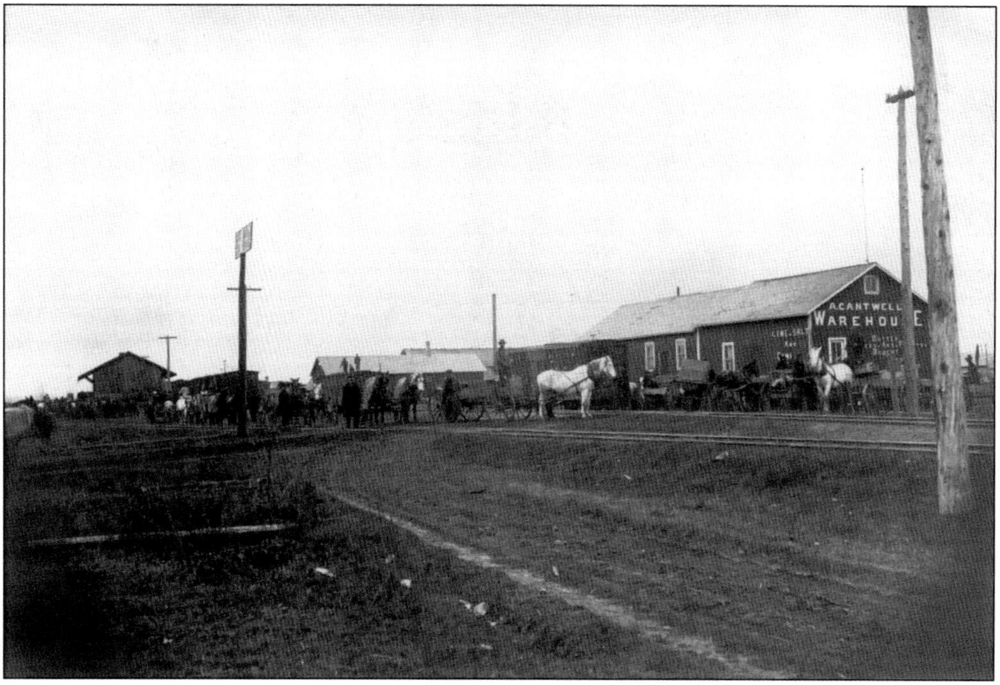

Albert Cantwell opened his own grocery and bazaar store in Chesaning in 1886. He expanded in 1892 with a shipping business, distributing local farm produce, and built two large warehouses near the Michigan Central Railroad tracks, as shown here in 1899. He developed Cantwell Driving Park, which is now known as Showboat Park.

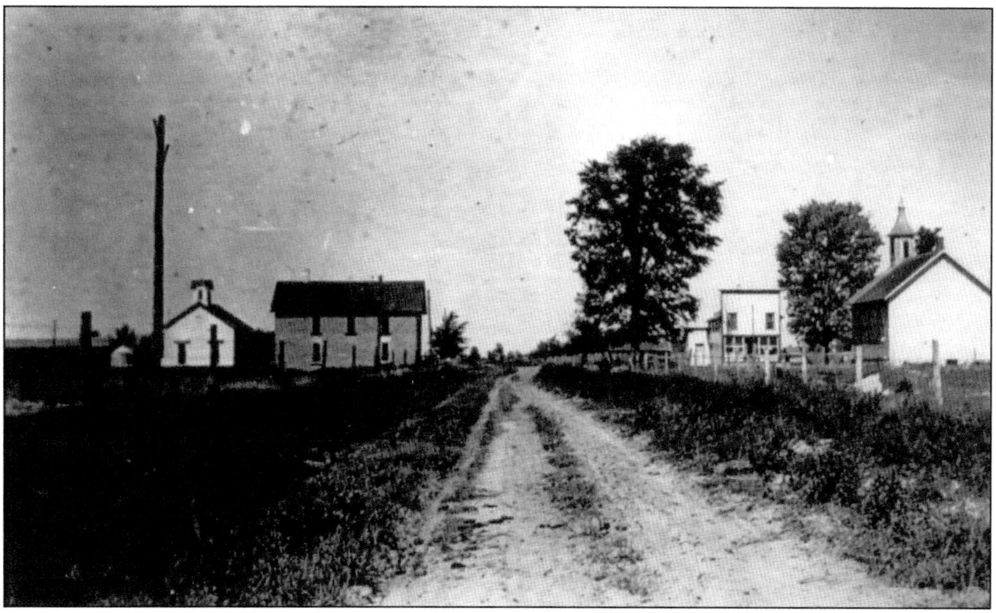

This view of Brady Center was taken in 1890 on Peet and Hemlock Roads south of Chesaning. On the left in this self-sufficient village are a township hall, a horse and farm supply store with upstairs hotel rooms, and a schoolhouse. To the right are a general store with upstairs living quarters and the Brady Evangelical Church. Today a Lutheran Church stands on the northwest corner.

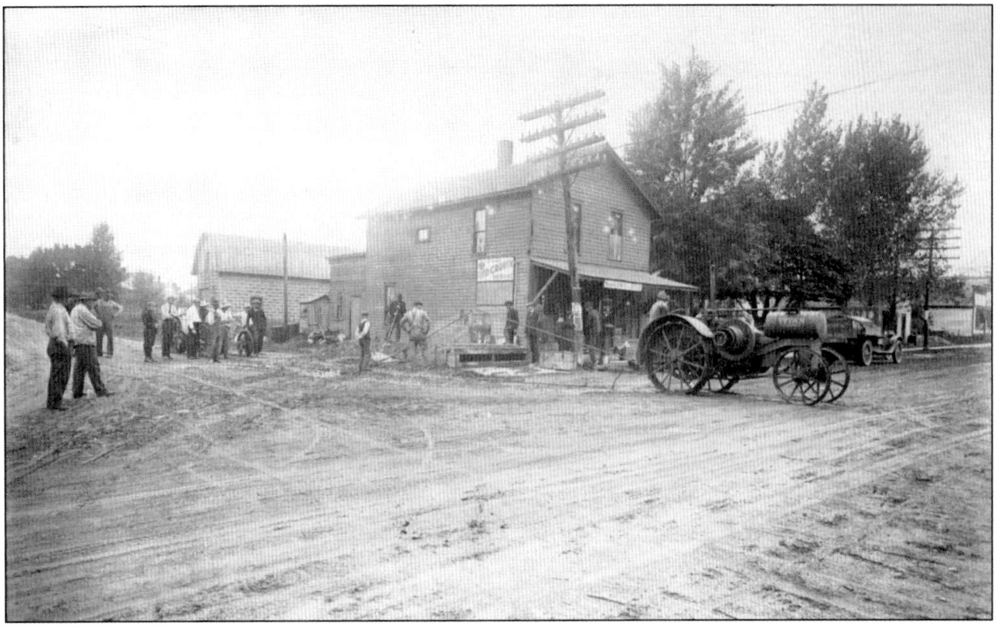

This building on the southwest corner of Gratiot and Hemlock Roads had been used for William McBratine's store, Nerwick Drugs, and the *Hemlock News* before John Rick's Garage occupied the site in the late 1910s. Rick later established his Ford dealership across the road on the southeast corner. Dr. Manzoni's Veterinary Clinic operated there in later years.

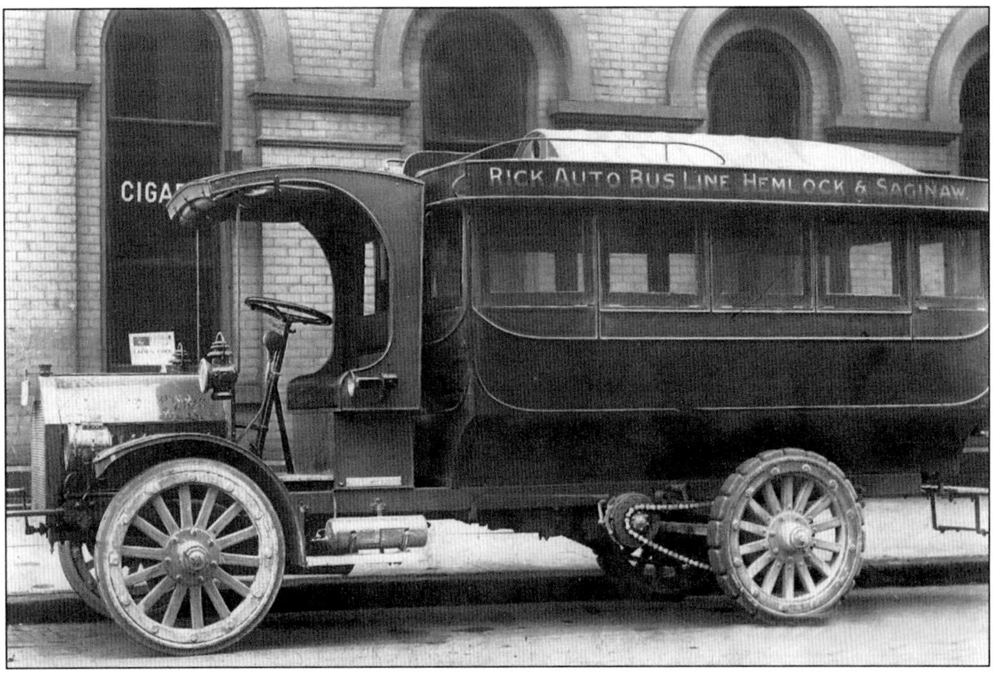

In addition to his garage, John Rick also ran regularly scheduled trips with his Auto Bus Line between Hemlock and Saginaw. This service furnished fast, efficient transportation for Hemlock residents who would go to Saginaw for shopping, business, or recreational activities and return the same day.

Three

Making a Living

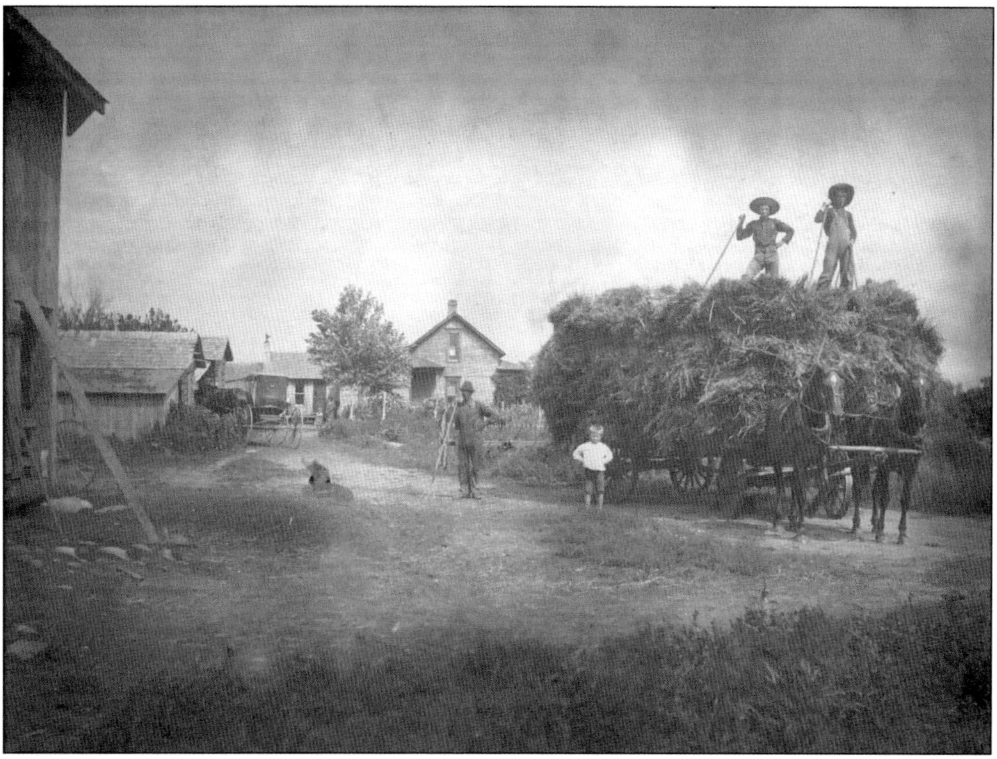

Farm scenes such as this Birch Run hay harvest in the 1800s and early 1900s occurred all over Saginaw County in July and August. As timber was cleared, more land was opened for farming. Horses were used for transportation and work in the fields, sawmills, and industries. Hay was needed to feed the many horses and cattle in the county and in Saginaw.

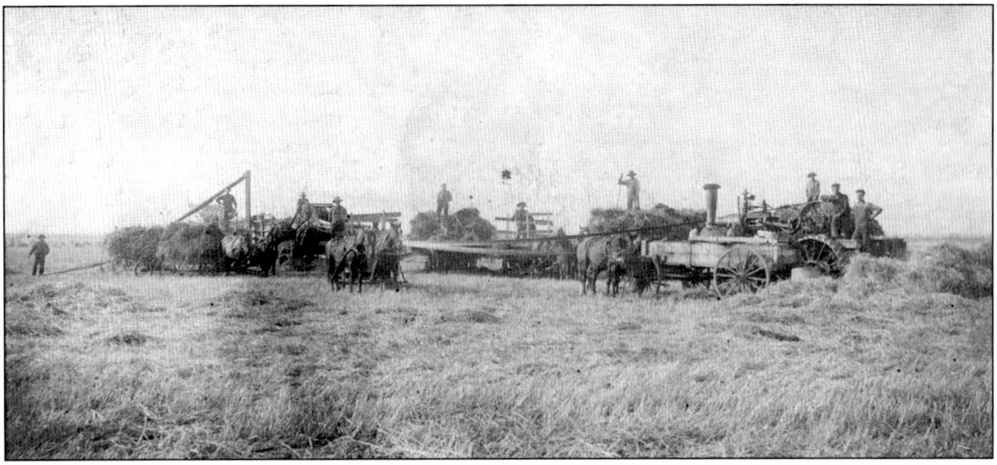

Birch Run was primarily an agricultural township in the 1800s and early 1900s. Neighbors brought their own equipment and helped each other with cutting, gathering, and threshing their wheat, rye, oats, and barley crops. This Birch Run scene was repeated throughout the county in July and August.

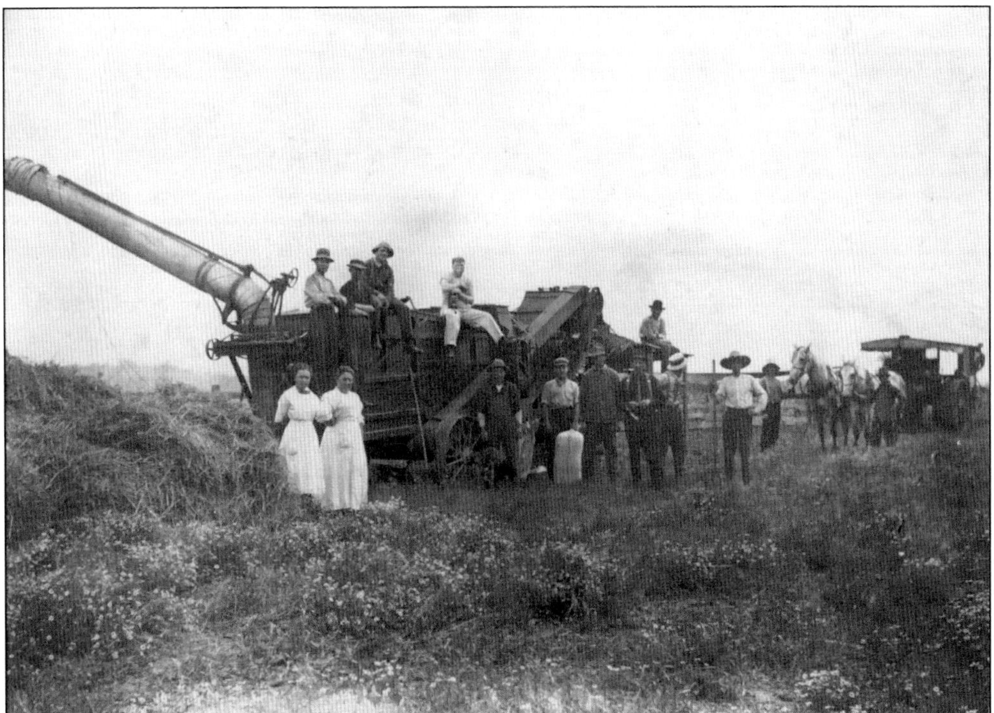

Harvesting involved the neighboring farmers and the entire family. This Tittabawassee Road scene might have occurred in Tittabawassee, Kochville, or Saginaw Townships but was a familiar summer scene all over Saginaw County. Farmers brought their horse teams and equipment to help each other. The women spent the day cooking large meals.

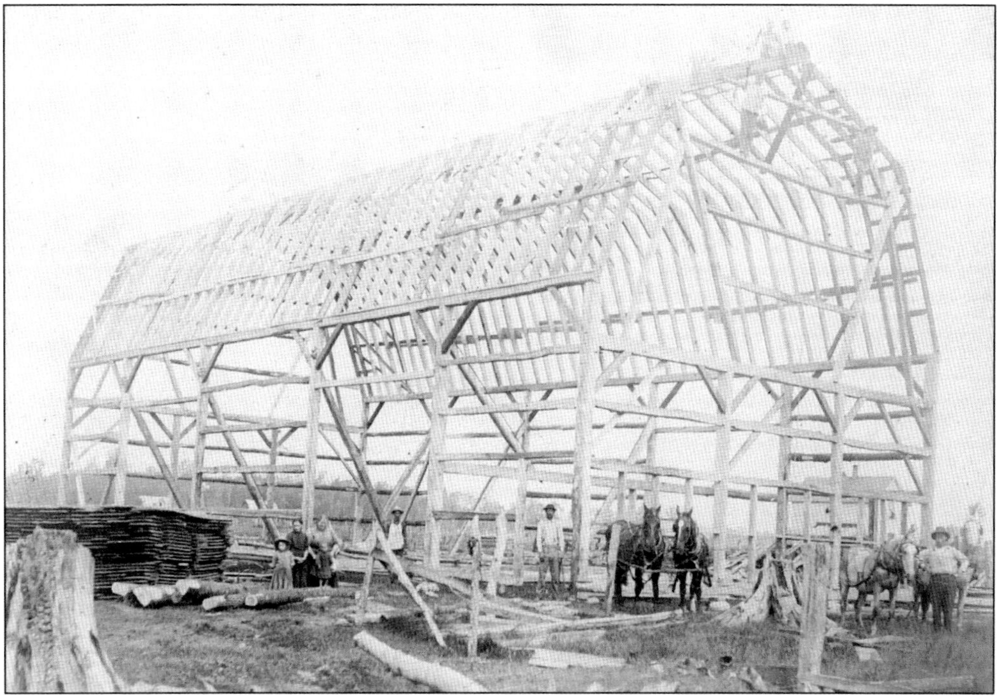

Large barns to house horses, cattle, livestock, grain, and hay dotted the rural landscape throughout the county. Joseph Ederer built many barns, such as this one in Saginaw, in James, Swan Creek, and Thomastown Townships in the 1800s and early 1900s. Barn raisings brought several farmers and their families together to finish the construction.

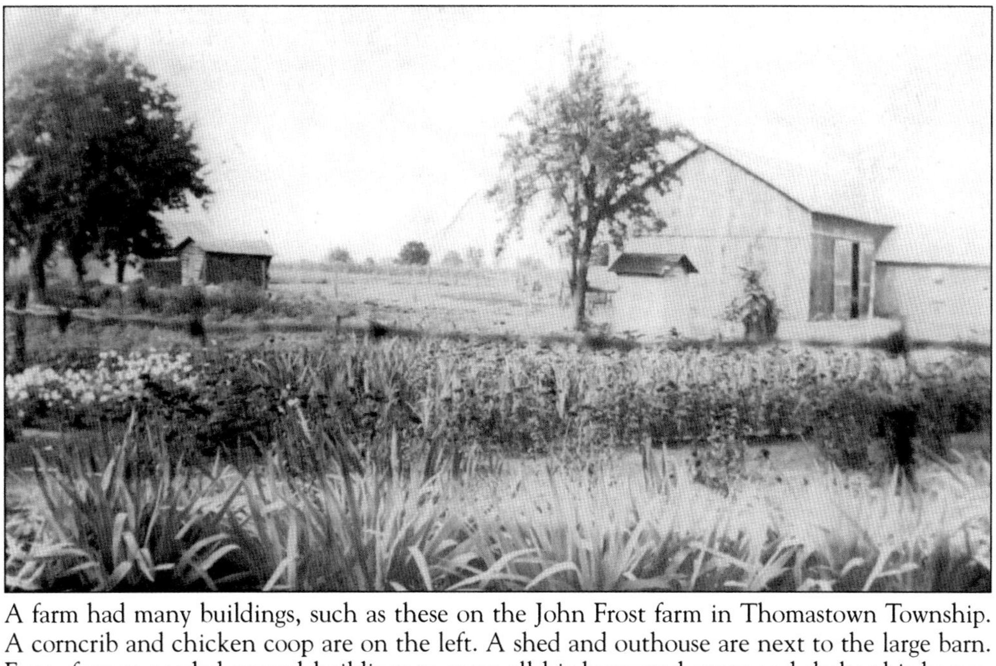

A farm had many buildings, such as these on the John Frost farm in Thomastown Township. A corncrib and chicken coop are on the left. A shed and outhouse are next to the large barn. Every farmer needed several buildings to store all his harvested crops and shelter his horses, cattle, swine, chickens, or sheep. Rural homes had no indoor plumbing.

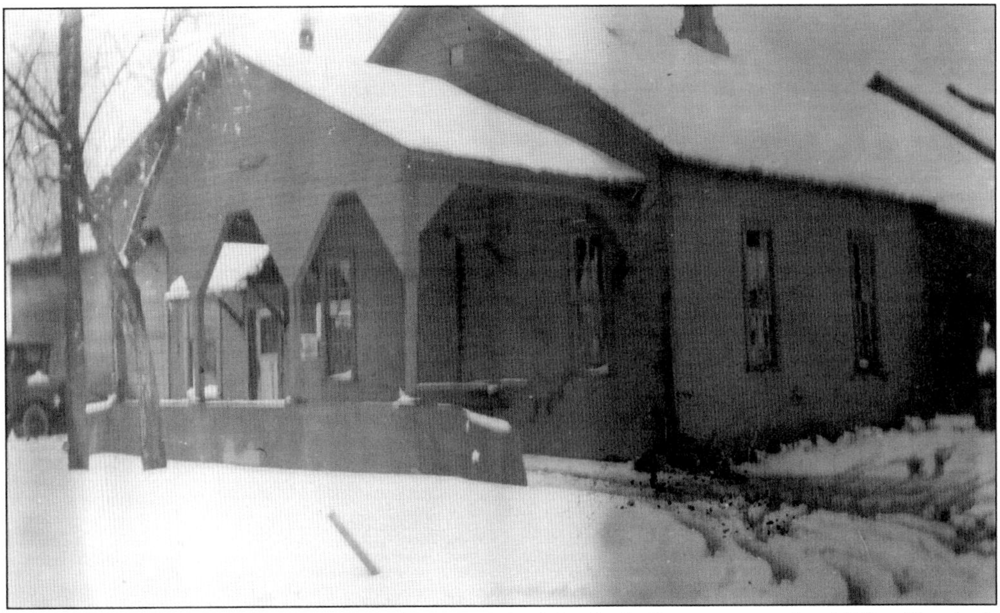

Local farmers brought their cream and eggs to the Hemlock Creamery in the 1800s. Hemlock Brand Butter was made here for decades and sold to the United States Army during World War II. Located on South Hemlock Road, it became the Hemlock Co-op, but the building remained for years until it was eventually replaced.

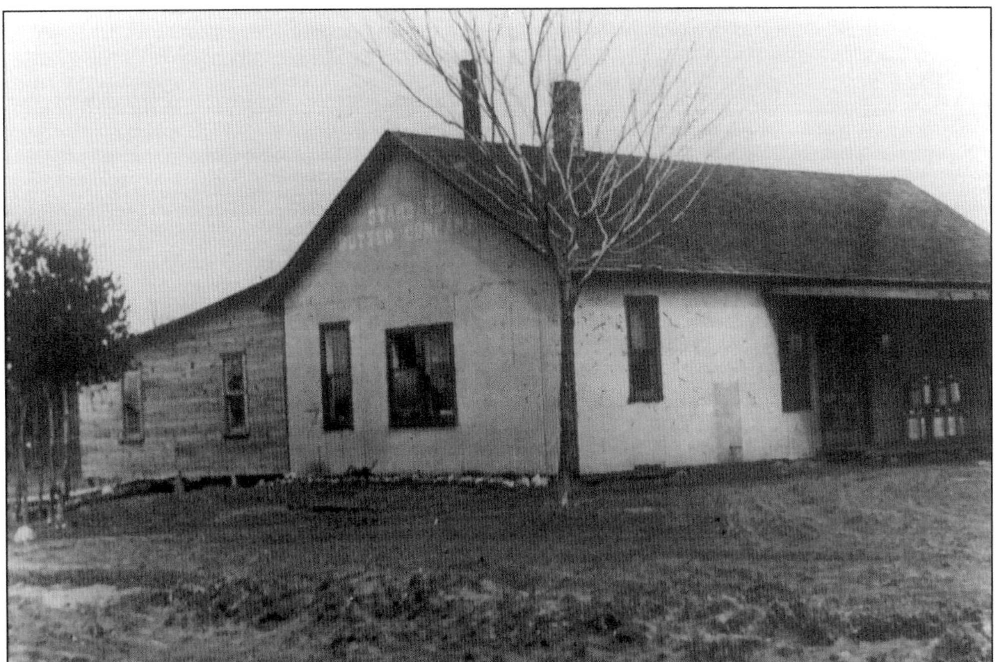

Harry Ammerman & Brother operated the Standard Butter Co. from 1907 to 1927. Every dairy farmer would sell his surplus milk to the cheese factory and his cream to this Burt creamery. Until cream separators were used, milk was set in crocks until the cream rose to the top. Then it was skimmed off and sold to the creamery for butter making.

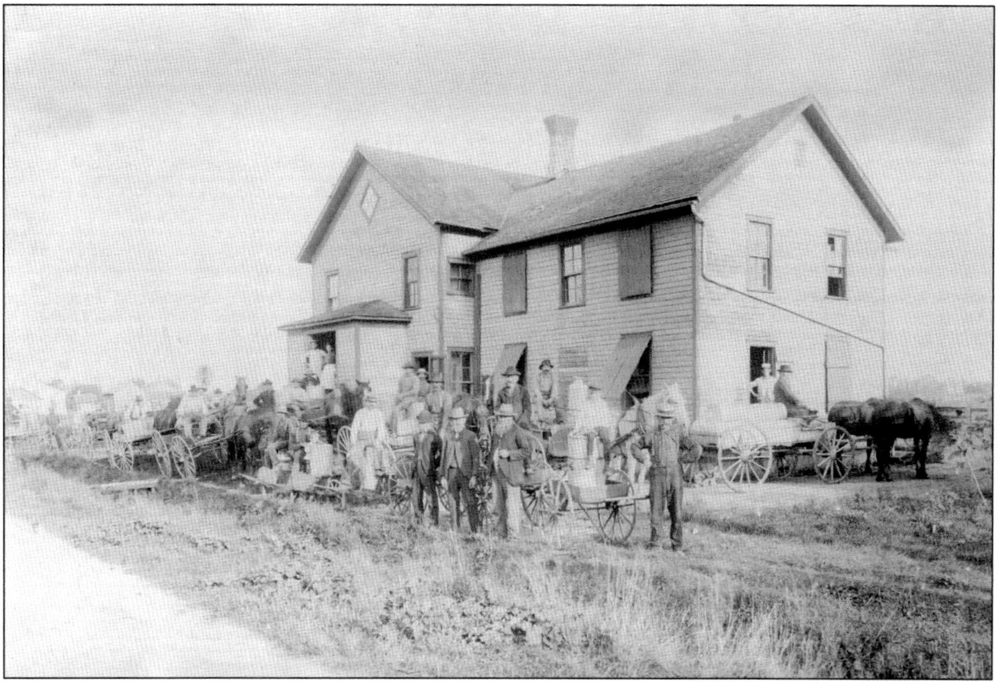

Herman Kueffner lived upstairs over his creamery and cheese factory in Frankentrost Township. Several local farmers with their horses, wagons, and milk cans are socializing while waiting their turn to sell their milk and cream. Kueffner made butter and more than 2,500 loaves of cheese annually until this factory burned in 1908.

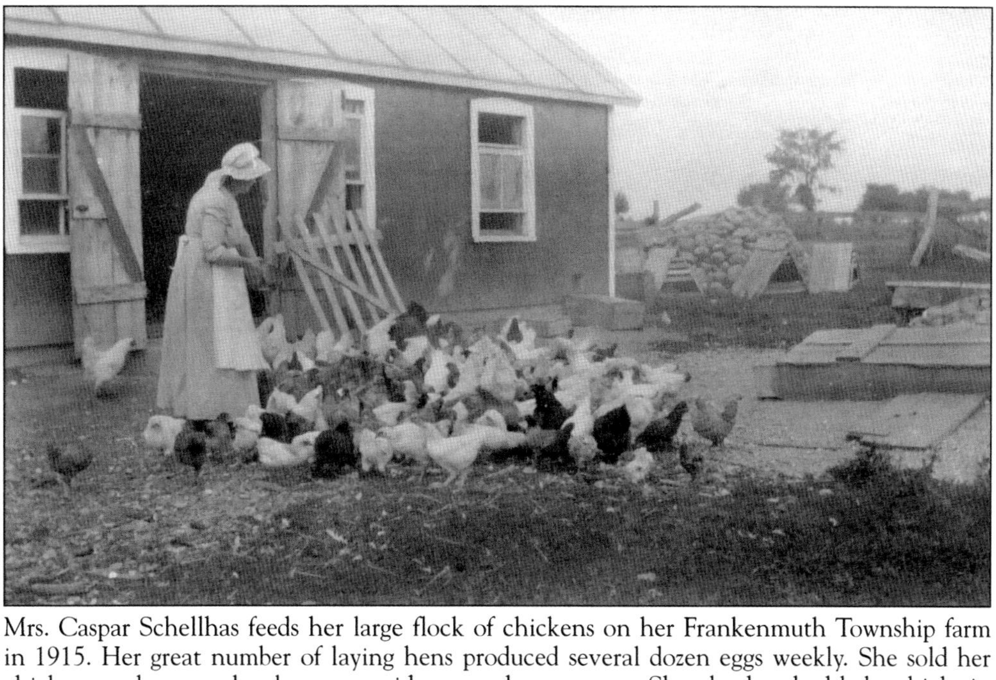

Mrs. Caspar Schellhas feeds her large flock of chickens on her Frankenmuth Township farm in 1915. Her great number of laying hens produced several dozen eggs weekly. She sold her chickens and eggs to local stores, residents, and restaurants. She also hatched baby chicks in the teepee-wood huts next to the rock piles on the right.

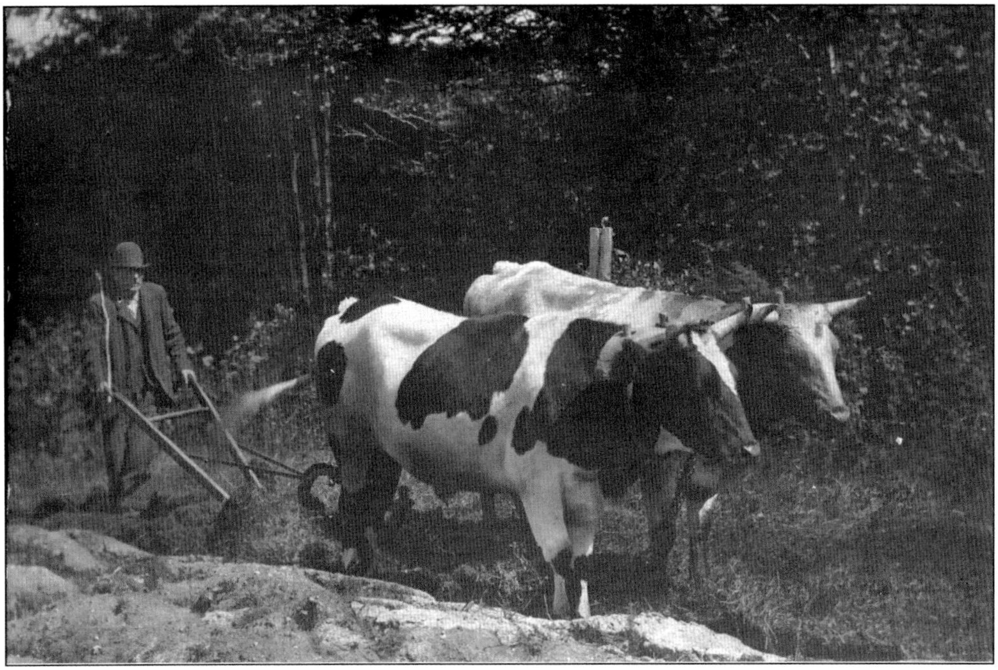

Albert Bates plows his Washington Road farm field with two oxen in 1877. After arriving from New York in 1854, he lived in South Saginaw and worked on the Saginaw River until 1861 when he bought his 107-acre Bridgeport farm. Early county settlers often used oxen for their farm and lumber work.

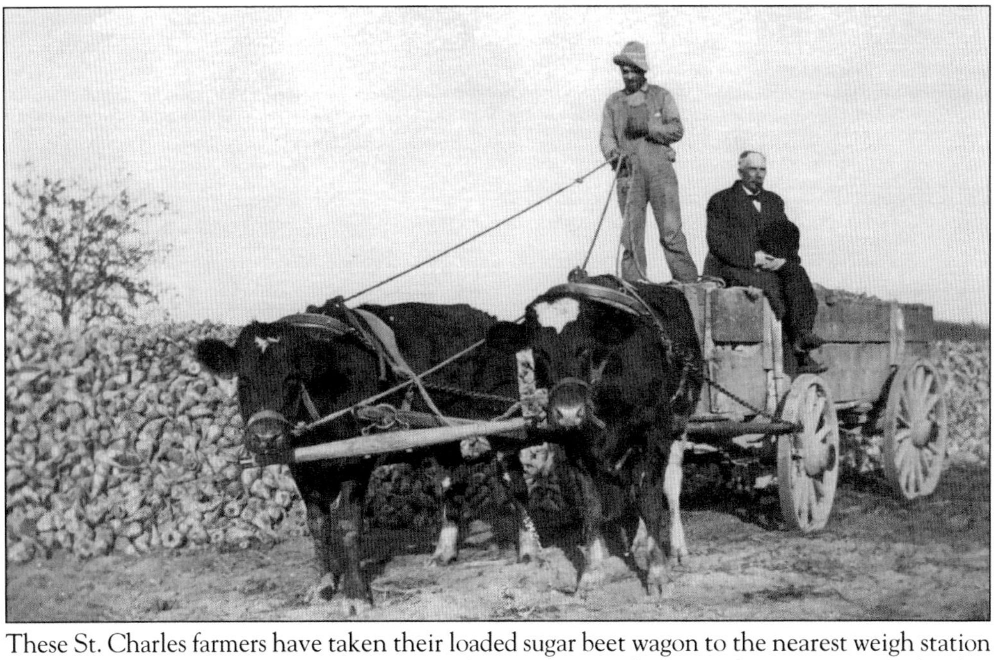

These St. Charles farmers have taken their loaded sugar beet wagon to the nearest weigh station to be transported by freight train to a sugar factory in Carrollton or Alma. Farmers used either oxen or horses for this heavy farm work. Beets were loaded and unloaded manually. Loading and delivering one load of sugar beets took an entire day.

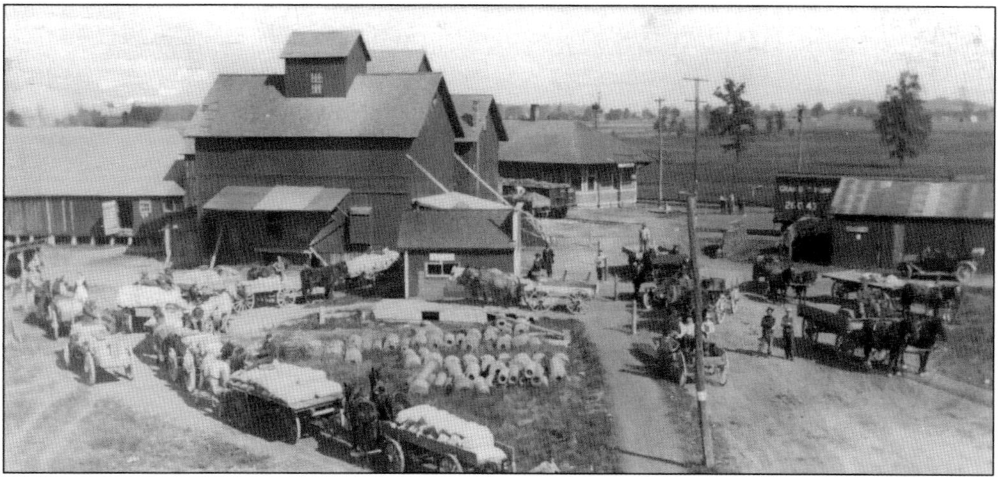

Farmers with their teams and wagons are queued outside the Old Feed Mill on Sixth Street in Freeland. Built in 1893 by Bay City Grain Co., ownership changed frequently—the facility was subsuquently a part of the Dietiker-Howd Elevator, the Freeland Elevator Co., Wolohan Elevator, Wickes Agriculture, and Pillsbury. Since 1985, Berger and Company has operated it as ConAgra Company. After local farmers hauled their sugar beets to the elevator, they piled them next to the street as shown below. Across the street is a residence. The railroad located in the rear of the elevator delivered the beets to Michigan Sugar Company in Carrollton.

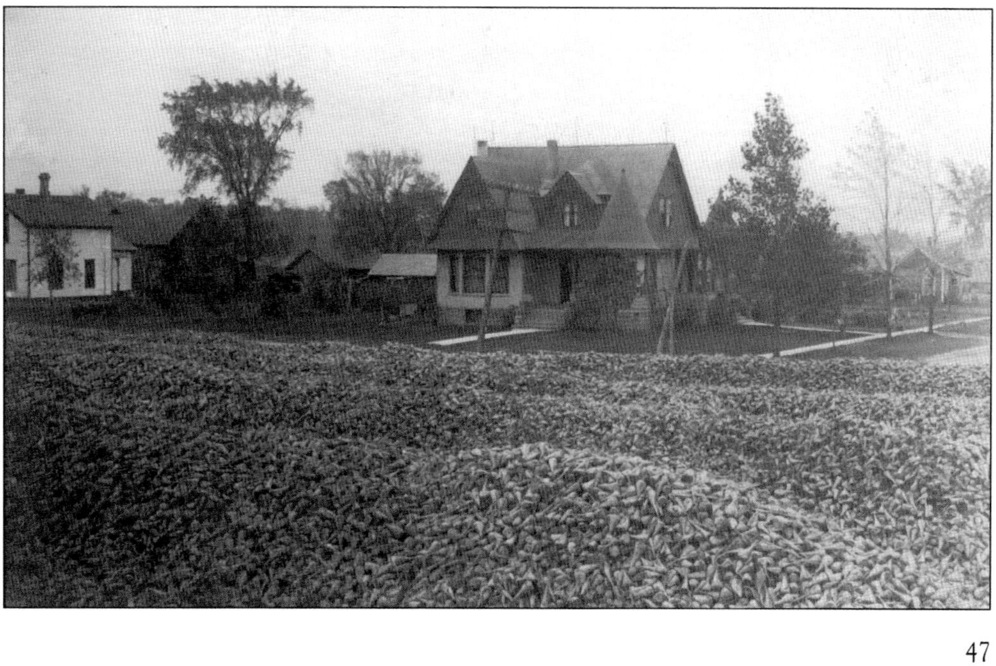

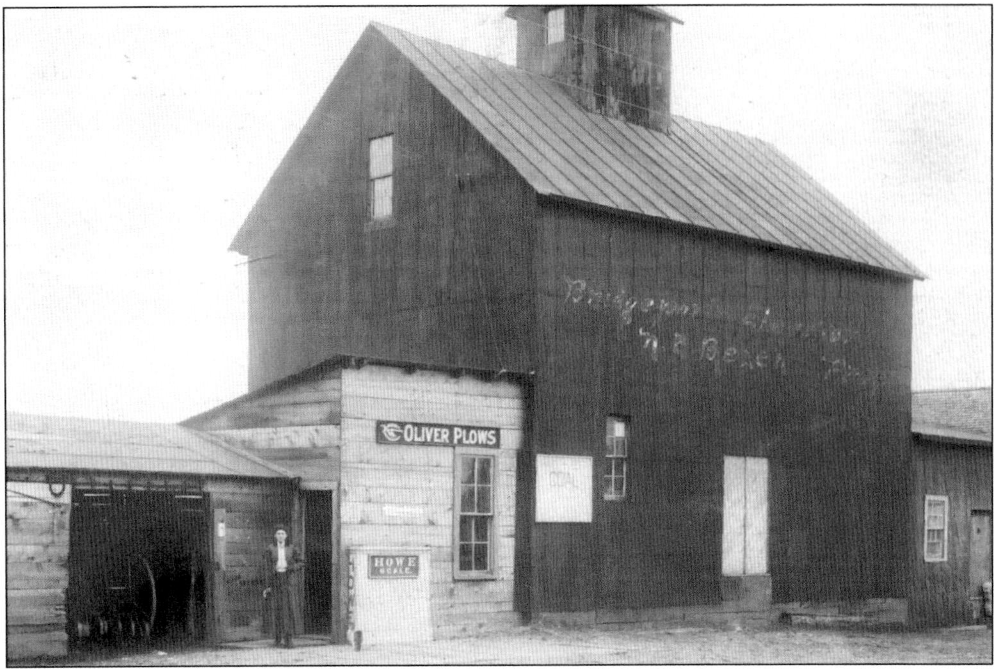

Olive Beach is standing in front of the Bridgeport Elevator Co., managed by her husband, Noah E. Beach, *c.* 1900. Local farmers brought their grain to this elevator to be sold or milled. Noah was a grandson of the Honorable Noah Beach who settled in Bridgeport in 1842, helped organize the township, and served as Democratic Senator in Lansing.

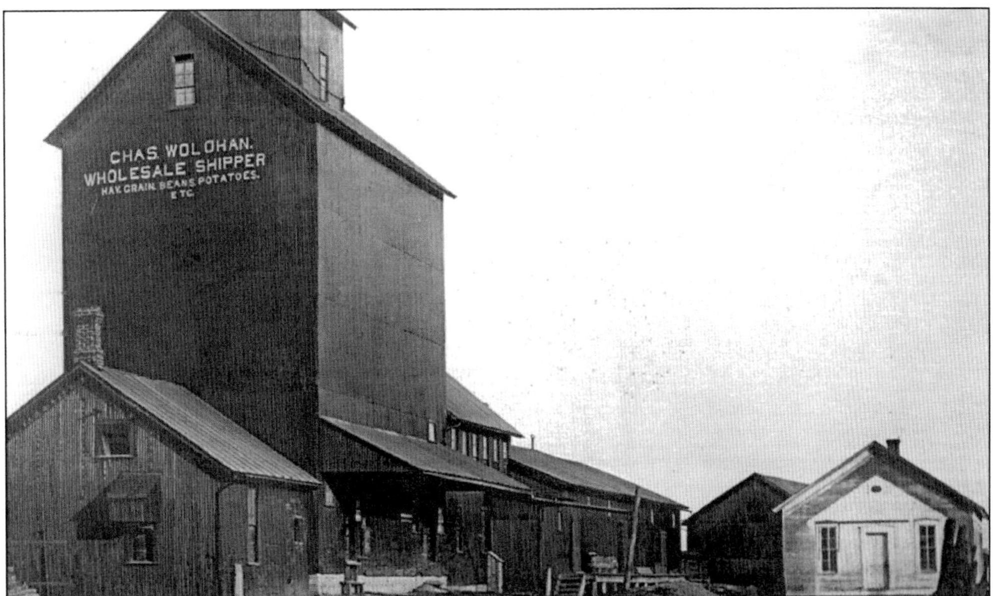

Charles Wolohan taught school and worked in a hardware store before purchasing the Birch Run elevator in 1896. After the elevator burned in 1898, he built the grain elevator shown here. He moved the school where he taught to the site on the right. The Wolohan Grain Elevator was Birch Run's main business. Wolohan also owned other county elevators.

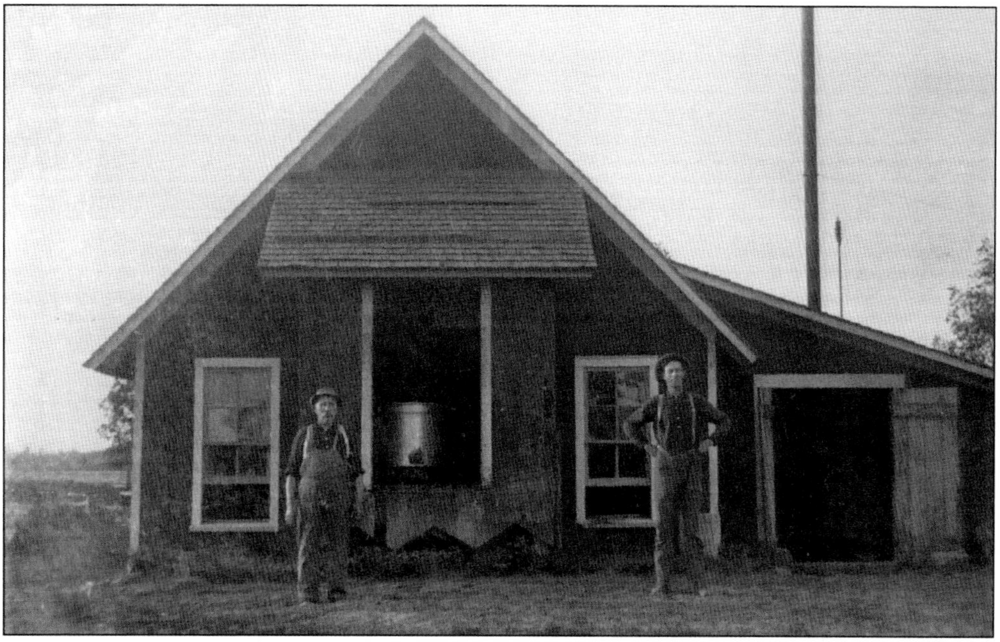

The Blackmar Village began with Abel T. Blackmar's sawmill, shingle mill, and salt works in Taymouth Township in 1852. A general store, cheese factory, post office, and Pere Marquette Railroad flag station followed. Postmaster Sylvester Judd ran the post office and flag station from his home. Benton Glasser and George Judd stand in front of the cheese factory above. Farmers brought their milk and traded in George Judd's adjacent store (below) on a daily basis. In the 1898 photo, shown below, the Judd family poses, from left to right: (on the porch) Will, Ola, Mary, Marion, Annie, and Raynor; (on the horse) Margaret; and (in the buggy) Clarence and Sylvester.

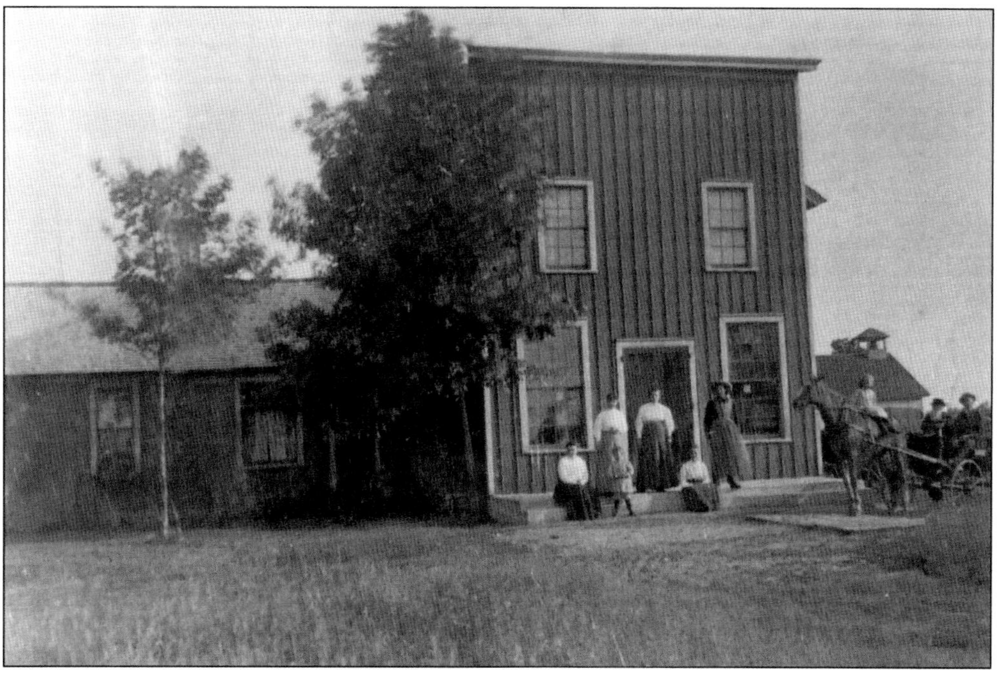

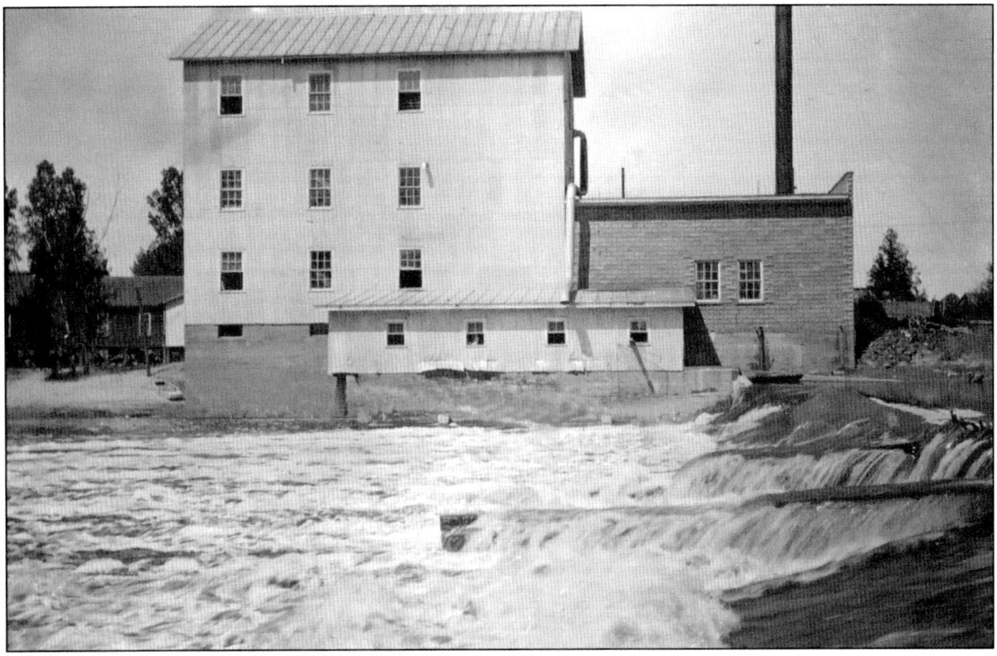

The Hubinger Brothers built the first gristmill and dam in Frankenmuth in 1848. Wheat, oats, and corn were ground for the local farmers. The mill burned in 1910. The Frankenmuth Milling Company built the above mill. In 1920 it became the Star of the West Milling Company. Since 1912, the Power Company and then the village used the dam.

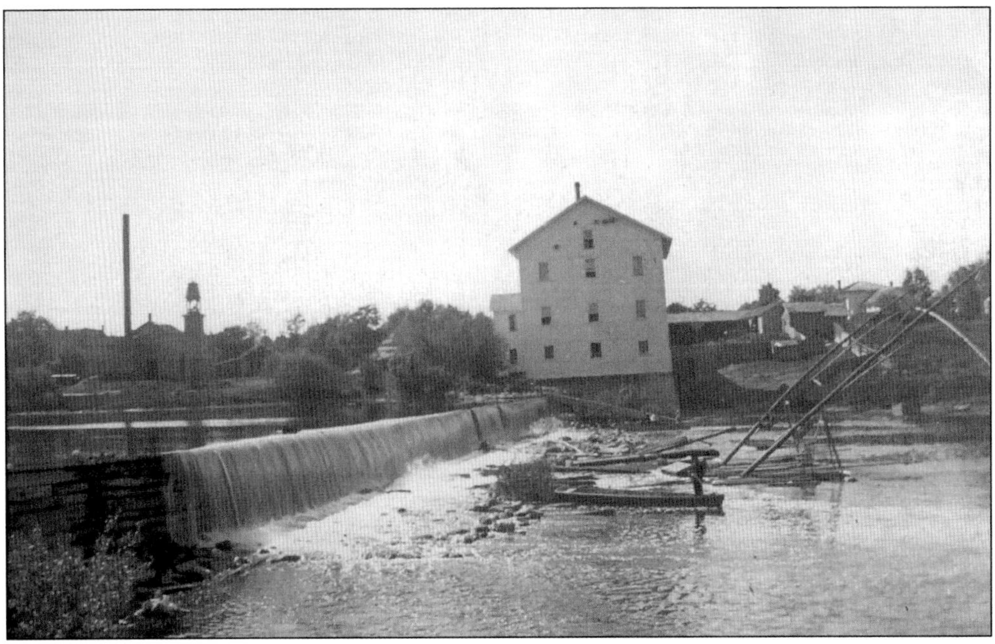

The Chapman Brothers bought Chesaning's first flourmill built in 1867 and added the roller system to process local grain into flour and corn meal. The village offices, water works, and electric light plant were built in 1895, shown in the distant left. The man in the boat is scraping gravel from the Shiawassee River to sell as washed stone. The mill burned in 1953 and Sarah's Attic was built.

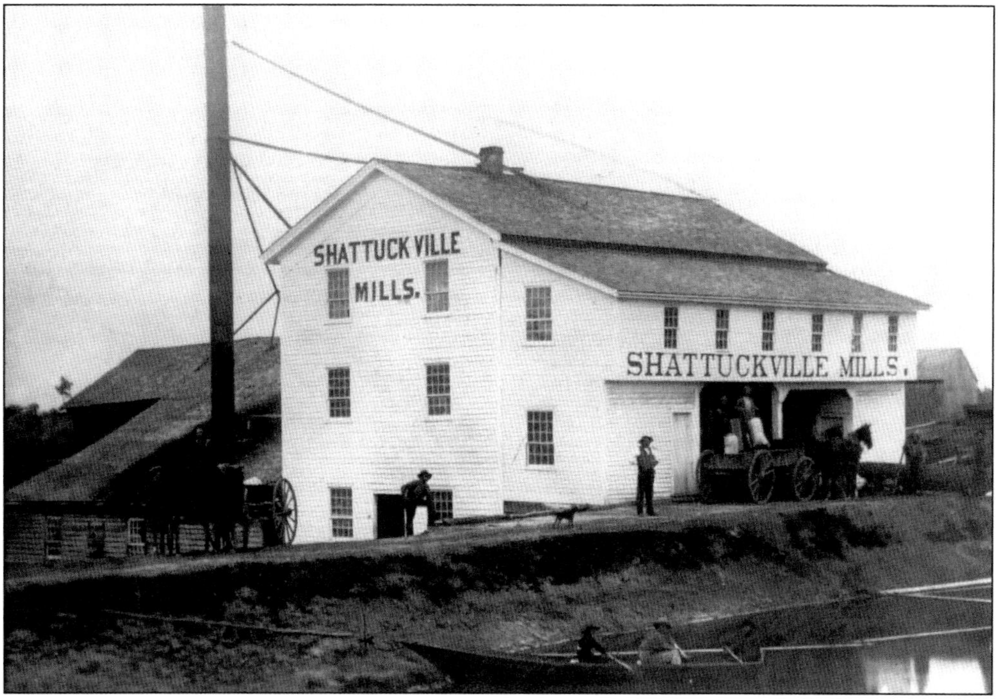

Samuel Shattuck and his new bride, Catherine Beach, established a sawmill and gristmill in Saginaw Township in 1842. A millpond and dam on Shattuck Creek supplied the waterpower. Shattuckville emerged with several farms, five streets, a creek bridge, wagon shop, cider mill, blacksmith, general store, and post office. Farmers from Thomastown, Tittabawassee, and Saginaw Townships brought their grain to be milled and traded at the store. The mill shown above stood where Shattuck and Midland Roads intersect today. The bottom photo shows the Shattuck home and millpond.

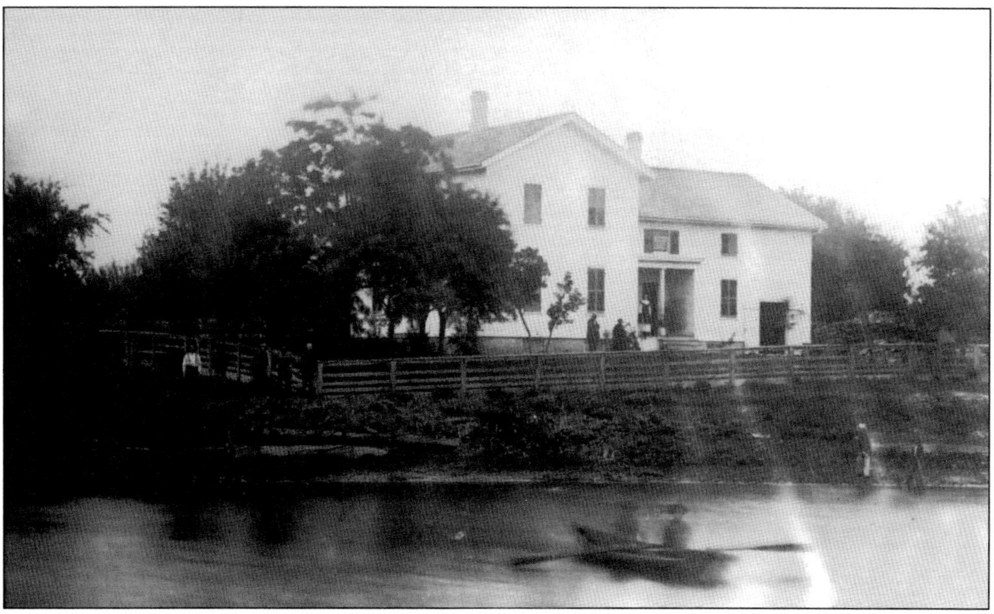

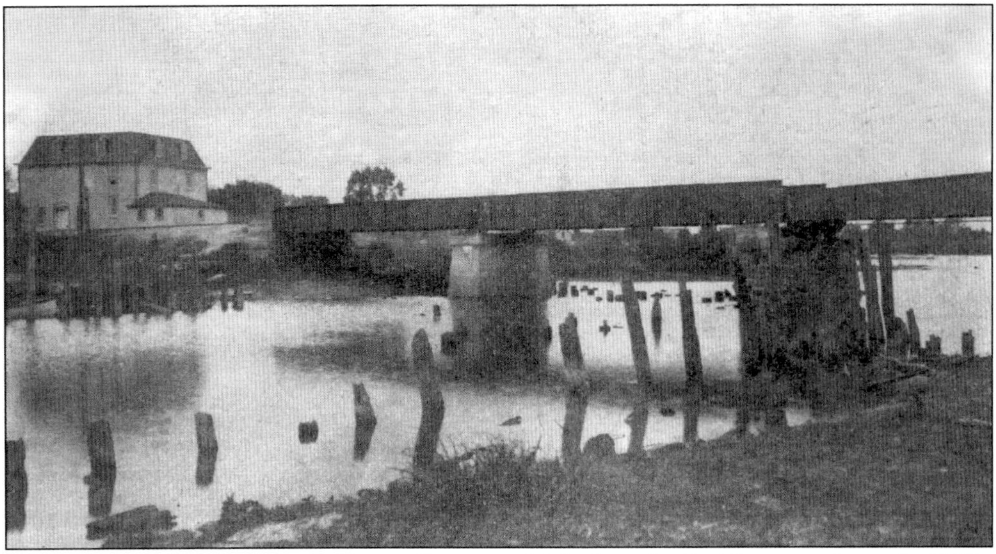

This St. Charles Roller Process Flourmill was established on the Bad River in the early 1900s. Michigan Central Railroad's old logging drawbridge extended to the mill. The swing span opened for passing boats. Farmers brought their grain and beans. Young women were hired as beanery workers cleaning beans for 1¢ per pound.

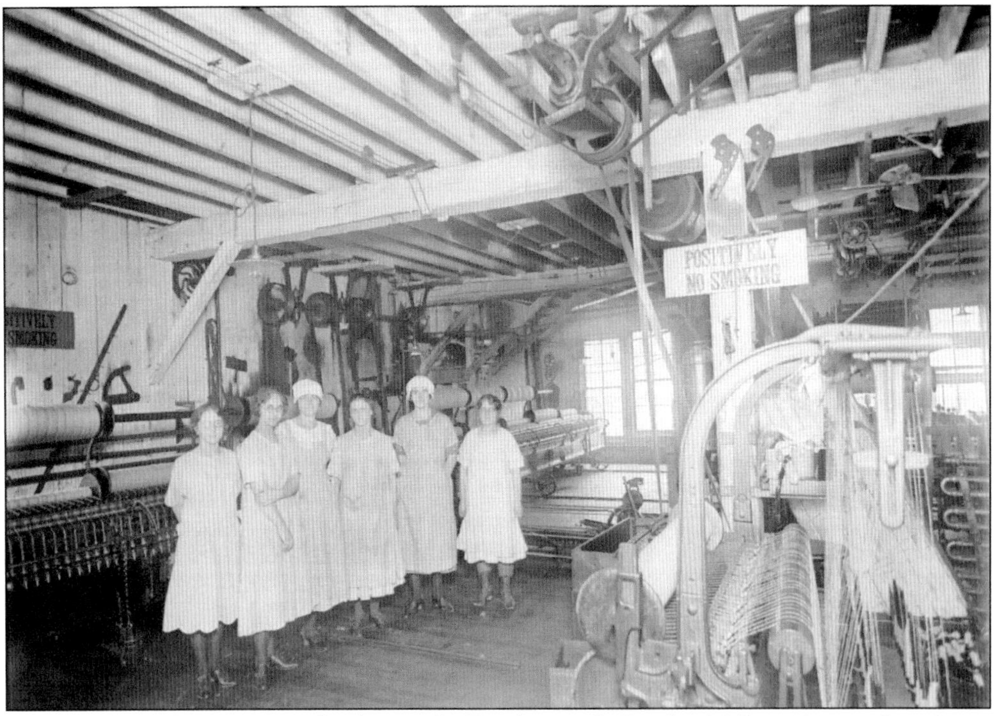

Franz Ranke and George Grueber began the Frankenmuth Woolen Mill in 1894, making horse blankets, lumbermen's mittens and socks, and wool comforters. Shown in this 1922 photo, women who ran the knitting machines are, from left to right: Nina Felgner, Molly Schmidt, Florence Eischer, Laura Kueffner, Meta Rodammer, and Elle Uebler. Mill products were shipped around the country.

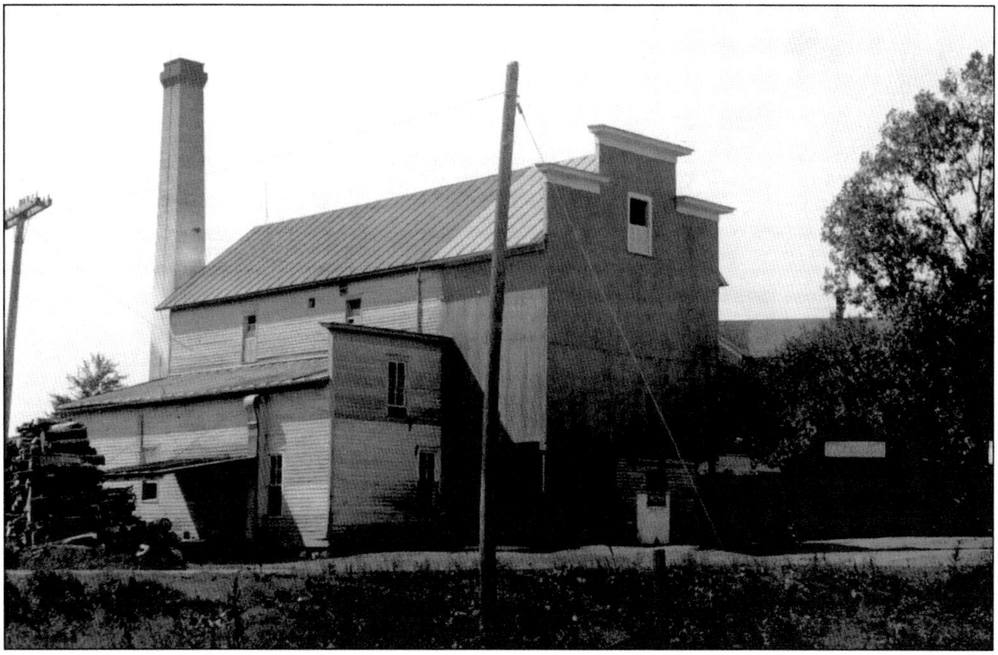

In the 1870s, John M. Hubinger built this roller flourmill on the Cass River. Lorenz Hubinger ran the mill until the Star of the West Milling Company took over in 1903 with John G. Hubinger Sr. as president. Rebuilt in 1911, the plant mills Michigan wheat into pie, cracker, and cookie flours, trucking both the wheat and flour in and out of Frankenmuth.

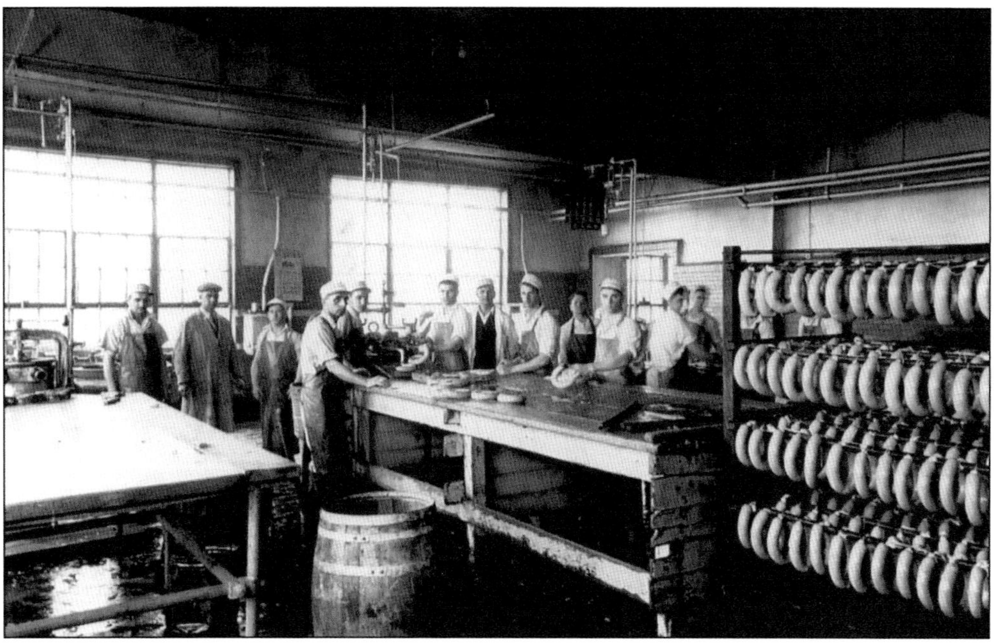

George Peet began his retail meat market store in Chesaning in 1885, buying and selling livestock locally. He also purchased livestock to ship to Chicago and Detroit. He built Peet Packing Plant in 1901 to purchase and process meat for his ham and veal specialties. In 1920 the corporation distributed nationwide. Farmer Peet's employed local residents.

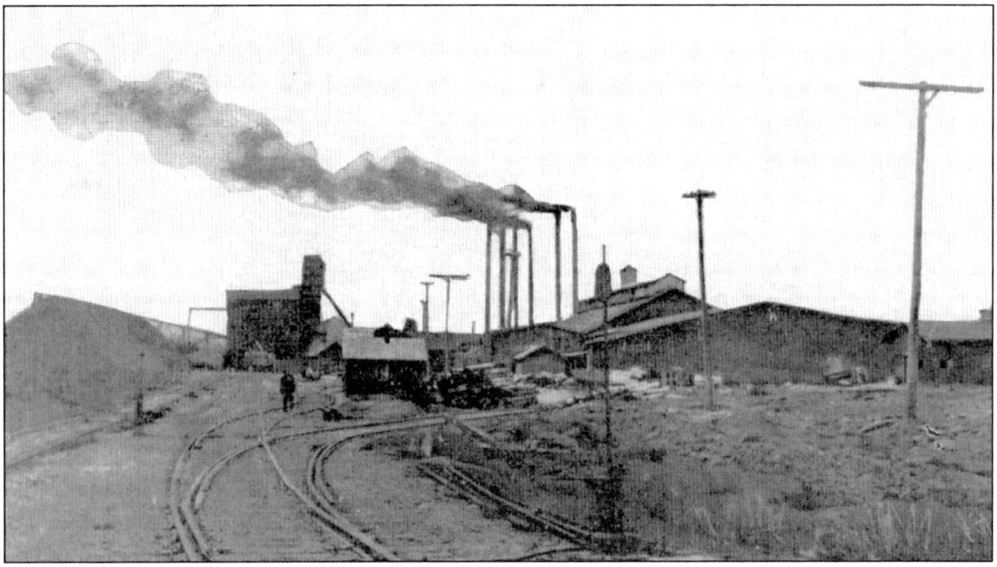

St. Charles' first coal mining activities began in 1896. The Robert Gage Coal Mine shown above began in 1900, employed 200 men, and mined 500 tons of coal daily. Miners carried their own carbide lamp, pick, shovel, and lunch pail, going underground in the tipple's cages. Coal was mined with the "Room & Pillar" method, with individual rooms assigned to each miner who broke up the dynamited coal chunks from the previous evening, as shown below. The last county mine closed in 1952 in Swan Creek Township.

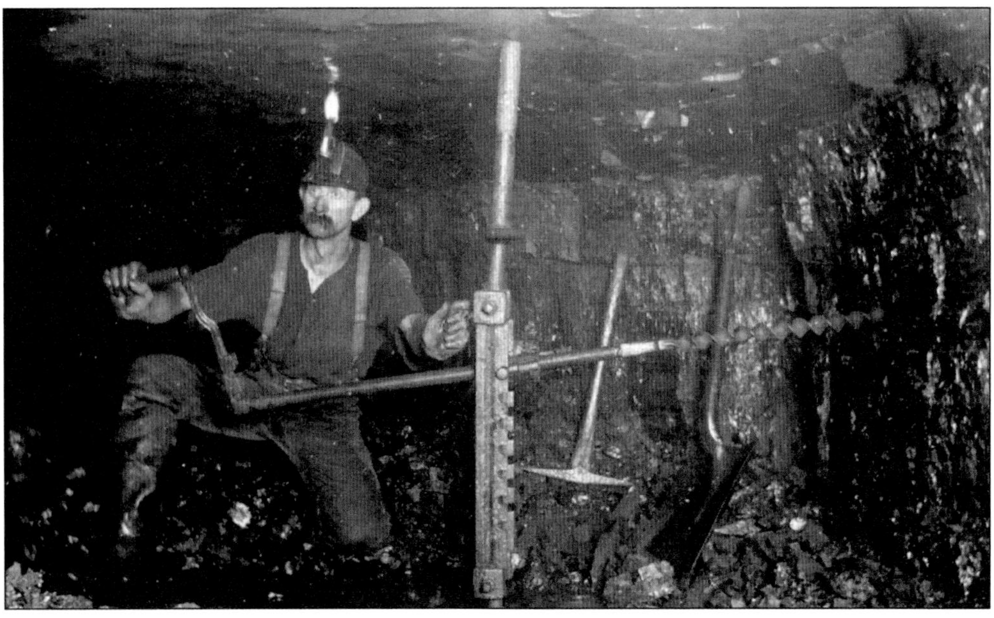

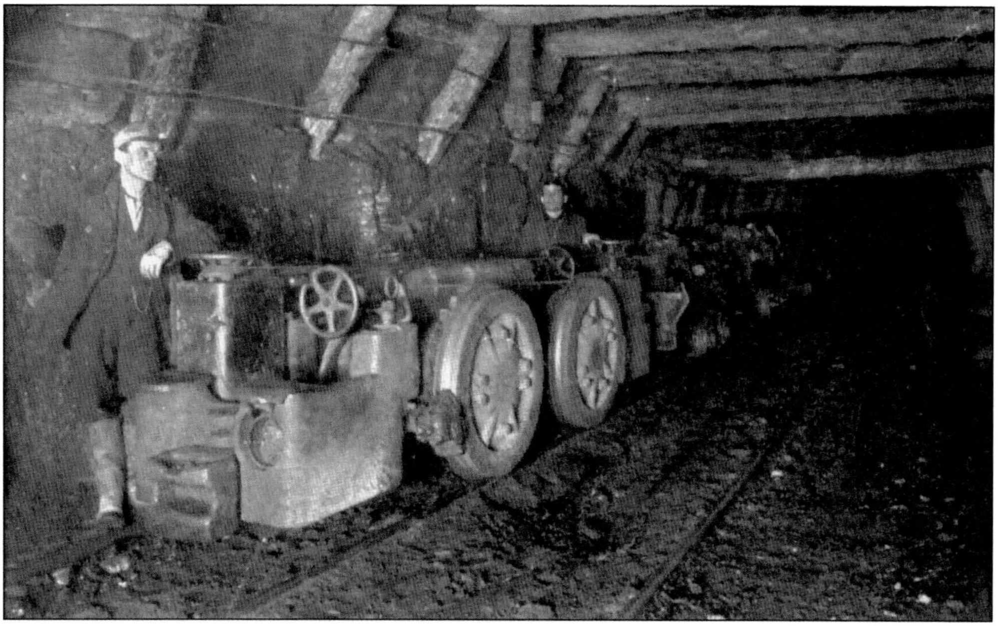

Coal miners loaded their coal chunks into small underground rail cars. Before electricity, little mules that lived underground would pull the cars. The electric rail cars were moved mechanically underground. All cars were pulled above ground in the tipple's cages. Miners could see in the black underground only by their head lamp. All coal miners were unionized.

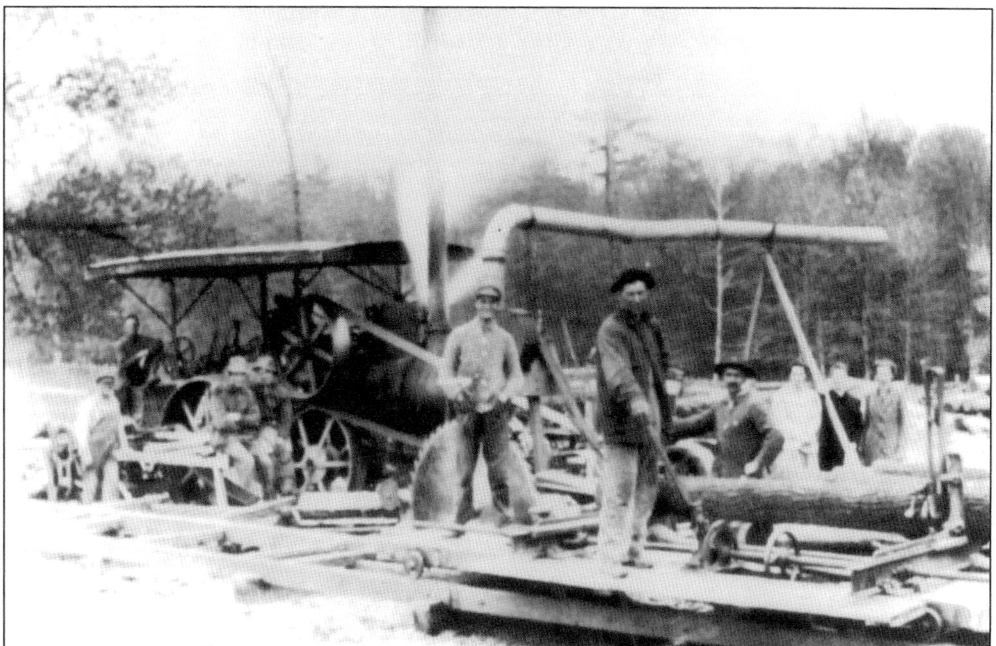

F. Hood & Company owned Oakley's only Steam, Stave & Heading Mill that was run by Daniel Mahoney. George Sackrider built Oakley's sawmill in 1870. A portable sawmill traveled to farms in the wooded Brady Township, cutting logs inaccessible to rivers. On the left, Ed Stickle and Frank Fickies are cutting a log, while on the right Maud Byam and friends watch.

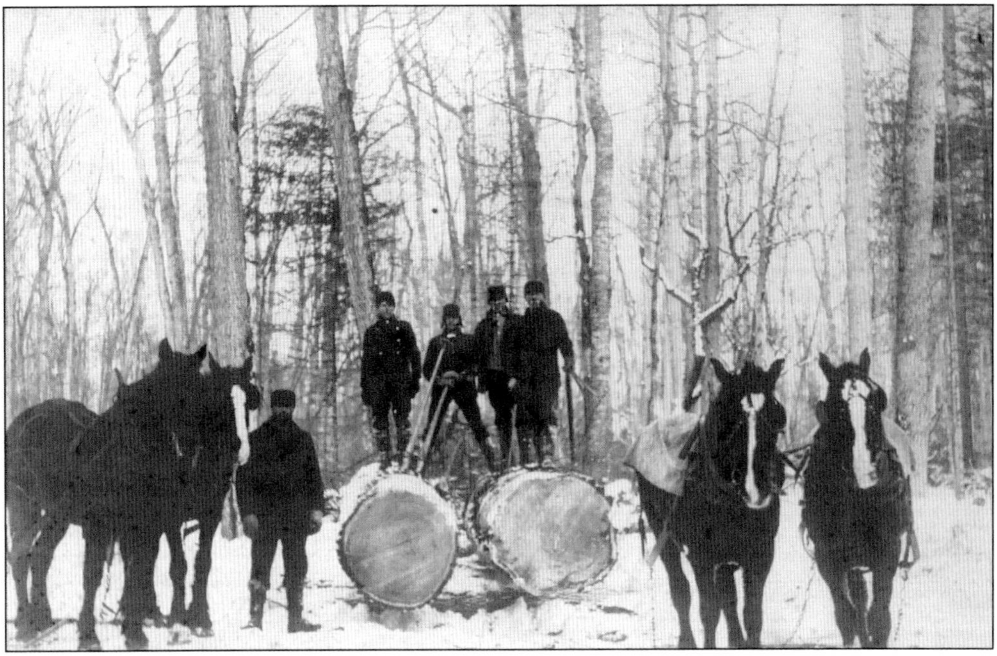

Every Saginaw County township was heavily timbered. Both of these Chesaning area scenes were repeated many times throughout the county during the1800s. Timber harvesting was done during the snow season from November through February. Shanty boys are loading logs for the horses to haul to a riverbank; the logs will be floated to a sawmill in the spring. The lumber camp crew has posed outside their log shanty. A husband, wife, and children lived at the camp and did all the camp cooking.

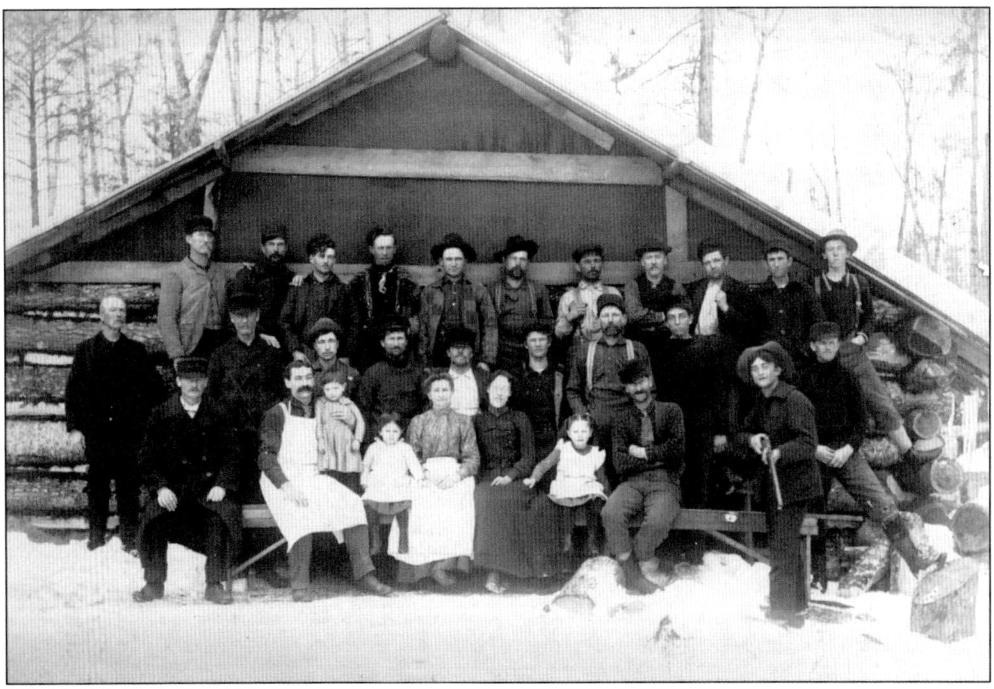

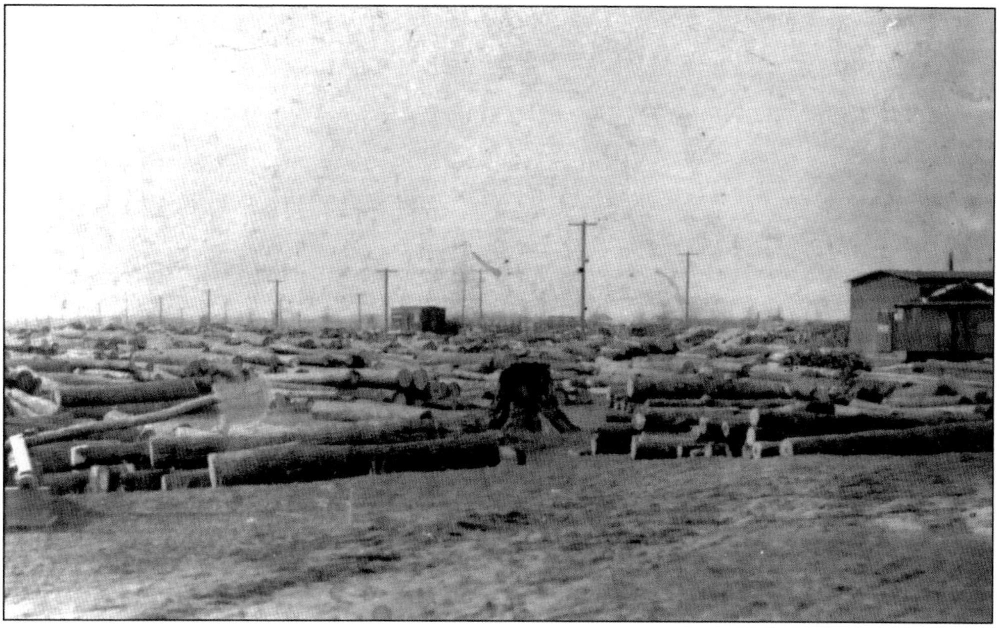

Hemlock City was named after its heavy timber tracts. Because no logging rivers ran through Richland Township, Plank Road (now M-46) was built to transport logs to Saginaw sawmills. These logs were cut on the James Henry Sawmill in 1880 and were loaded to be transported on Plank Road or the railroad to Saginaw City or St. Louis.

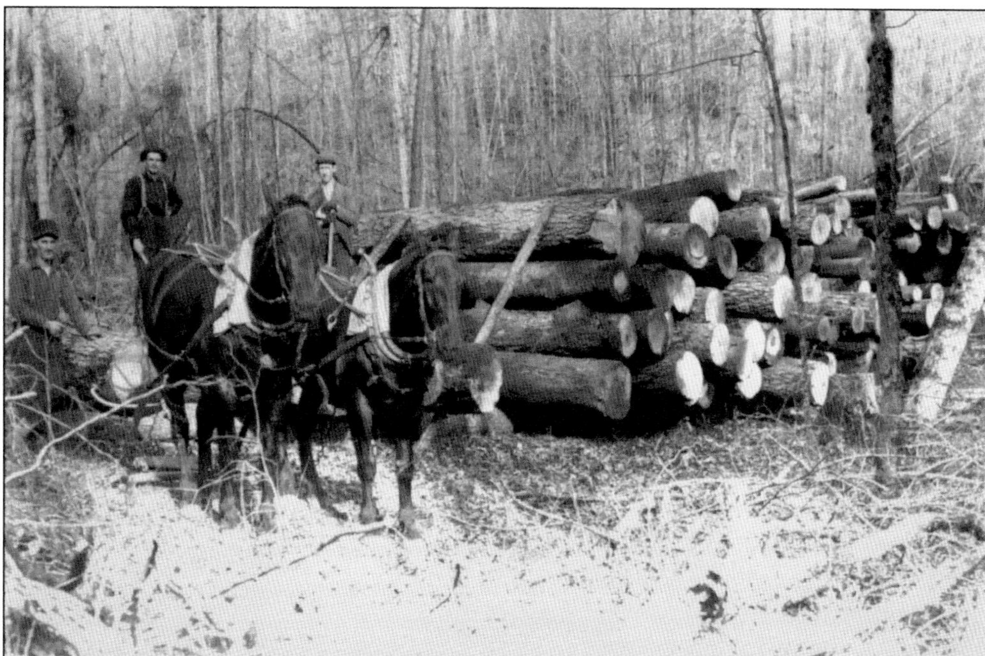

These men are hauling logs with their horses for the Richmond Lumber Company on Sharon Road in St. Charles *c.* 1894. Because of its dense forest, St. Charles' earliest settlers could arrive only on the Shiawassee and Bad Rivers. As more land was cleared, the only remaining timber was inland or away from the logging rivers.

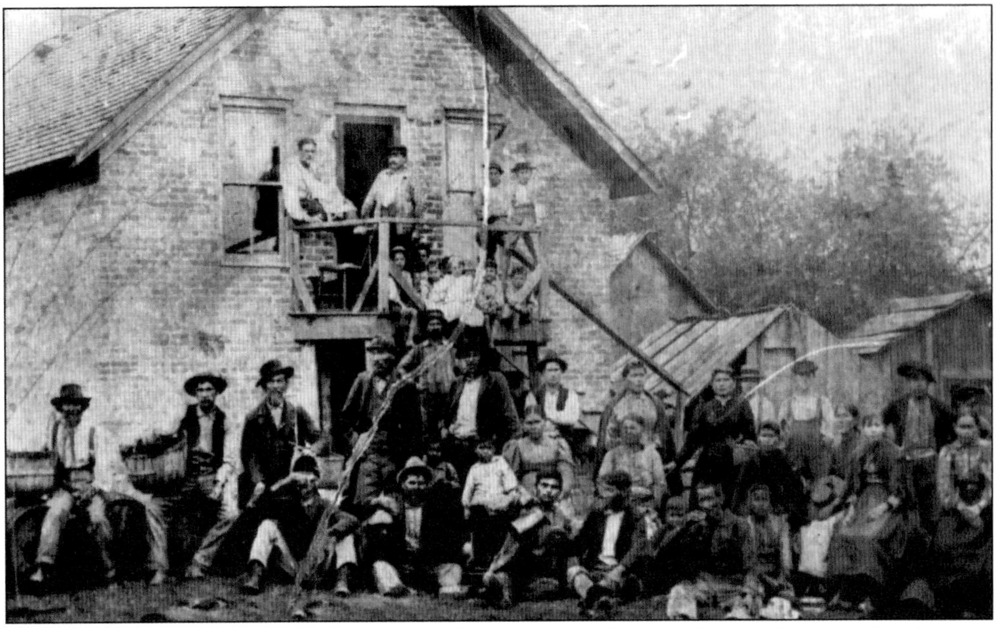

Born in Saginaw City in 1831, Gardner W. Foster bought his Taymouth Township farm in 1861. His seven children built homes on his farm. Fosters Village emerged. Gardner and Edward built "Foster's Wine Cellar" buying grapes from local Indians, and making and selling wine to Saginaw saloons or locally for 25¢ a gallon. The dance hall was upstairs.

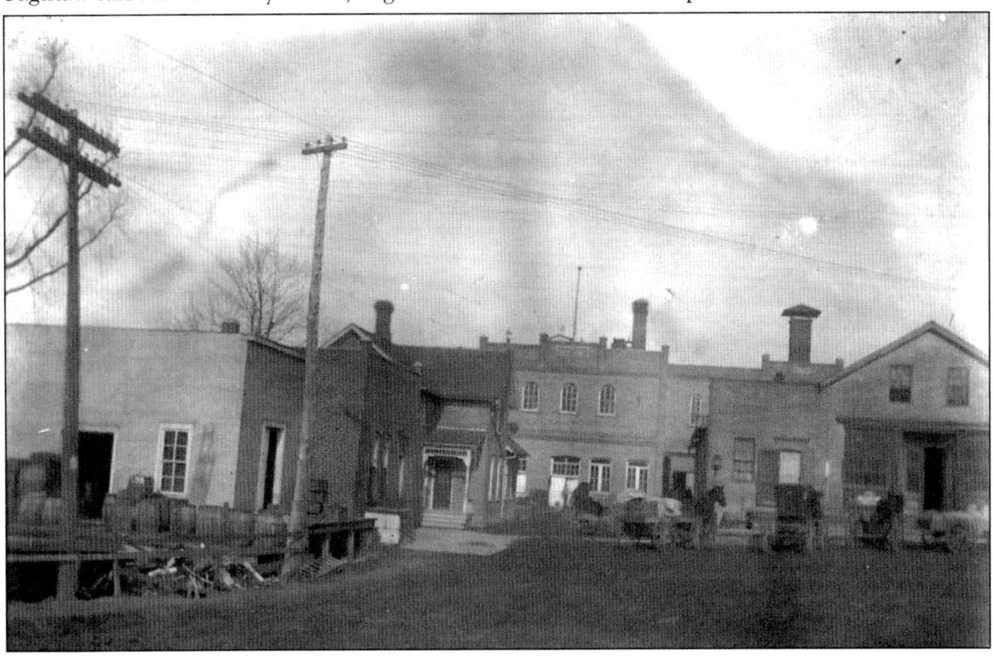

Unlike the family-owned Frankenmuth breweries, which had existed since 1857, the stockholder-owned Frankenmuth Brewing Company was organized in 1899. Farmers sold their grain here to be brewed into the "Gold Medal Beer." On the left is the brewery, then the brick house offices, and Block's/Zucker Saloon is on the far right. It became Carling's in 1956. Today it is Riverplace.

Four

Strolling Down Main Street

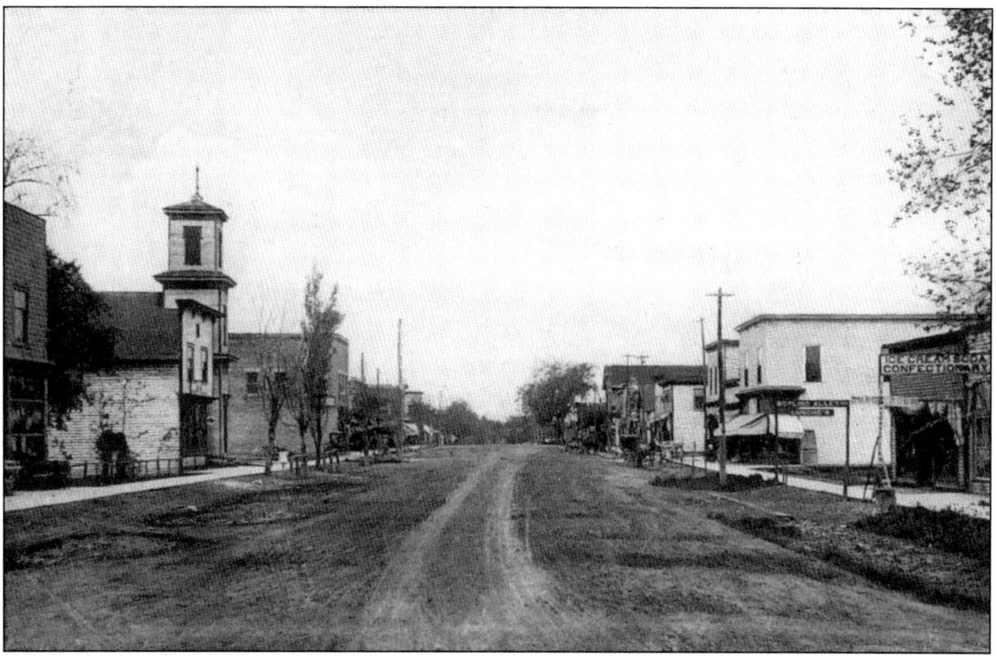

Every town had its Main Street for residents to shop, conduct their business, and socialize. Unpaved Saginaw Street in St. Charles had pine plank sidewalks in 1903. Looking north toward the bridge on the left are Armstrong's Shoe Store, Dr. McEwen's office, the Methodist Church, and Clinton Street. On the right, the empty lot is Mrs. Nickels' Flower Garden, or the town park, and the three Nickels' and Rogers' stores.

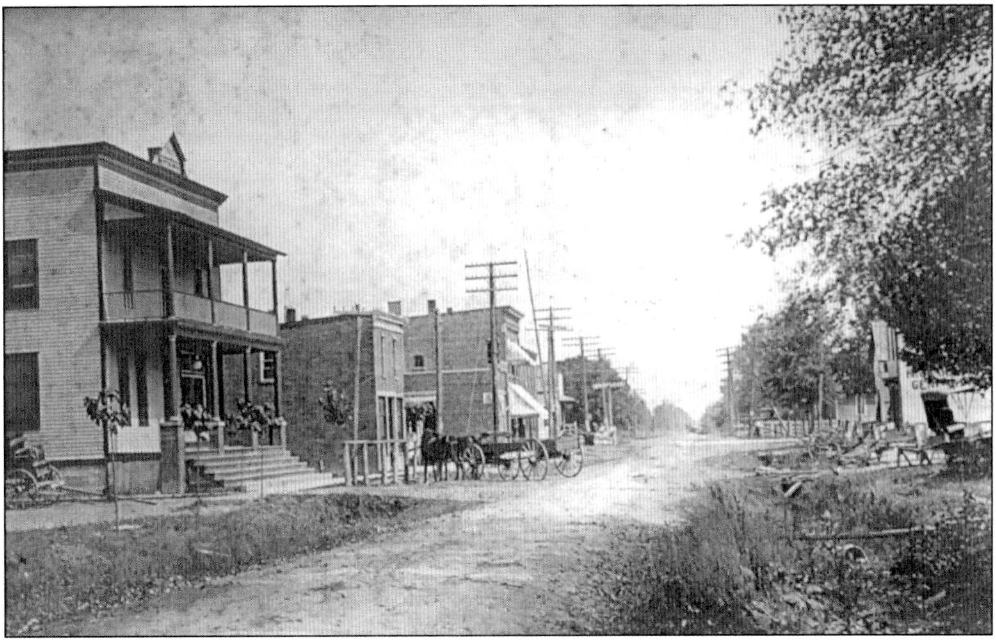

Schmitzer's Center House, on the left, was the main attraction on Birch Run's Main Street in 1909. Since it was near the Railroad Depot, travelers could stay overnight or visit the saloon. The village was becoming a bustling trading center for area farmers with its general store, blacksmith, bank, dry goods, drugs, and furniture store.

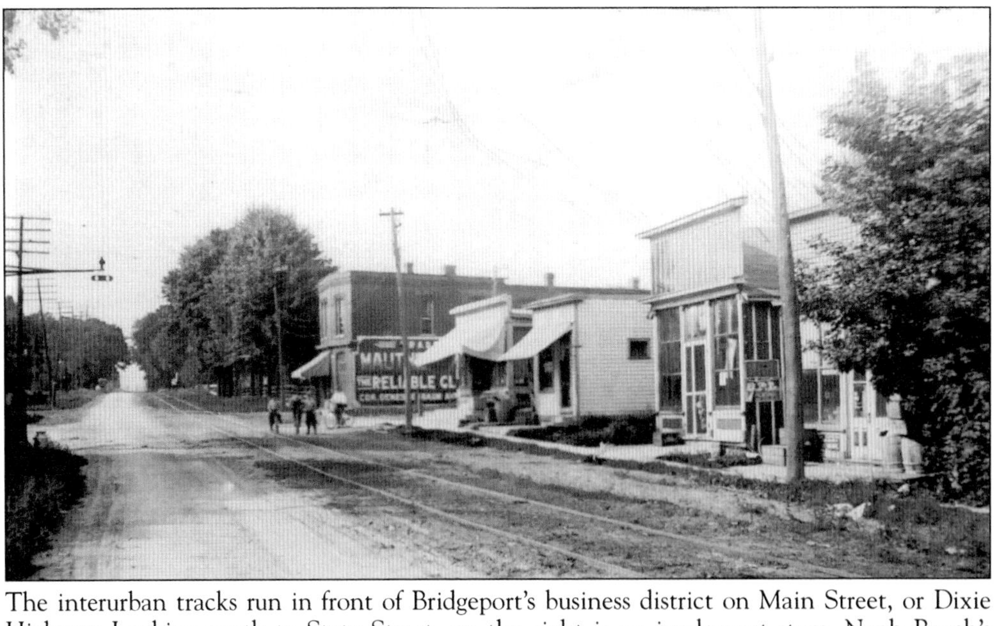

The interurban tracks run in front of Bridgeport's business district on Main Street, or Dixie Highway. Looking north to State Street, on the right is an implement store, Noah Beach's Hardware and Post Office, a barbershop, a grocery store, the State Street intersection, and Krause Saloon. Frederick Brueck originally built the saloon as a general store.

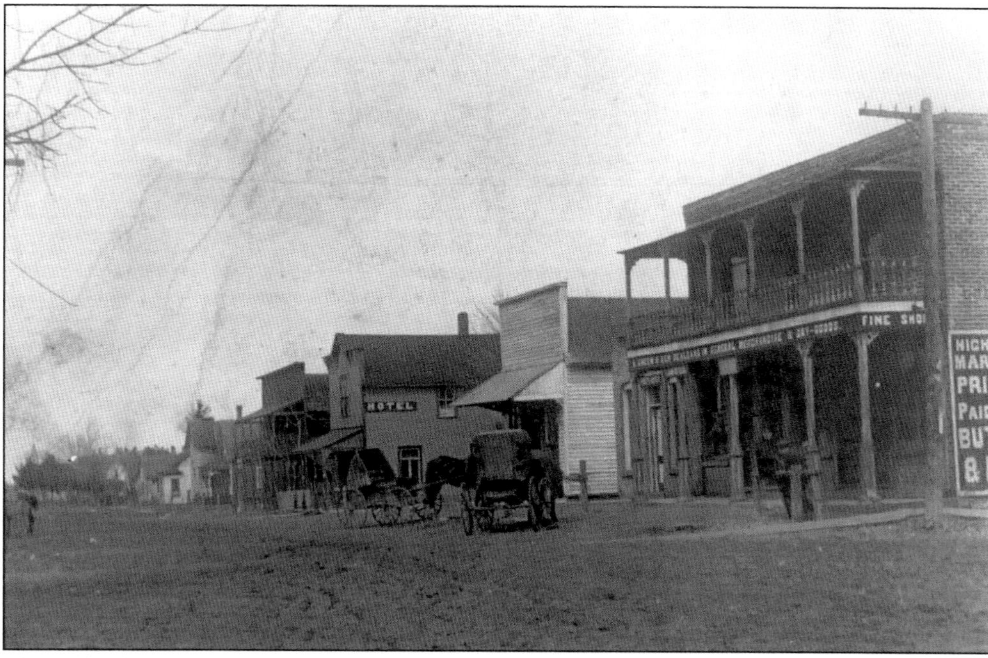

The self-sufficient village of Burt emerged in 1888 when Wellington R. Burt influenced the Cincinnati, Saginaw & Mackinaw Railroad to pass through Burt instead of nearby Morseville. Burt's Main Street had its saloon, store, hotel, post office, drug store, undertaking and furniture business, dressmakers, cigar maker, barber, and blacksmith shops.

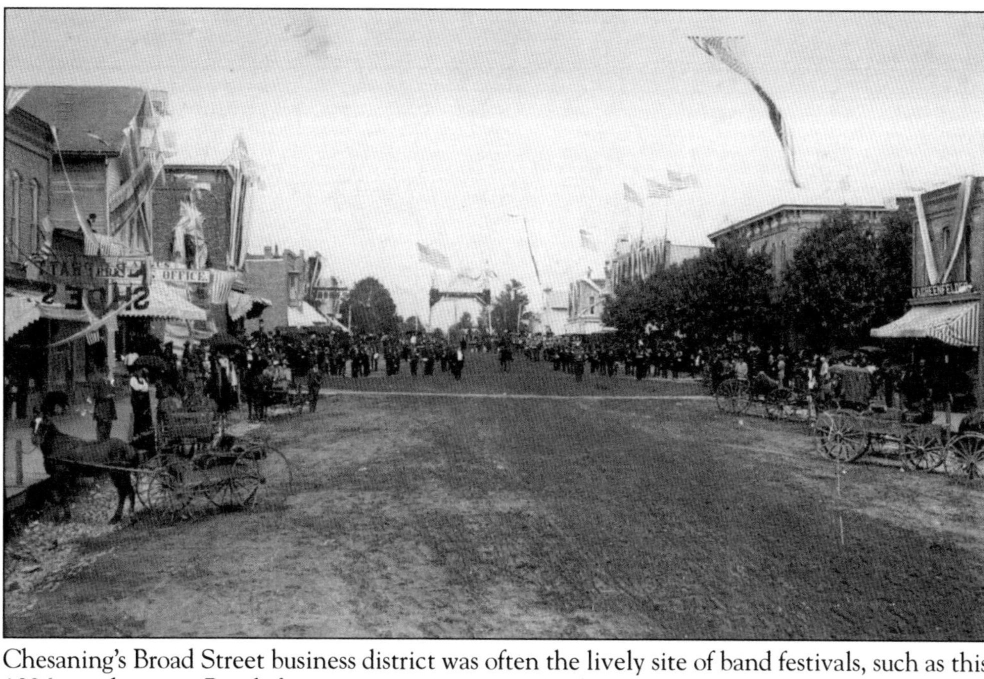

Chesaning's Broad Street business district was often the lively site of band festivals, such as this 1896 parade scene. Bands from area communities came by train for an enjoyable day of parades, concerts, and fun. A gazebo was brought out of storage and placed in the middle of Broad and Front Streets during Friday night concerts.

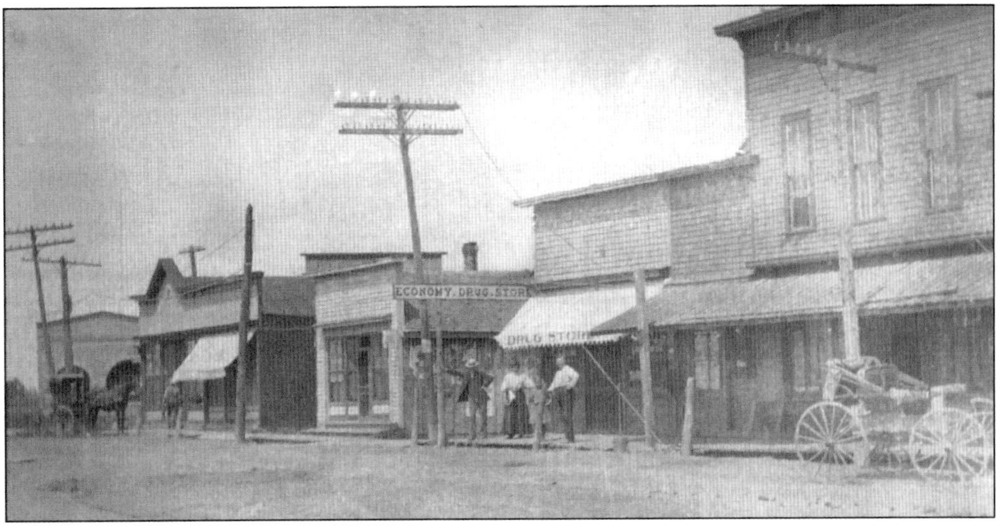

This early 1900s photo of the east side of Freeland's Main Street shows the bank in the far distant corner, as well as Dietiker's Store and Post Office, Valley Telephone office, Barbarin Drug Store, and Thurber's Restaurant. Trade from the riverboats, stagecoaches, railroad, and local residents made Freeland a very busy, growing community.

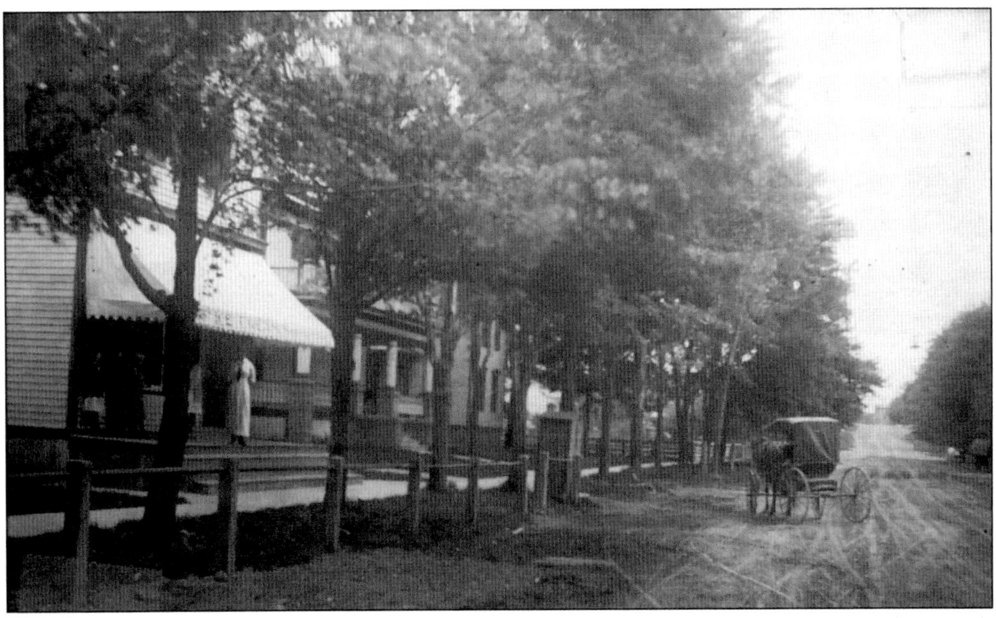

Dr. Hohn's Drug Store and Ice Cream Parlor on Frankenmuth's Main Street is always busy with local residents and travelers. Hitching posts outside the store make it convenient for visitors to park their horses and buggies. Pine plank sidewalks line the entire block. Wooden rail fences keep livestock from entering residential yards.

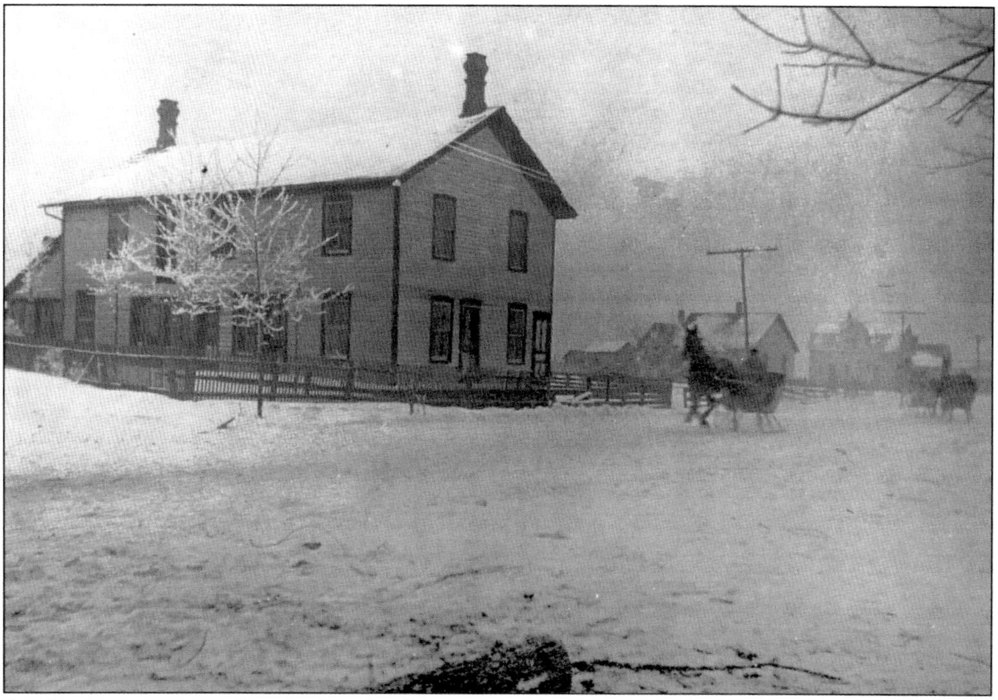

Freeland was named after the Freeland House run by Garrett and Elizabeth Freeland on Main and Washington Streets in 1857. Lumbermen and other travelers stopped often at "Mammy Freeland's." Eventually the town was called Freeland. The busy town had several hotels such as Trickey Hall (above) on the southeast corner of Church and Main Streets.

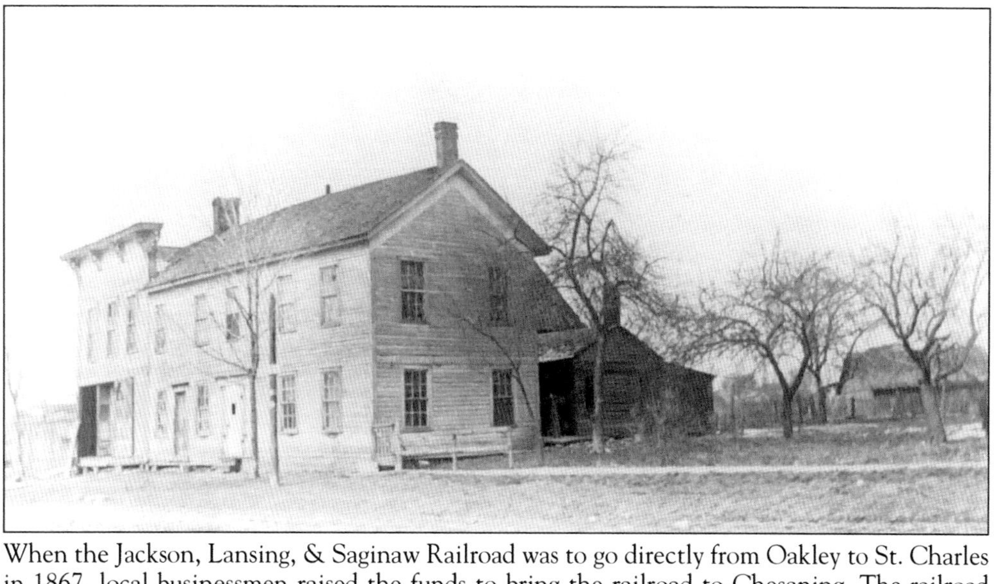

When the Jackson, Lansing, & Saginaw Railroad was to go directly from Oakley to St. Charles in 1867, local businessmen raised the funds to bring the railroad to Chesaning. The railroad brought travelers to Chesaning. This 1890s view of Post's Hotel, also known as Waverly House, was on top of the hill across the river from the business district.

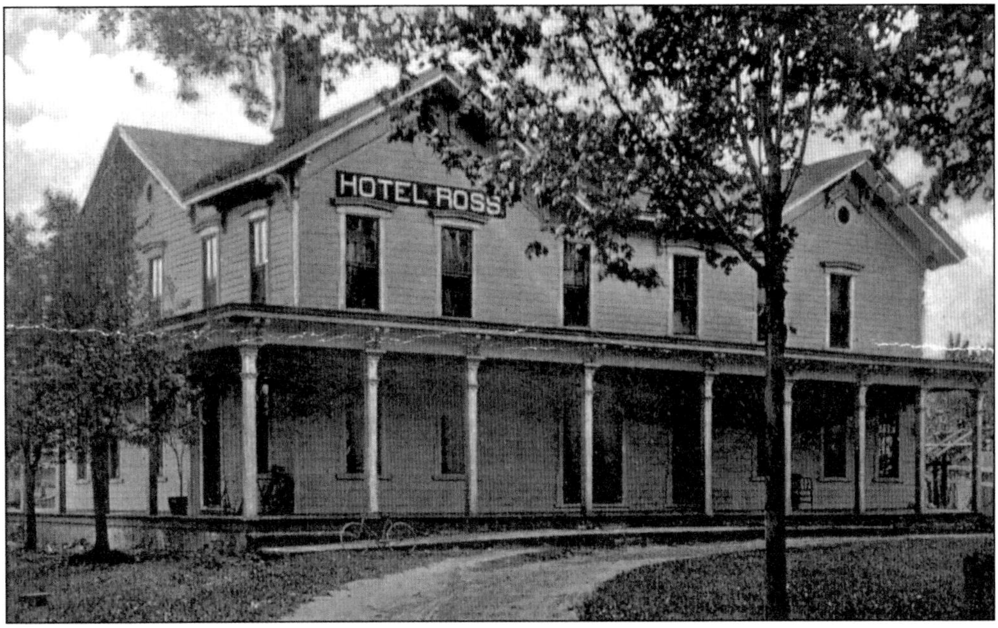

When Hiram Davis built his five-room log house at the junction of the South Branch and North Branch of the Bad River in 1852, it served as both his family's home and St. Charles' first hotel. More hotels were needed when the railroad arrived. Hotel Ross with its spacious wrap-around porch was another early downtown St. Charles hotel.

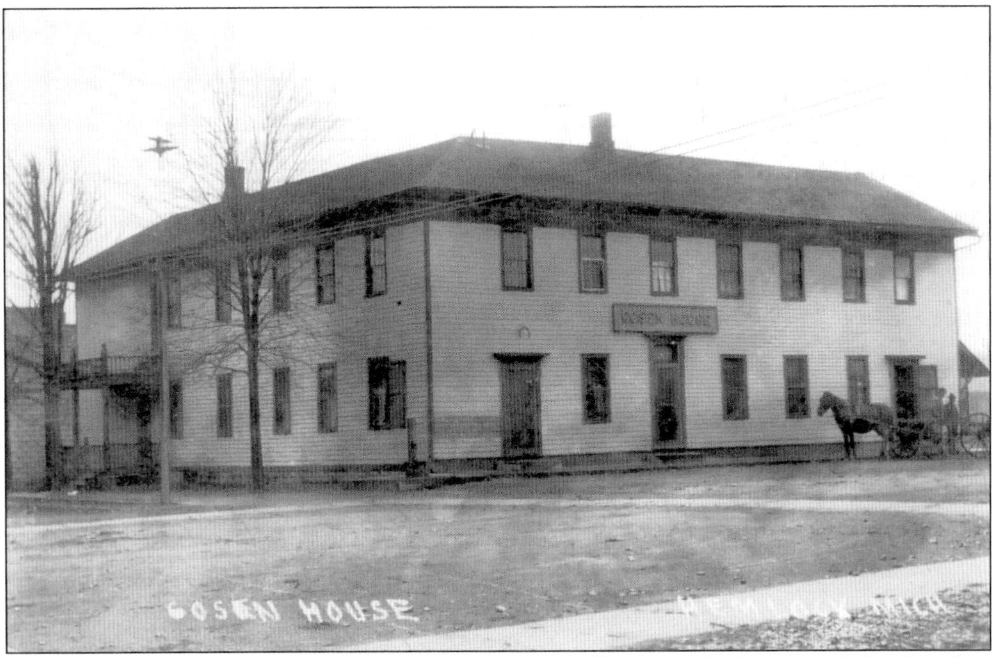

William F. Glasby built the Plank Road, several sawmills along the Road, and this hotel in Hemlock. It was owned or managed by Henry Bemish, Mr. Bennett, Cass Gosen, and Matt Stroebel. It was the halfway point for travelers going to Saginaw City or to St. Louis. It featured an inside garden. The horse barn was replaced with a brick livery.

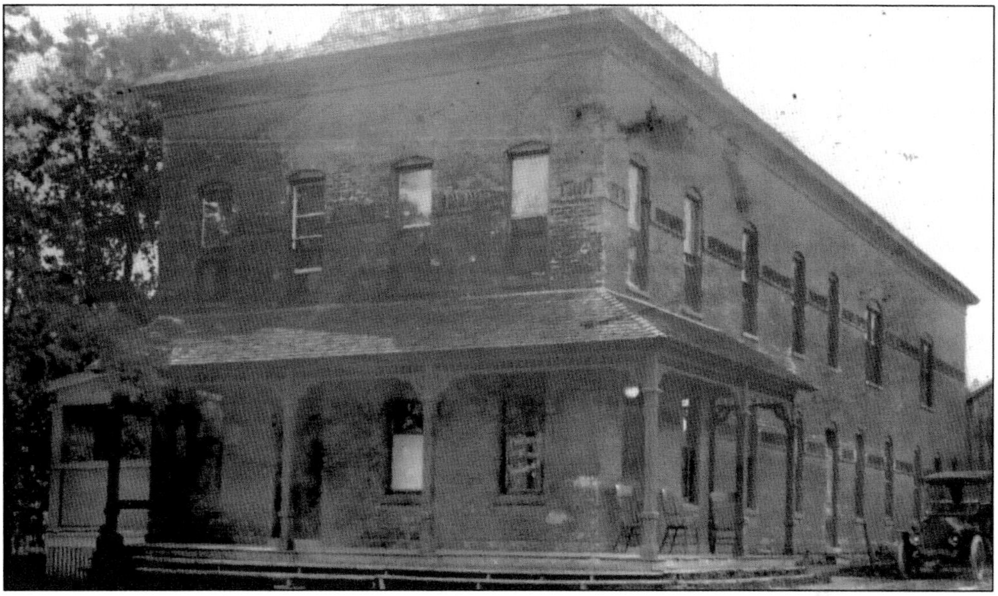

The first settlers settled at "Cass Bend." The bridge was the "Cass Bridge." Charles Lull built a hotel, the "Bridgeport Center House," because he wanted Bridgeport Village to be located there. The village was called Bridgeport but moved to State Street and Dixie Highway. This photo of the Center House was taken in 1912.

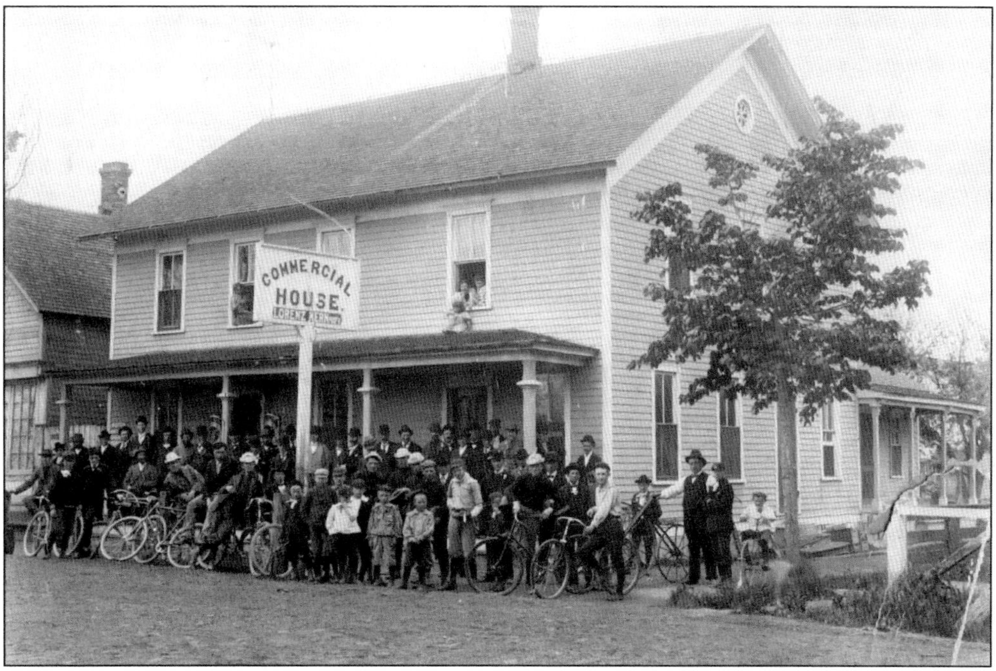

Innkeeper Heinrich Rau built this Commercial House on Frankenmuth's Main Street in 1882. In 1894 Lorenz Kern ran the hotel, dining room, and saloon. His family lived in the hotel, and rooms were rented to local bachelors. In 1905 a brick addition was added. The frame front was moved to the back. The *Frankenmuth News* occupied the building from 1943 until 1972, when the Historical Museum took over.

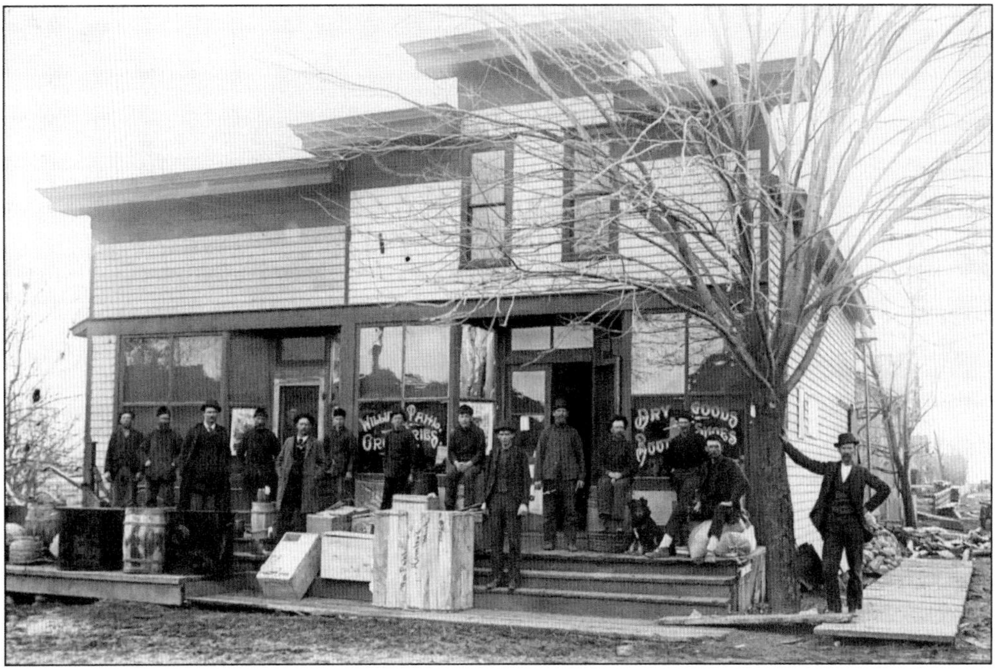

Every town had its general store. Several customers and the clerks have gathered outside William Pahl's General Store in Hemlock. Pahl sold groceries, dry goods, boots, and shoes. Many items were sold in barrels or kegs. Wooden plank sidewalks lined the store on two sides. Cut up wood was stacked outside, ready to be used for heating the building.

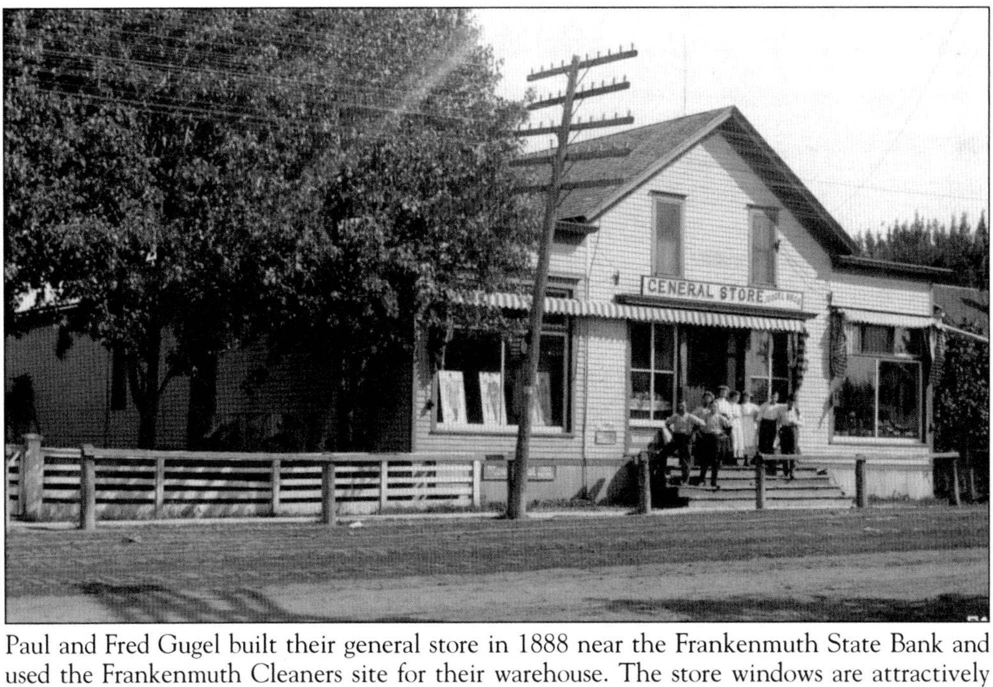

Paul and Fred Gugel built their general store in 1888 near the Frankenmuth State Bank and used the Frankenmuth Cleaners site for their warehouse. The store windows are attractively decorated with fashion posters. China, crocks, and harness are neatly arranged. The hitching post makes it convenient for customers to park their horses.

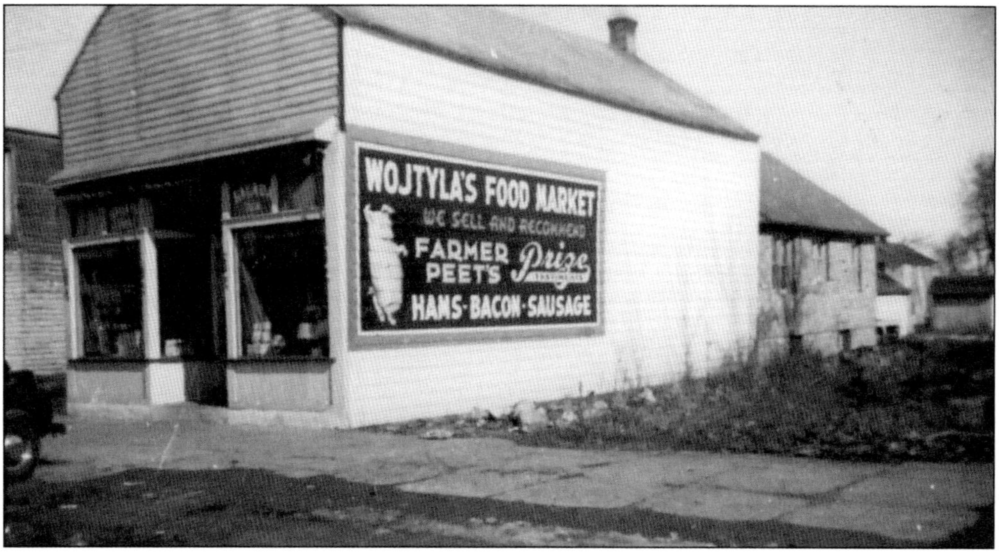

The store shown above was built on Oakley's Main Street in the early 1900s. In the early 1920s it was known as Wojtyla's Food Market. Chesaning's Farmer Peets meats were sold locally in grocery stores and distributed nationally. The store had a dual business as shown in the photo below. Groceries and meats were sold on the left side, and the drug store operated on the right-hand side of the store. The building still stands today, but it is a Biergarten.

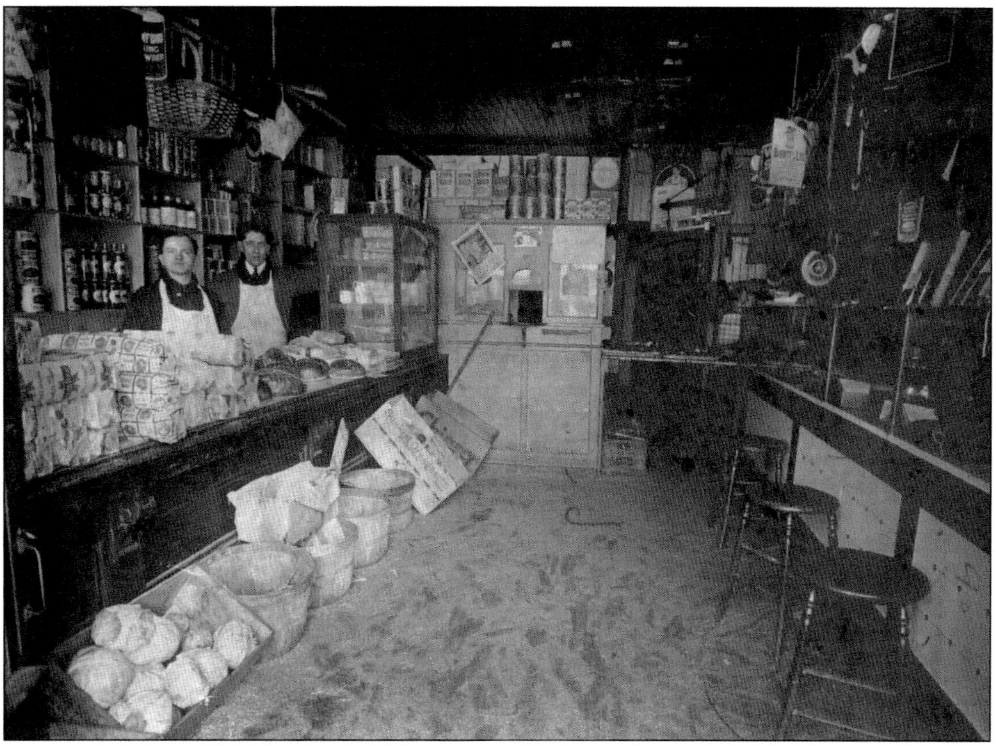

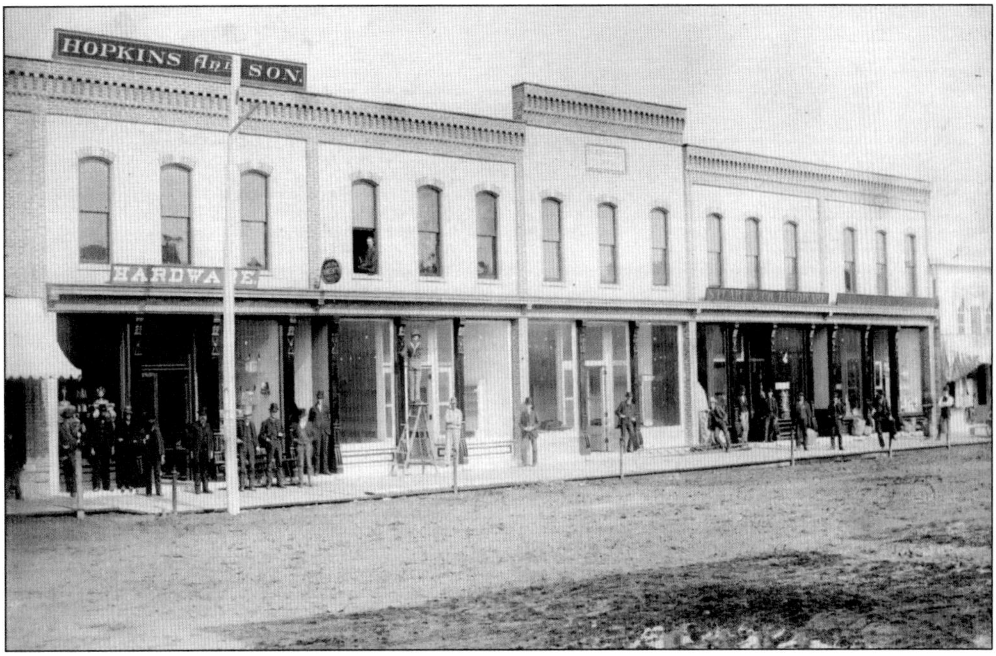

Named for Rufus P. Mason, Chesaning's first storeowner, postmaster, and township official, Mason Block was built in 1887. This view of 144 to 126 West Broad Street shows the Chesaning Bank with the white awning at far left, a hardware store, and Dredge Harness Shop on the far right. Hitching posts, cobblestones, and wooden sidewalks line the block.

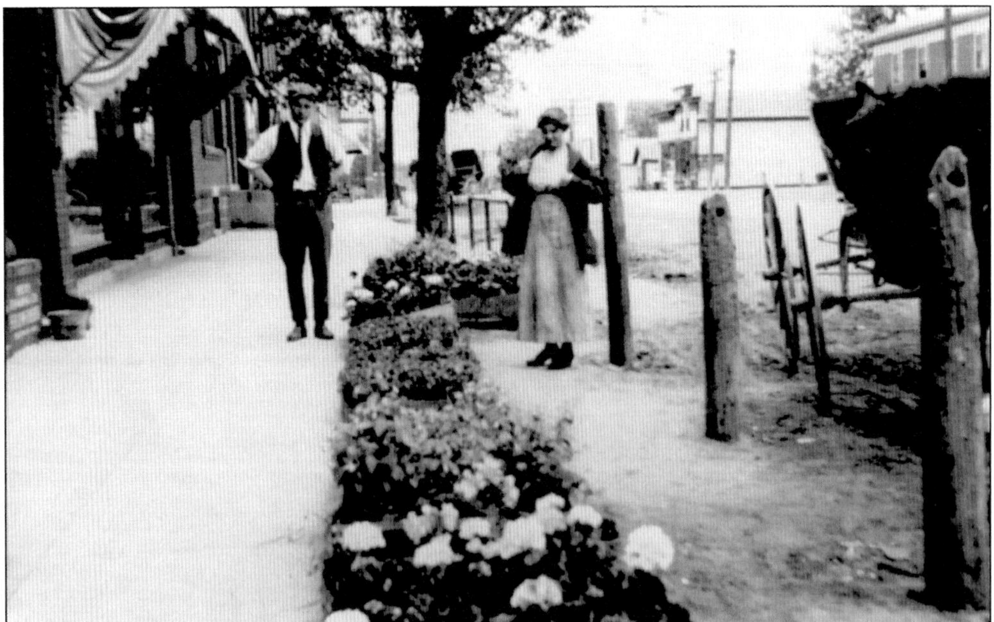

Watson & Warner displays their spring flower flats on the sidewalk in front of their store on Hemlock's Main Street. A customer has tied her horse and buggy to the hitching post on the right while she looks over the assorted flowers. The storeowner is helping her. On Decoration Day, residents planted flowers in their yards and on cemetery graves.

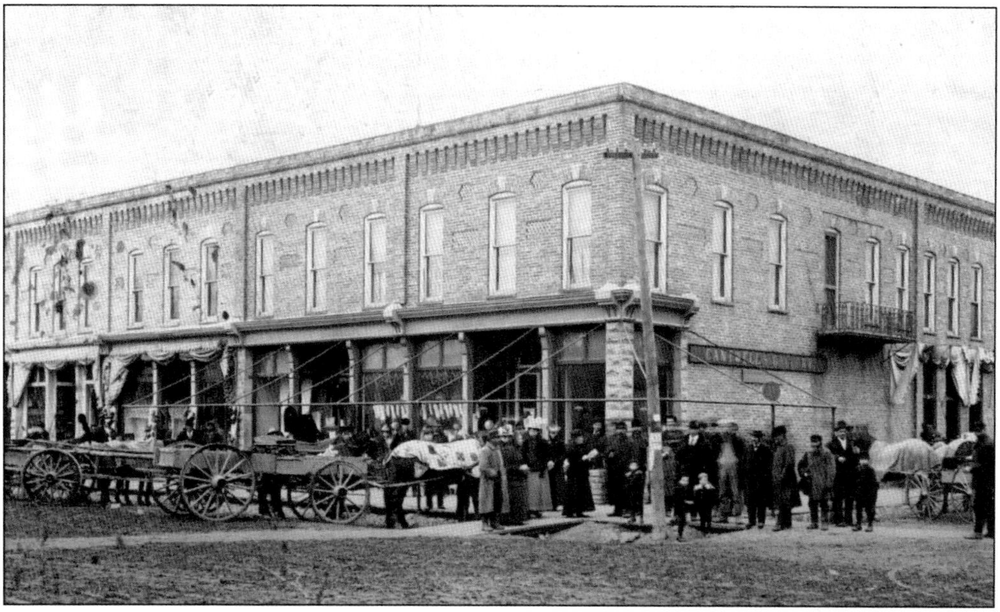

Several customers have gathered with their horses and wagons outside Cantwell's Grocery. Albert Cantwell built the Cantwell Block on Chesaning's Main Street in 1892 for his retail grocery store, Trestain's Drug Store, Watkins' Restaurant, and Conly & Haley's Saloon. The Cantwell family lived upstairs. Albert Cantwell owned Cantwell Driving Park and warehouses near the railroad tracks.

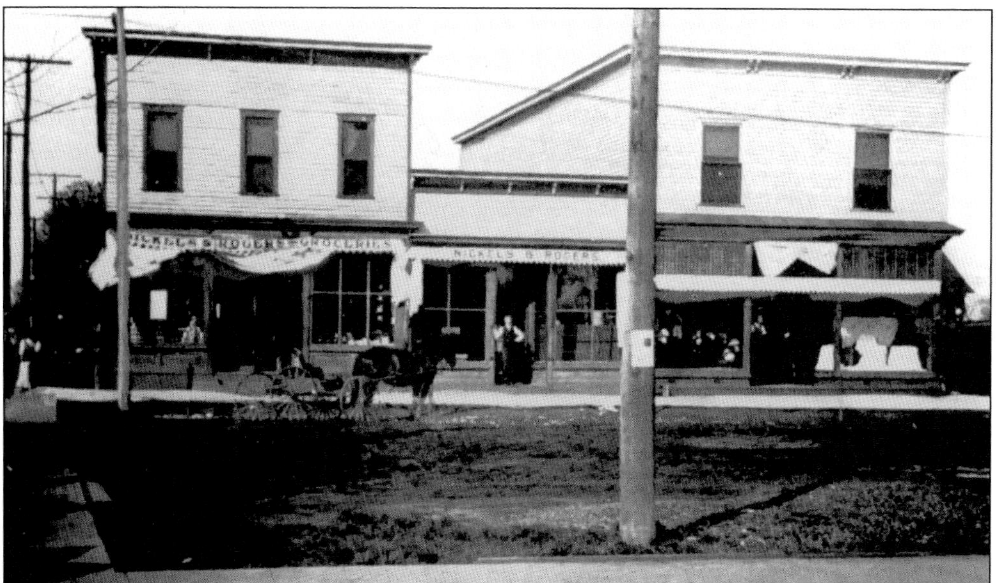

Nickels and Rogers' three adjoining stores were on the corner of Clinton and Main Street in St. Charles in the early 1900s. Two two-story buildings were connected to a one-story building. The grocery store and general stores displayed a mezzanine, rugs, dishes, and household items. Mrs. Nickels planted the empty lot next door with flowers and shrubs.

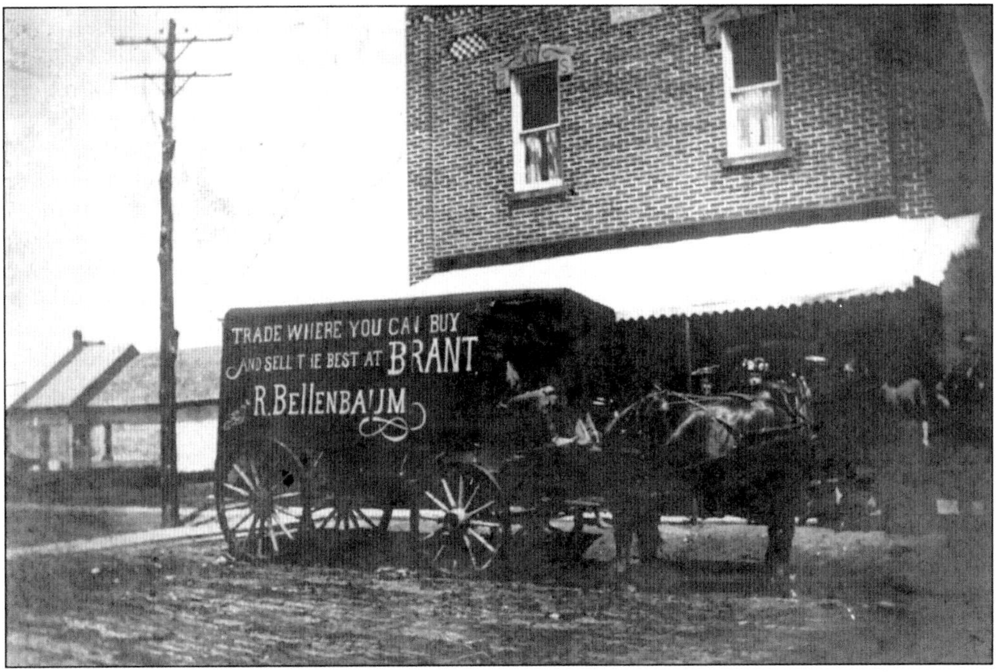

Because of its distance, located in the far western part of the county, Brant Township wasn't organized until 1858. The local merchant provided delivery service to those residents who could not travel to his store.

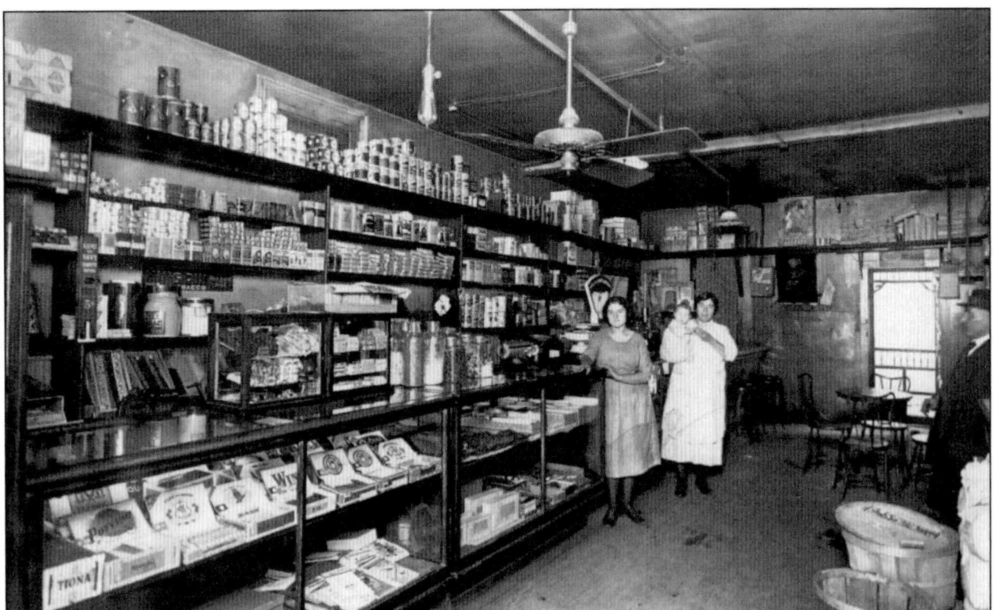

A tin ceiling, an electric light and fan, wood floor, neatly stacked shelves with a large display of cigars, wooden baskets, and a table and chairs for counter service make up the interior of St. Charles' A.J. Bertotte Grocery Store in 1916. Standing on the left are clerk Jennie Gerva, owner Jennie Bertotte, holding one-year-old Richard, and a customer at the far right.

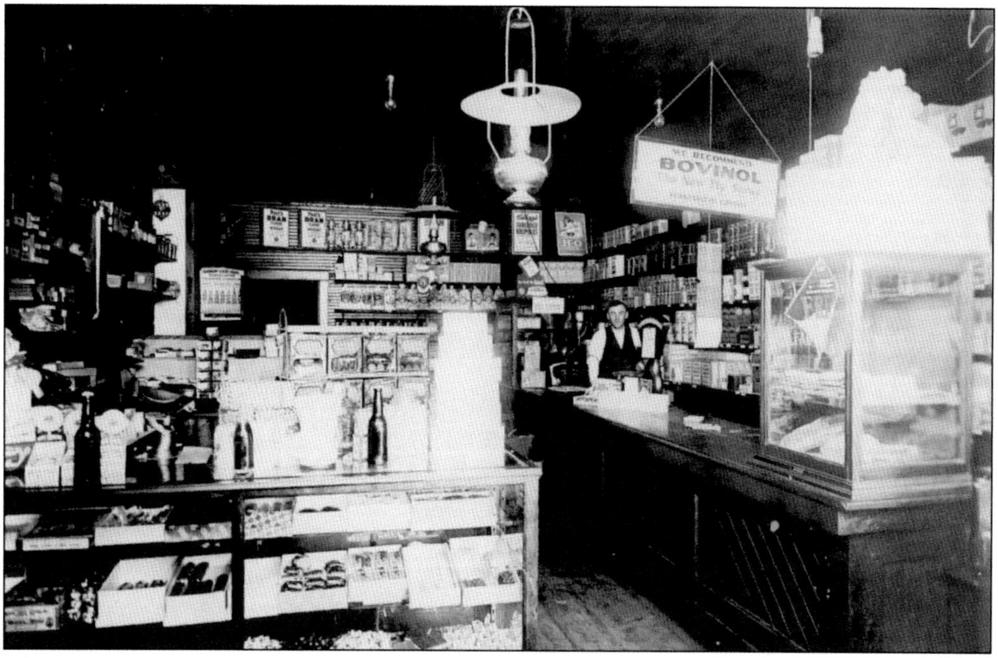

Charles A. Hannay stands behind the counter of the Hannay Store on Williamson and State Streets in Bridgeport in 1924. Built in the late 1800s, John Hannay bought the store in 1924. His family lived above the store. In 1945, the same location housed the Popps Store. Since 1974, Dale Meyer has operated his Lamplighter Flower Shop in the original building.

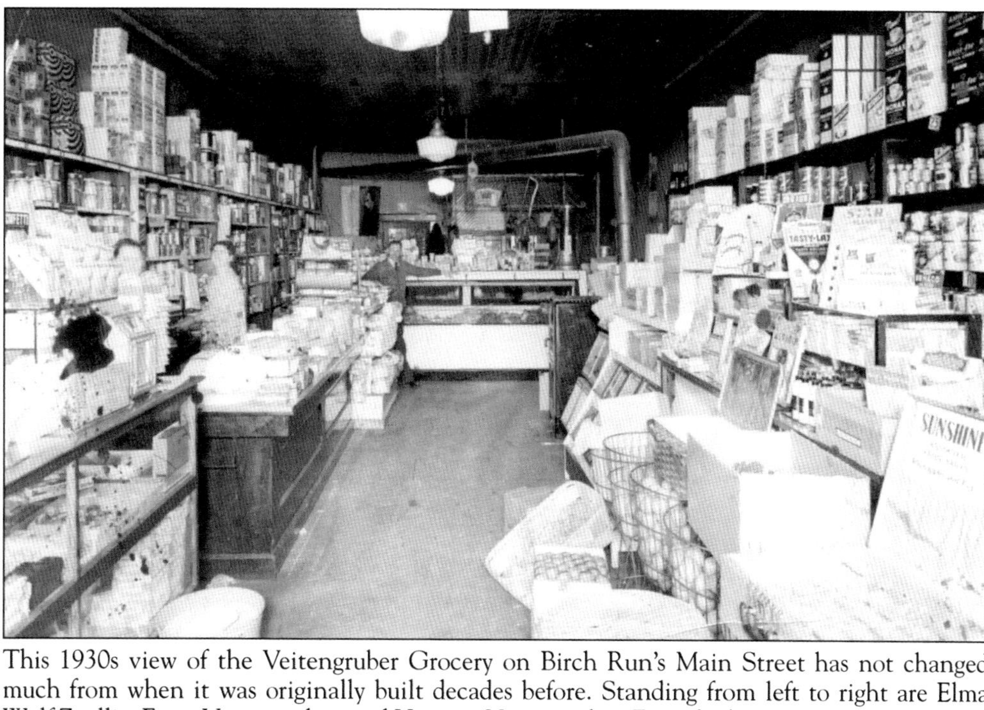

This 1930s view of the Veitengruber Grocery on Birch Run's Main Street has not changed much from when it was originally built decades before. Standing from left to right are Elma Wolf Zuellig, Erma Veitengruber, and Herman Veitengruber. Farm fresh eggs in wire baskets and produce in cardboard boxes and baskets are on the right.

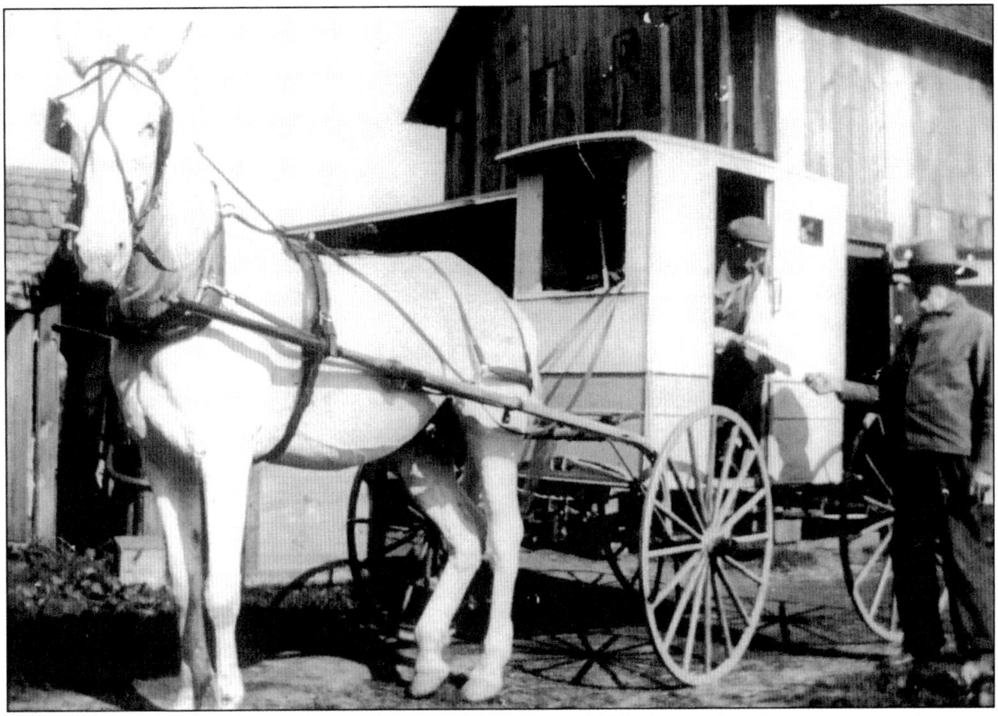

Taymouth Township has had several post offices since 1858, located in houses, general stores, and businesses. Each small village had its own post office. When Burt emerged with the railroad in 1888, its post office was located in the Hunt General Store. Rural carrier Dan Robertson delivers mail in 1903. Only the Burt Post Office remains today.

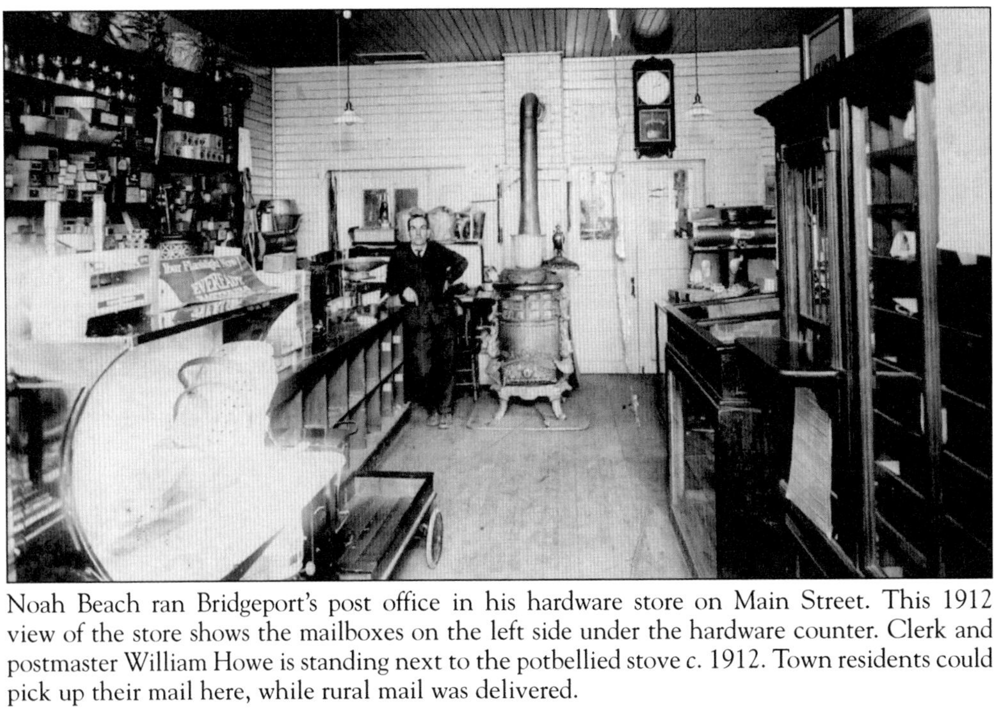

Noah Beach ran Bridgeport's post office in his hardware store on Main Street. This 1912 view of the store shows the mailboxes on the left side under the hardware counter. Clerk and postmaster William Howe is standing next to the potbellied stove c. 1912. Town residents could pick up their mail here, while rural mail was delivered.

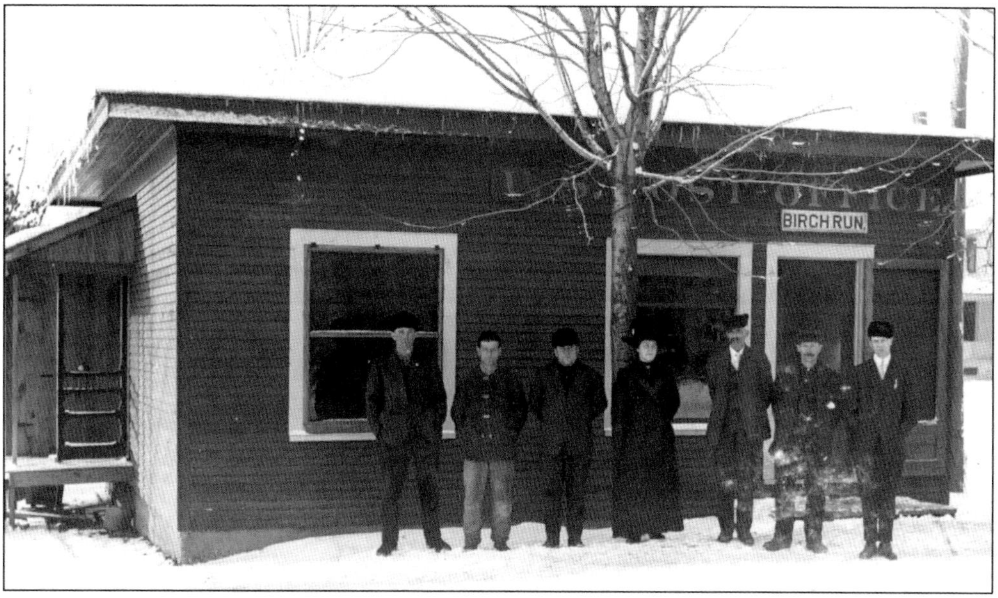

A mail carrier traveled weekly by horseback over Indian trails from Flint to Saginaw City, delivering mail in 1831. After the Pine Plank Road, now Dixie Highway, was completed between East Saginaw and Flint in 1852, the mail was delivered daily by stagecoach to East Saginaw. Birch Run was a fuel and rest stop, and an important post office station. The above photo shows the early Birch Run Post Office with its mail crew in the early 1900s. The postmaster and his letter carriers have posed for the photo shown below before starting their morning deliveries in the village.

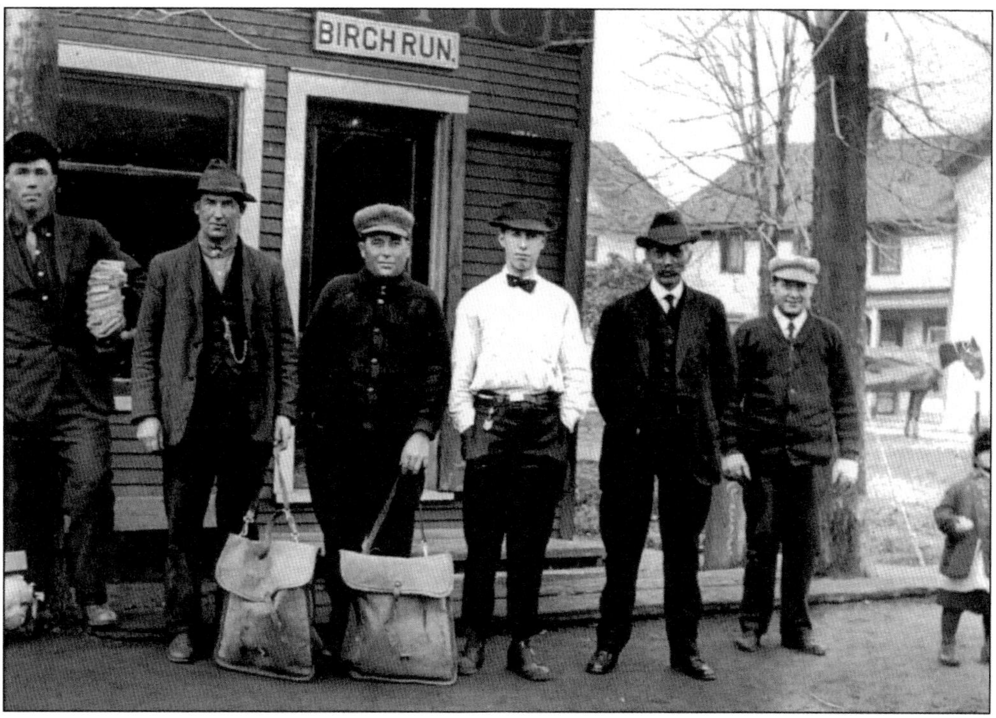

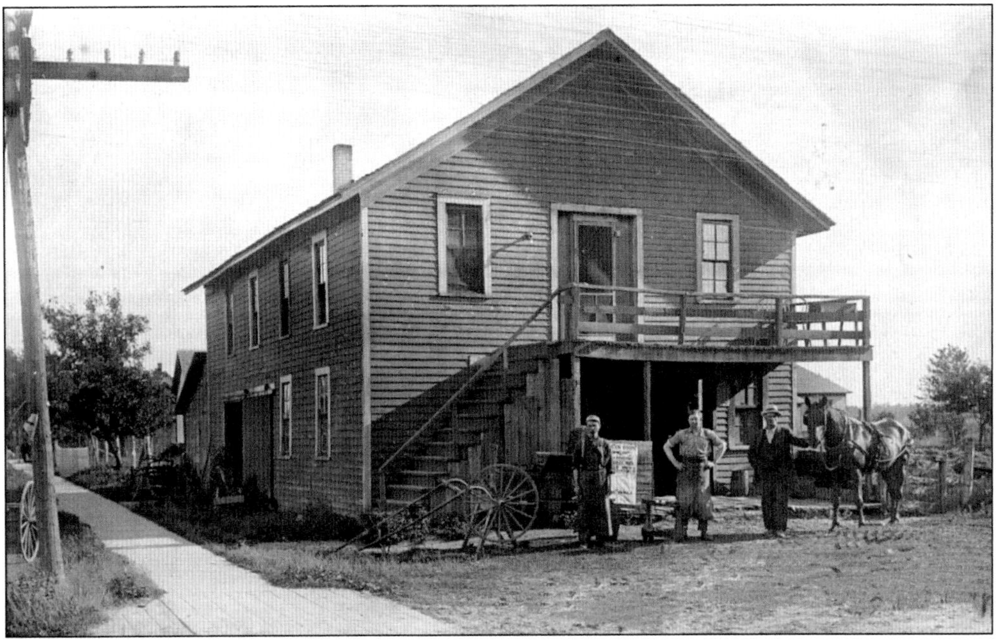

Philo Thomas built this Hemlock blacksmith shop in the 1870s on Saginaw Street. Waterman Blacksmith, and then Dungey Blacksmith occupied it. GAR and IOOF meetings and the Golden Slipper Ballroom dances were held upstairs. The County Road Commission, Carl's Auto Body, Greg's Wrecker, and Martin Chevrolet occupied it after it was rebuilt.

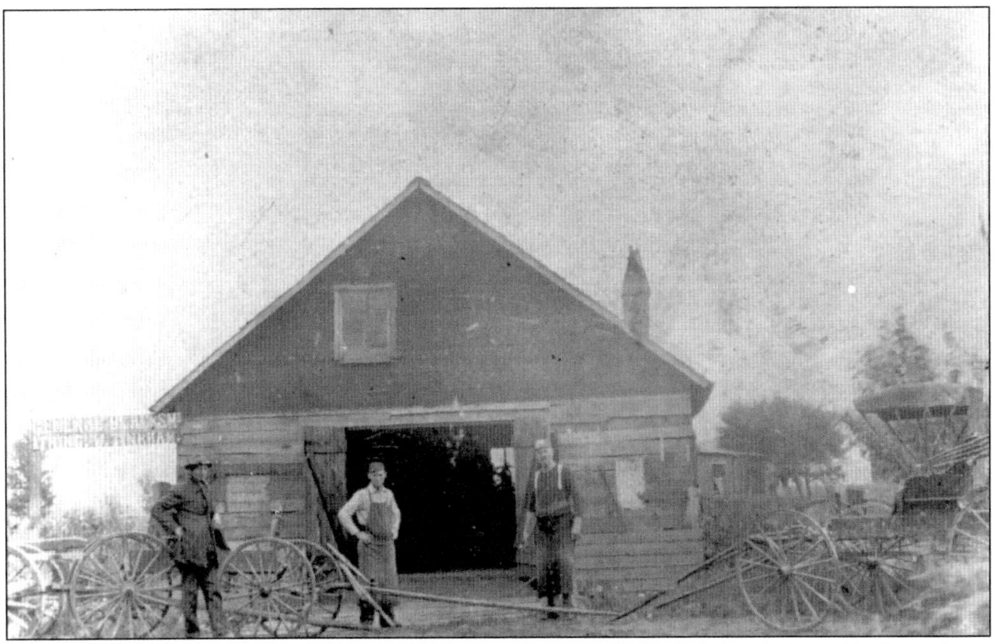

Every town had its blacksmith shop. The larger towns might have two or three blacksmiths at one time. W. Tinkham poses in front of his blacksmith shop in Burt in this early 1900s photo. Burt had a number of blacksmiths over the years. A blacksmith shop was kept busy shoeing horses and repairing broken wagon and buggy wheels.

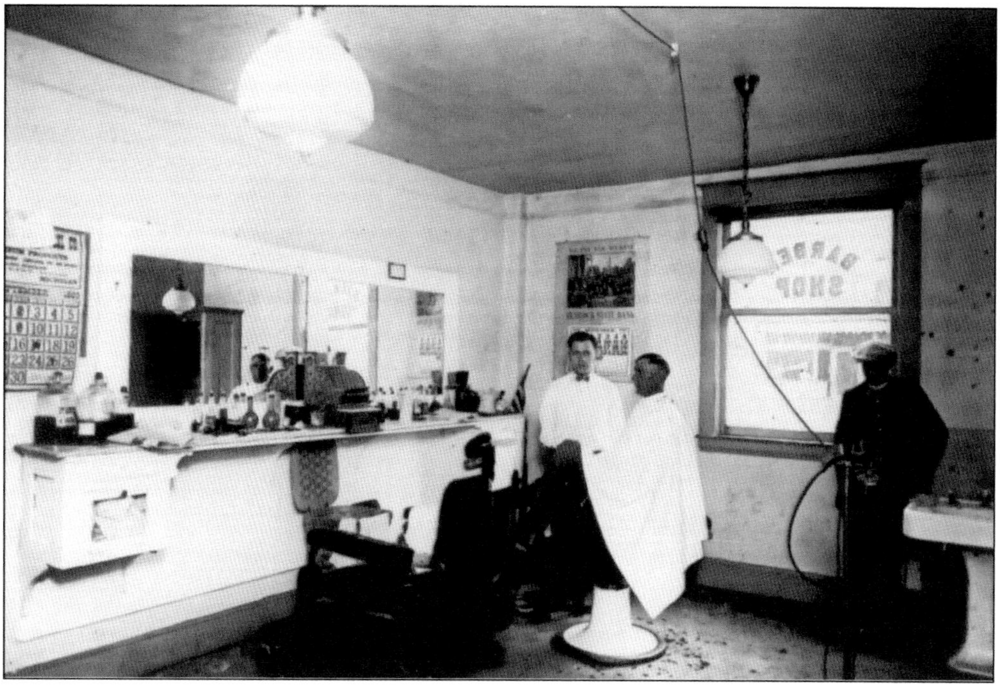

Every town had its barbershop, a place for haircuts, shaves, and socialization. Floyd Conger's Barber Shop, as well as the family's living quarters, are in the upstairs of the livery building. The restaurant across the street can be seen through the window in the 1925 photo above. Stroebel's Hotel in Hemlock replaced its wooden barn with the brick livery shown below. The livery boarded and sold horses and gasoline and serviced automobiles. The upstairs was also used for dance and pool halls. Hemlock Garage and Martin Chevrolet Garage also used the building at one time.

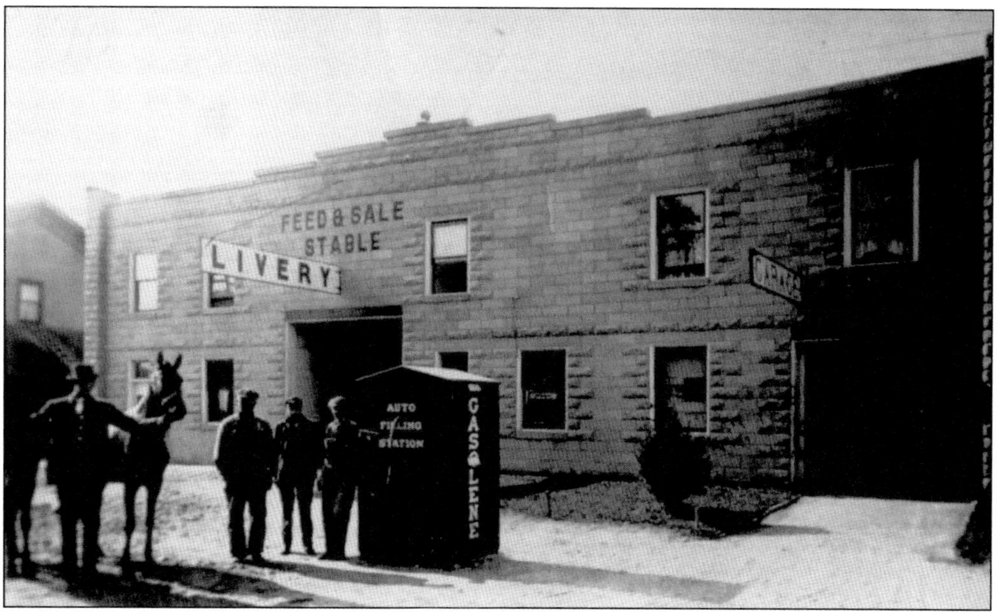

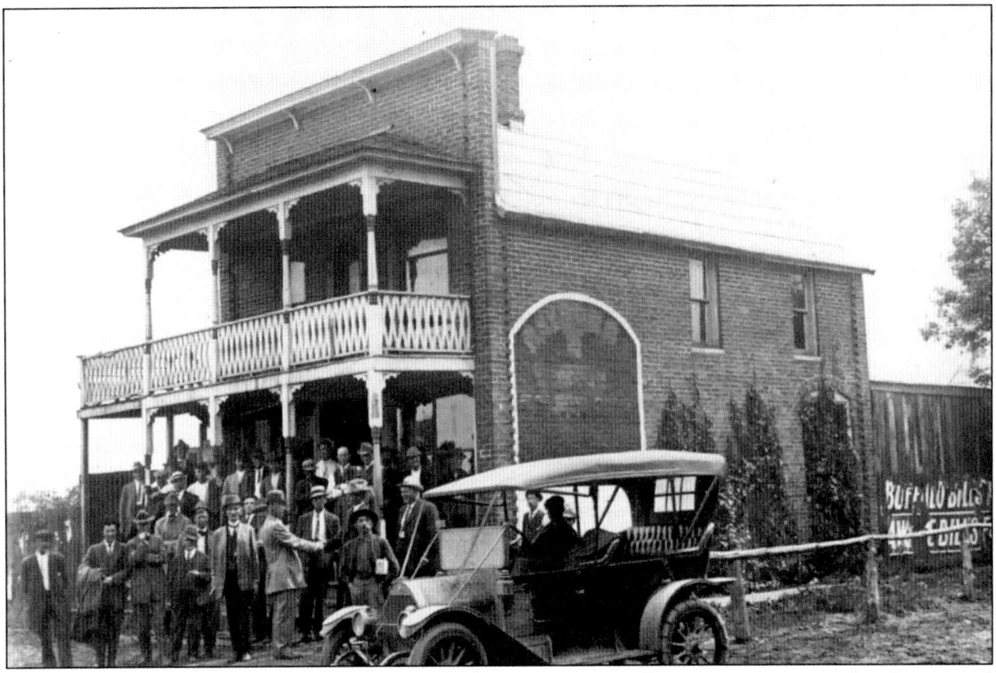

Over the years Burt businessman George Baker ran a general store, gas station, hardware and implements shop, blacksmith shop, mason, lunchroom, and saloon. Several town folks have congregated outside his popular Baker Saloon on Main Street. The site later served the business of Malone & Aldridge before being converted to the Latter Day Saints Church.

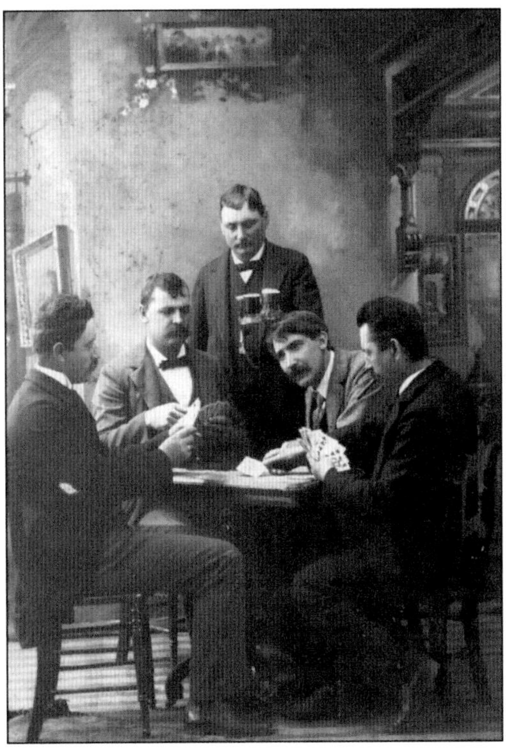

Lorenz Kern bought the Commercial House on Frankenmuth's Main Street in 1894. The hotel had a public dining room, saloon, and rooms for travelers. Lorenz Kern is shown serving Frankenmuth-made beer to Godfried Hubinger on his left, Carl Koboldt on his right, and two unidentified men who are playing the German card game "Skat."

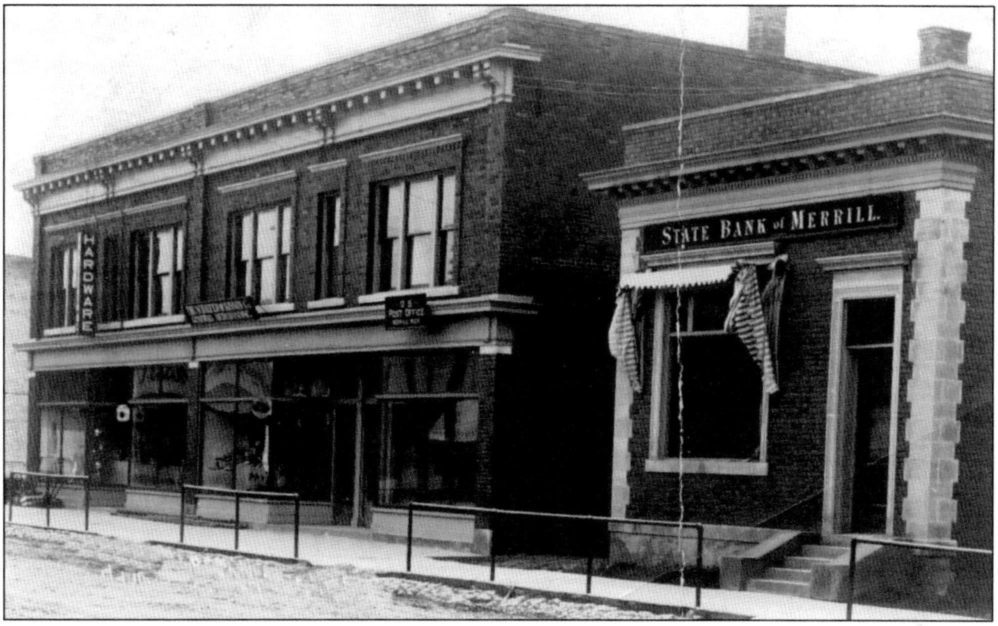

Edward and Catherine Jones were the first permanent settlers in Jonesfield Township in 1857. William E. Glasby built a sawmill in 1866, followed by the Green and West sawmills. Towns emerged around each sawmill. A.C. Melze moved his general store to the crossroads where a village began. Because lumberman N.W. Merrill kept a railcar nearby for evacuation in case of fire, the village was named Merrill. Stores, a bank, and a blacksmith were added to Merrill Village. The 1908 fire destroyed the following buildings on Midland Street: Packard's Drug Store, Whitney Hardware, Ward's Undertaking, and the Merrill Bank. All of these businesses, shown above and below, were rebuilt.

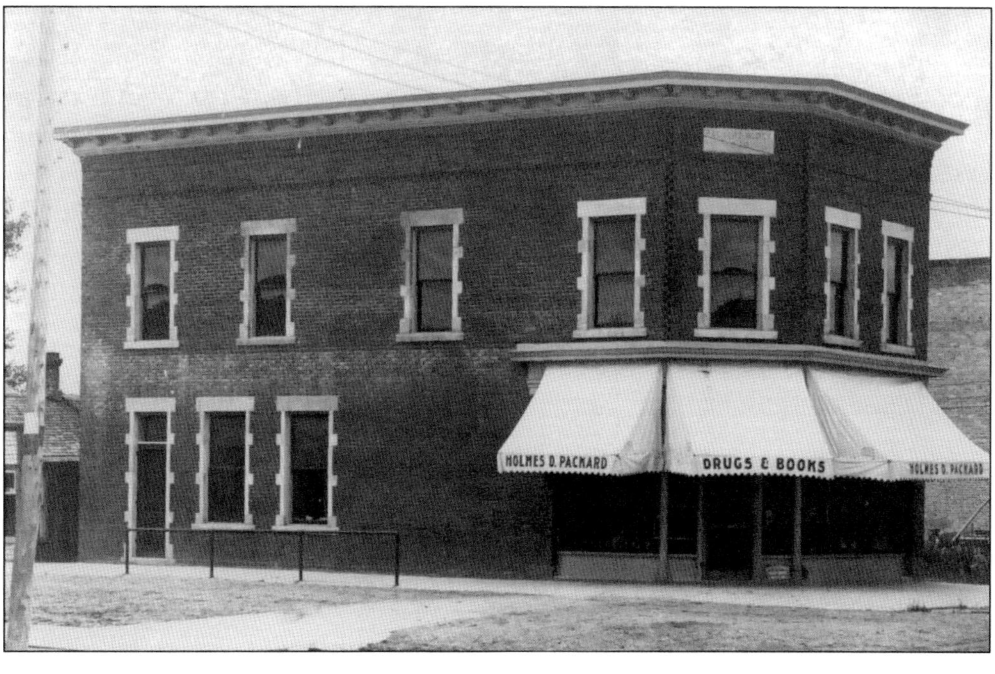

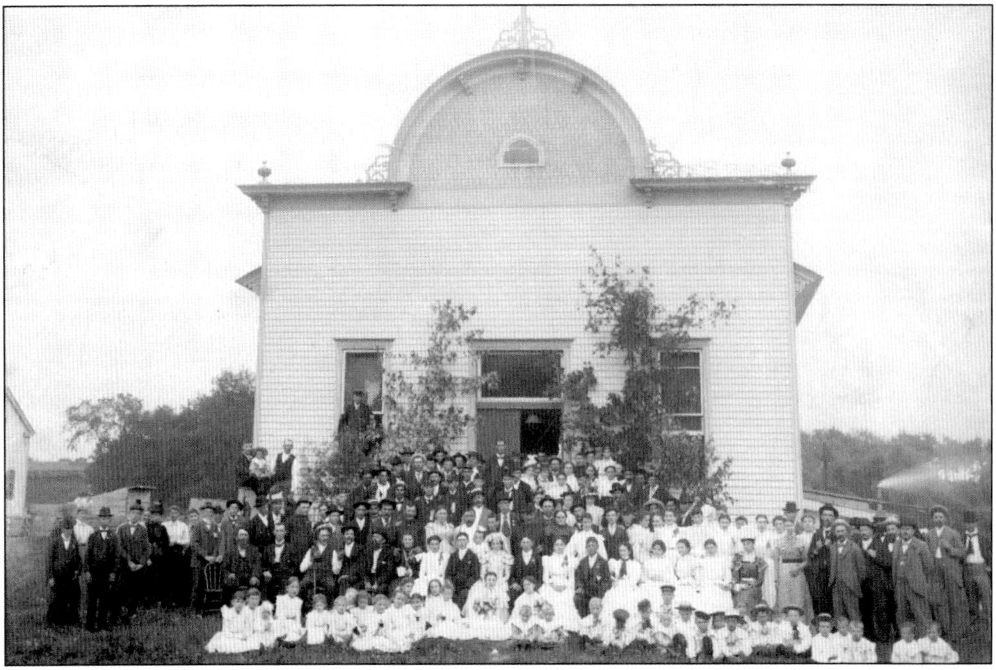

Theodore Fischer built Frankenmuth's Town Hall in 1894. This "Opera House" was the hall for weddings, concerts, social events, and town meetings. This July 1898 bridal party, band, and guests are celebrating the Max Rau and Emma Auernhammer wedding at the Town Hall. This Fischer Opera House has since been moved next door to the Historical Museum.

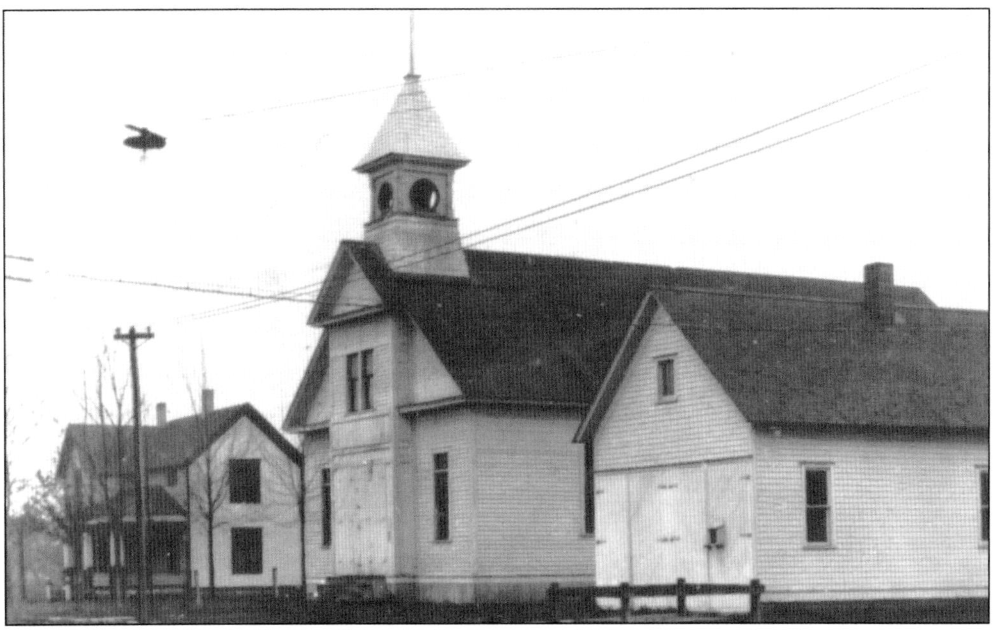

This old Richland Township Hall was built in 1891 with the volunteer fire department next to it on the right. The building was used for township meetings and social events until 1976 when a new Hall and Fire Department were built on North Hemlock Road. The old town hall is still used for Hemlock's senior citizens' activities and other social events.

Five

Nurturing The Mind

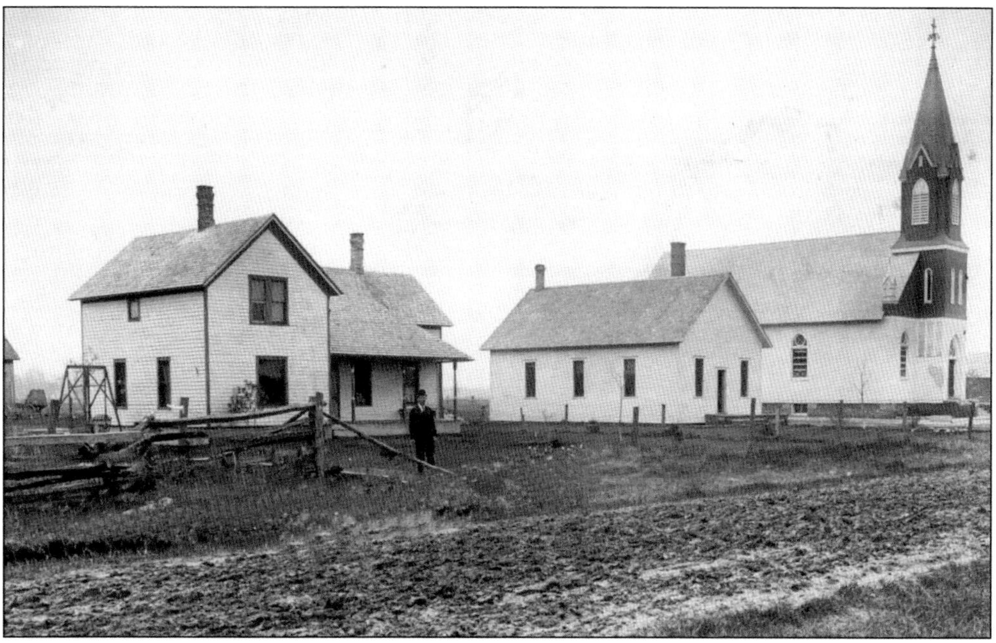

Amelith's minister came as a circuit rider preaching to Richland Township Lutherans in the Lunney School and private homes until St. Peter Lutheran Church was organized in 1880. Iva's Zion Lutheran Church was organized in 1895. Its first church, shown in the middle, above, became the school when the church on the right was built in 1908. The parsonage, on the left, was built in 1897. All buildings have since been replaced.

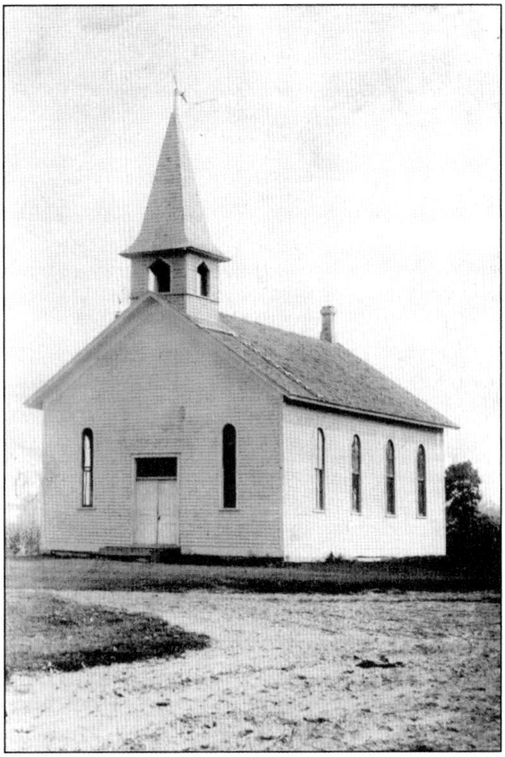

M. E. Cornell conducted lectures in private homes until this Seventh-Day Adventist Church was built on the northwest corner of Church and Second Streets in Freeland in 1867 for $1,200. The church was open for funerals to all denominations. The congregation had only 67 members, and the Church disbanded some time in the 1800s.

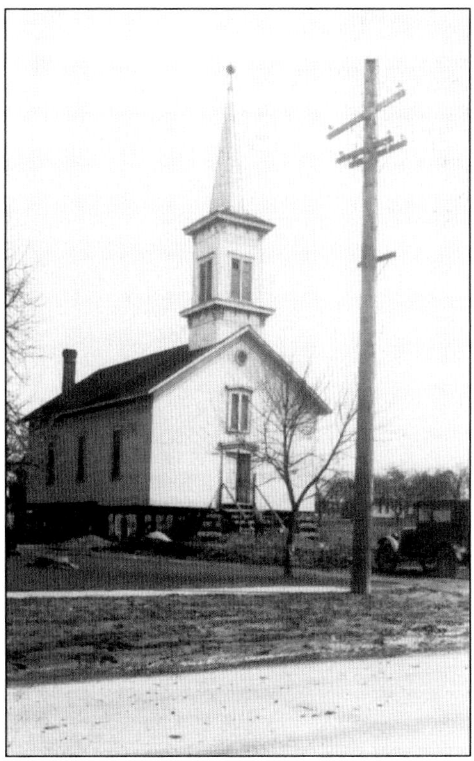

The Wesleyan Methodist Church, in 1844, was the first to organize in Bridgeport. The Methodist Episcopal Church, the Methodist Protestants group, and the Congregational Society joined together unsuccessfully. In 1866 the Peoples' Church organized and survived. This Bridgeport Community Church built in the 1800s still stood in 1932.

The Nelson United Methodist Church in Fremont Township was organized in 1877 but held its functions in houses and schools. When another denomination at Podunk Hill, two miles away, disbanded, the church was moved to Nelson Corners in 1910. Shown here, the church added a basement in 1924 and is still used by the Methodist Church today.

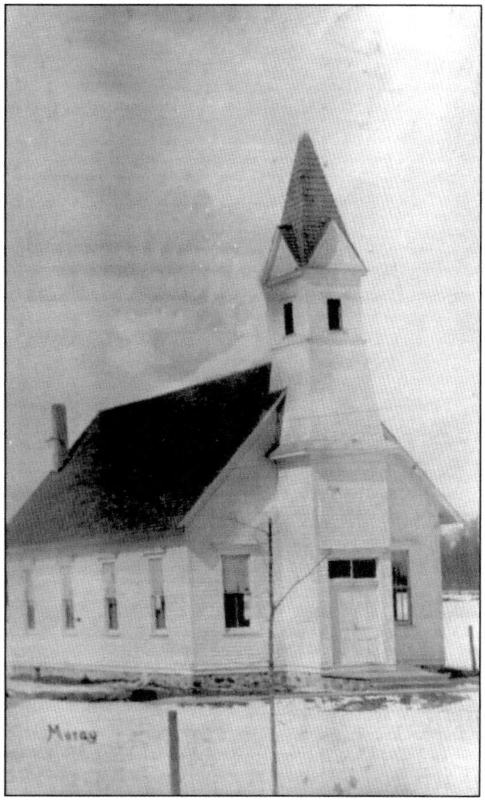

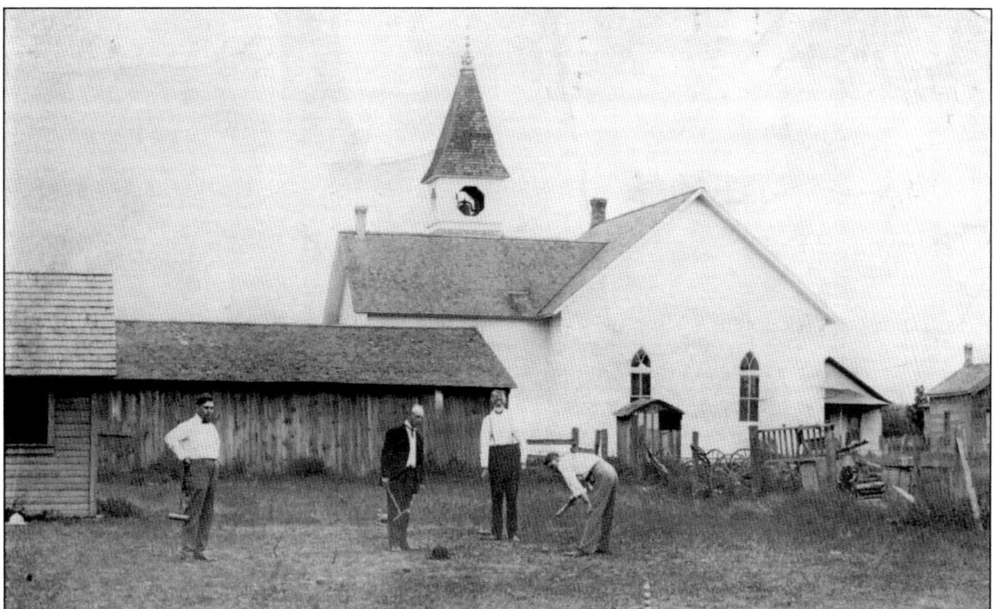

The Congregational Church was organized in 1891 in Freeland. The church shown above was built for $2,500 and could seat 200 people. Church members are enjoying a game of croquet in the back yard. An outhouse and a long horse shed, used during church services, complete the grounds. The Tittabawassee Township parking lot occupies the site today.

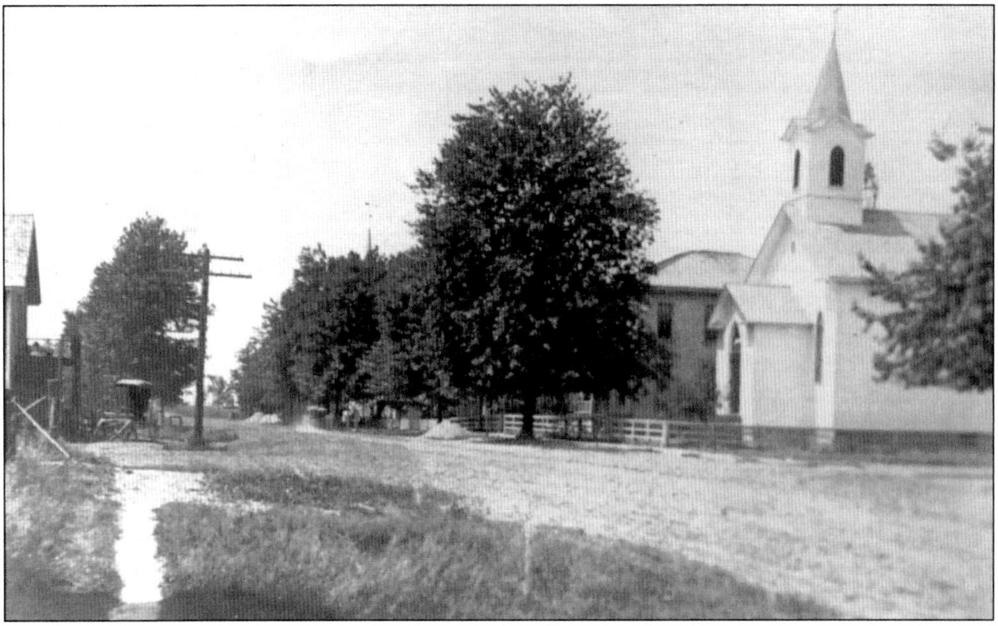

Catholics attended Saginaw's St. Andrew's Church or Midland's St. Brigid's Church until St. Mary's Catholic Church was organized in 1884. St. Mary's Church, with its parsonage on Saginaw Street in Hemlock, is shown above. The blacksmith shop is on the left. Wood rail fences surround the church grounds and houses along the street.

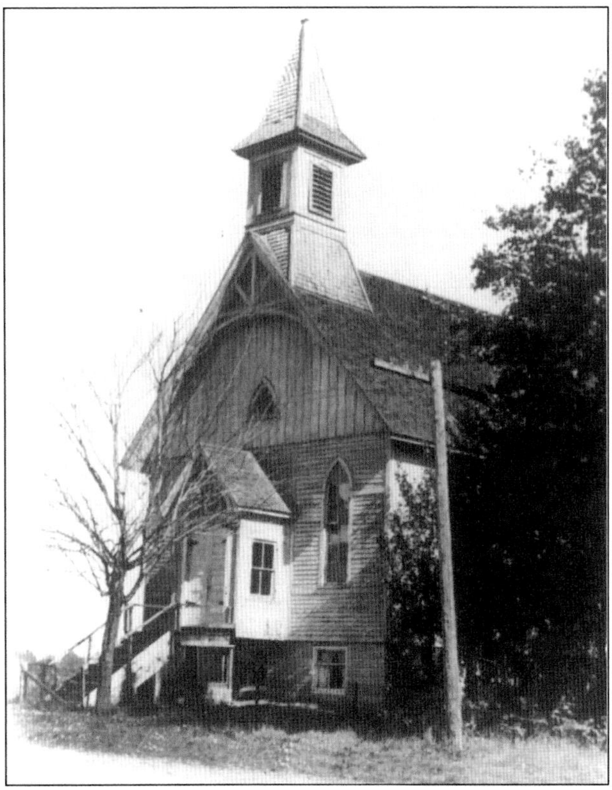

The First Presbyterian Church of Taymouth was organized in 1868. Services were held in schoolhouses until this church was built in 1871. The bell was added in 1882. A row of horse sheds was built in the back. Church pews were rented in the 1880s. A basement and other additions enhance the picturesque township church today.

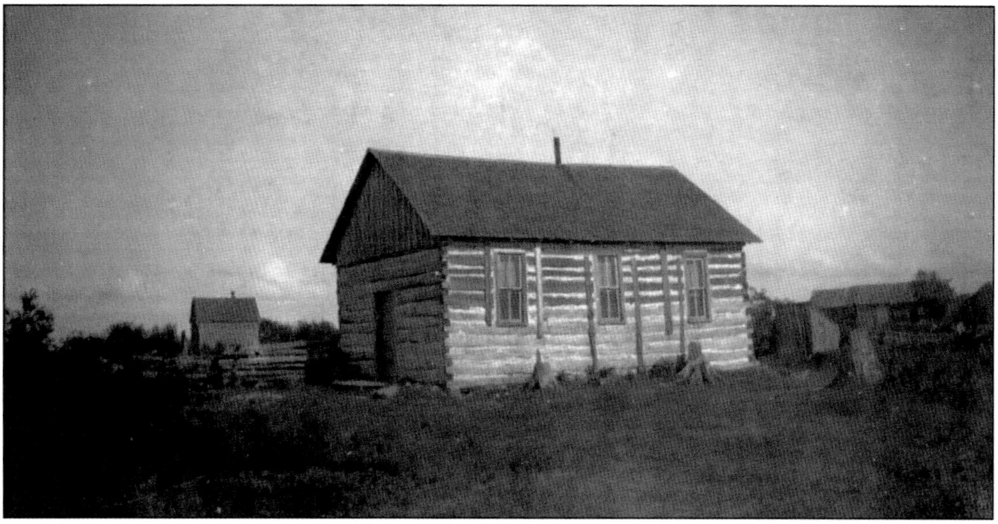

Several county churches had their beginnings as log churches as seen in this Methodist Church in Brant. Little villages, including houses, stores, saloons, blacksmiths, and churches, emerged around sawmills. Some villages survived and developed into larger towns. The Methodist Church no longer exists in Brant today.

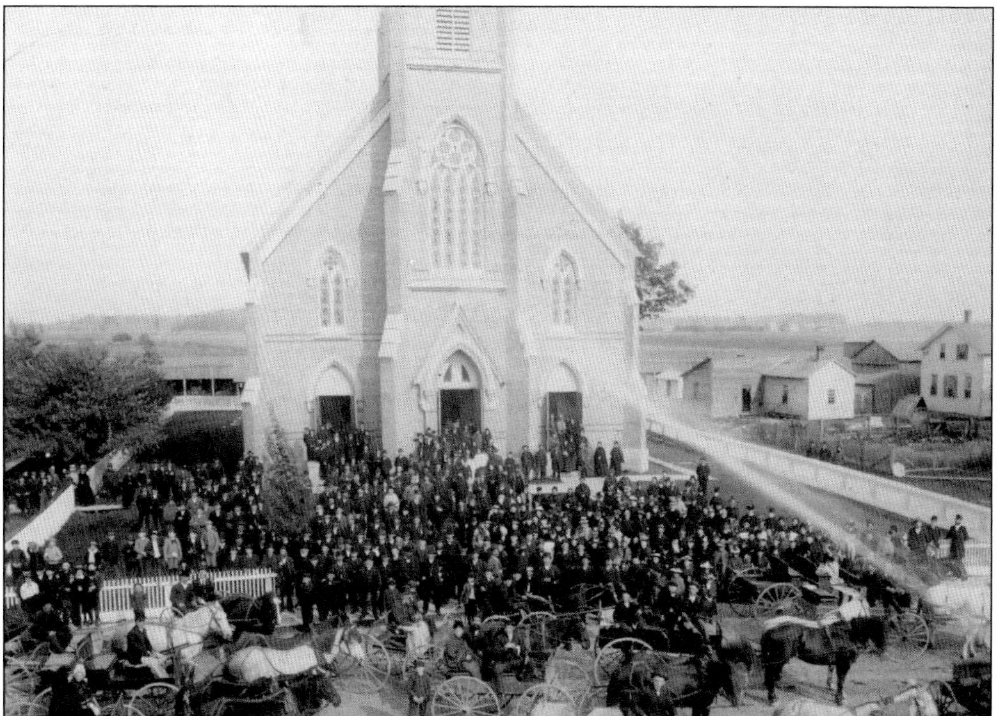

Franconian Lutheran Germans founded Frankenmuth in 1845. Their log cabin church was replaced with a frame church in 1852. The entire congregation gathers in front of the third St. Lorenz brick church on dedication day in 1880. The tree on the left is used in the ceremony. A white picket fence surrounds the churchyard and horse sheds in the back left. The Galsterer farm is on the right.

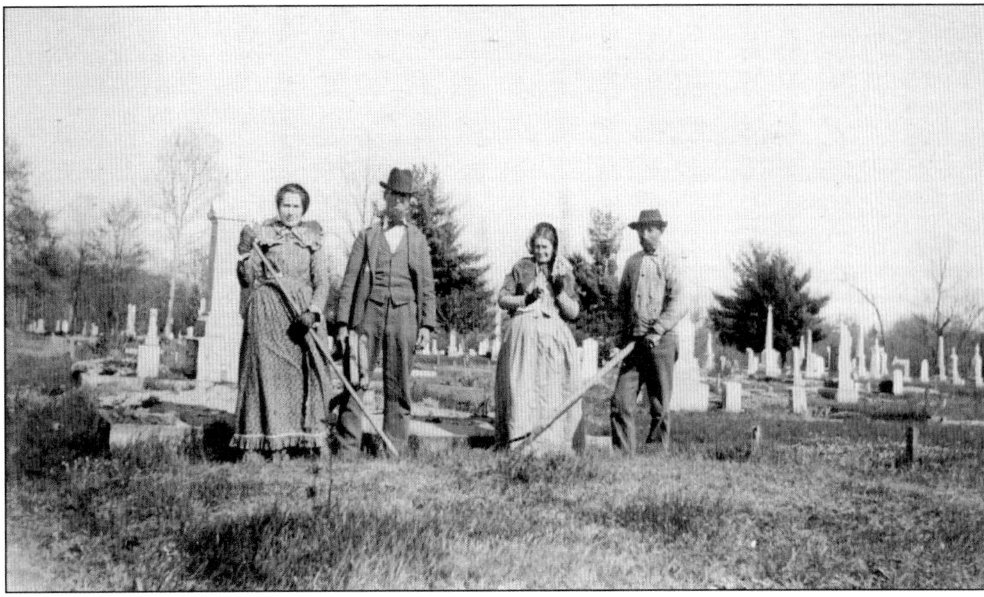

These Chesaning residents are tending their family's graves in the Wildewood Cemetery on Decoration Day in 1900. From left to right are, Stella Ormes Schwantz, Edward Waldron, Stella's mother Mrs. Ormes, and Sexton William Gunther. Decorating graves and planting flowers was an annual Decoration Day observance all over the county.

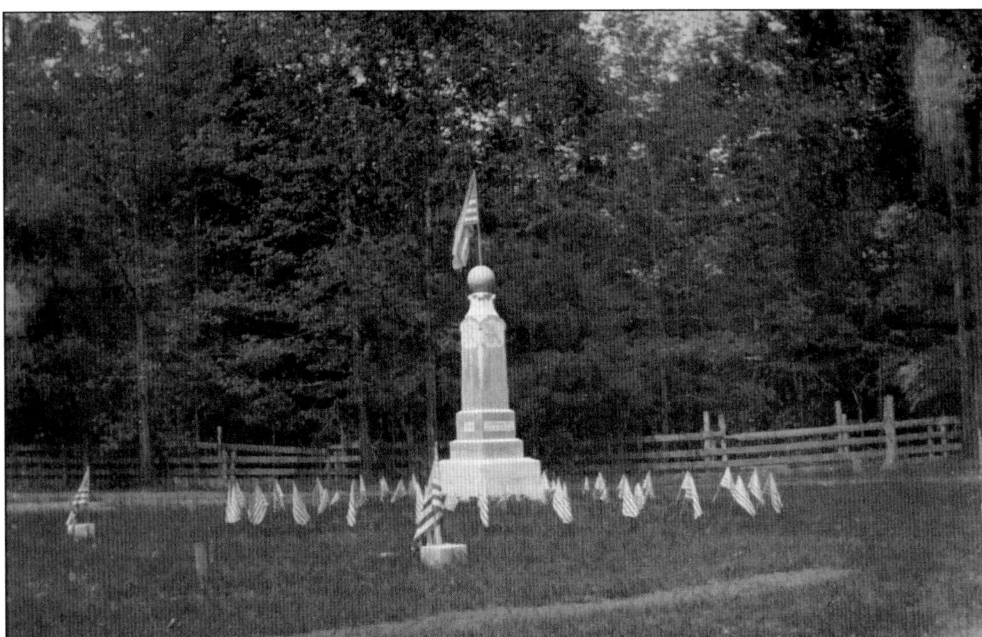

This soldiers' monument was dedicated on May 30, 1898 in Chesaning's Wildewood Cemetery near the Shiawassee River. On every Decoration Day the parade began at either the Township Hall, Methodist Church, or a schoolhouse and marched to the cemetery about three miles away where speeches, ceremonies, or memorial dedications took place.

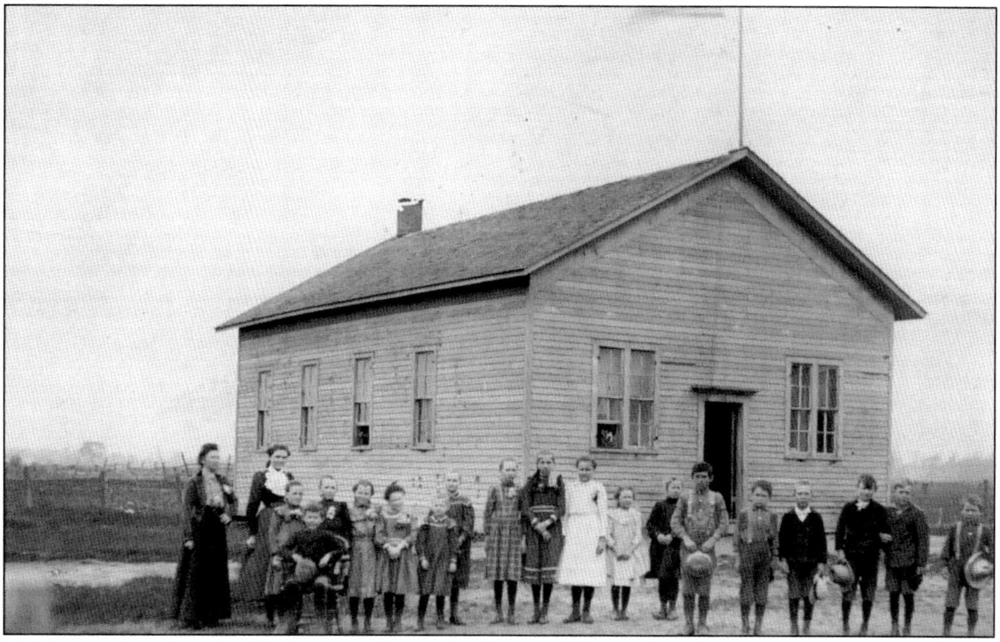

Tittabawassee Township had seven school districts: Munger (#1); Porter (#2); Freeland (#3); Law (#4); Whitman (#5); Vasold (#6); and Wellman (#7). The teachers and school children have gathered in front of the one-room Porter School at 6125 Garfield Road in this 1890s photo. The flag flies from the rooftop. All schools consolidated into the Freeland School District in 1945.

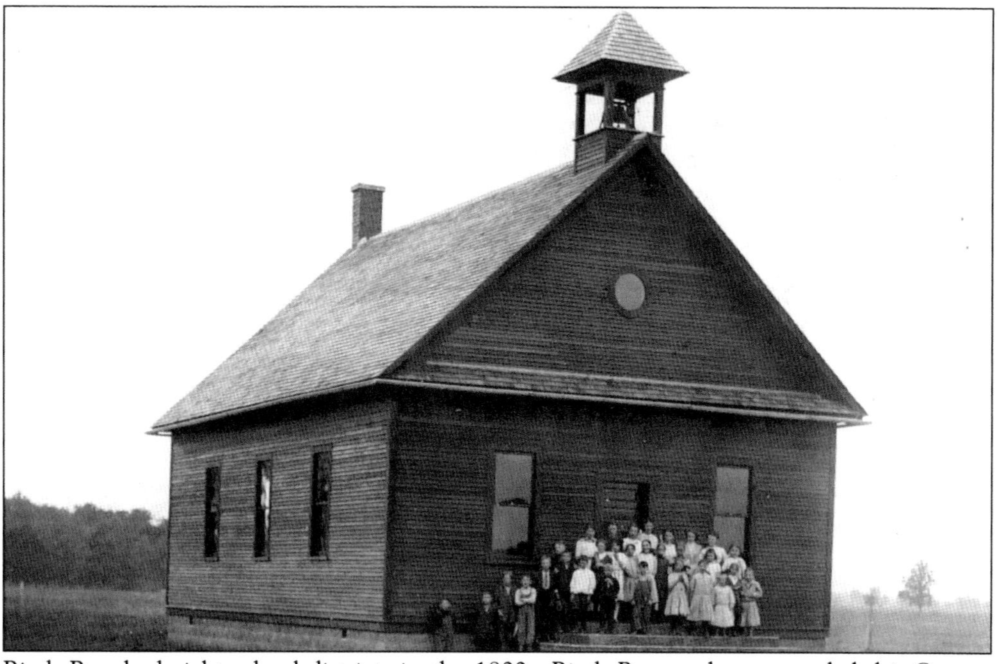

Birch Run had eight school districts in the 1800s. Birch Run students attended this County Line School next to Genesee County until the 1940s. After the school fell into disrepair, the Birch Run Historical Society purchased it, moved it from Willard Road to the Township Community Park, and restored it for its museum.

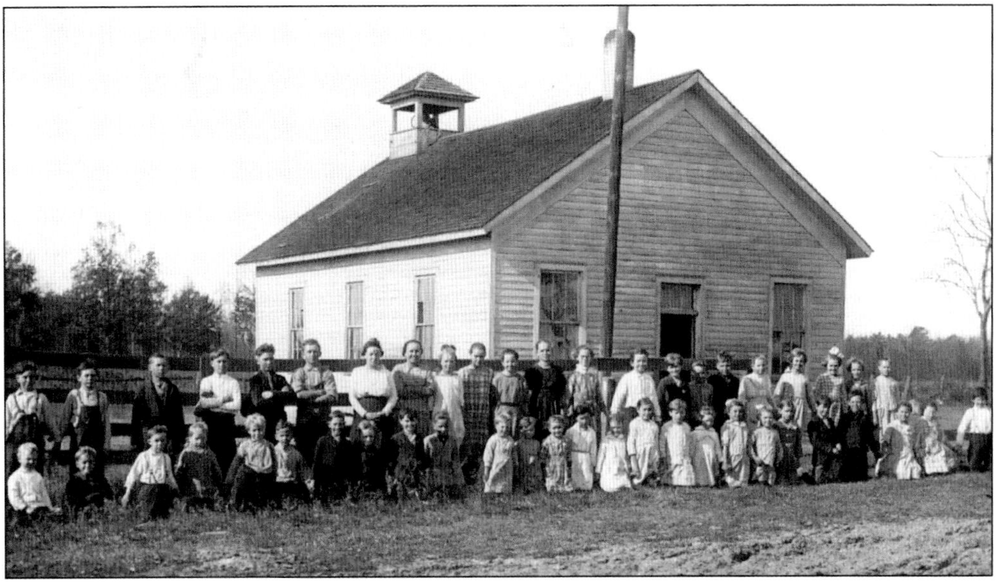

Taymouth Township had nine School Districts. The first Blackmar School District No. 6 log cabin was replaced in 1873 with the above school. Schoolteachers and children came from Blackmar, Fosters, and Birch Run. Congregational Church services were once held here. The children and teachers have gathered around the tall flagpole in this 1921 photo.

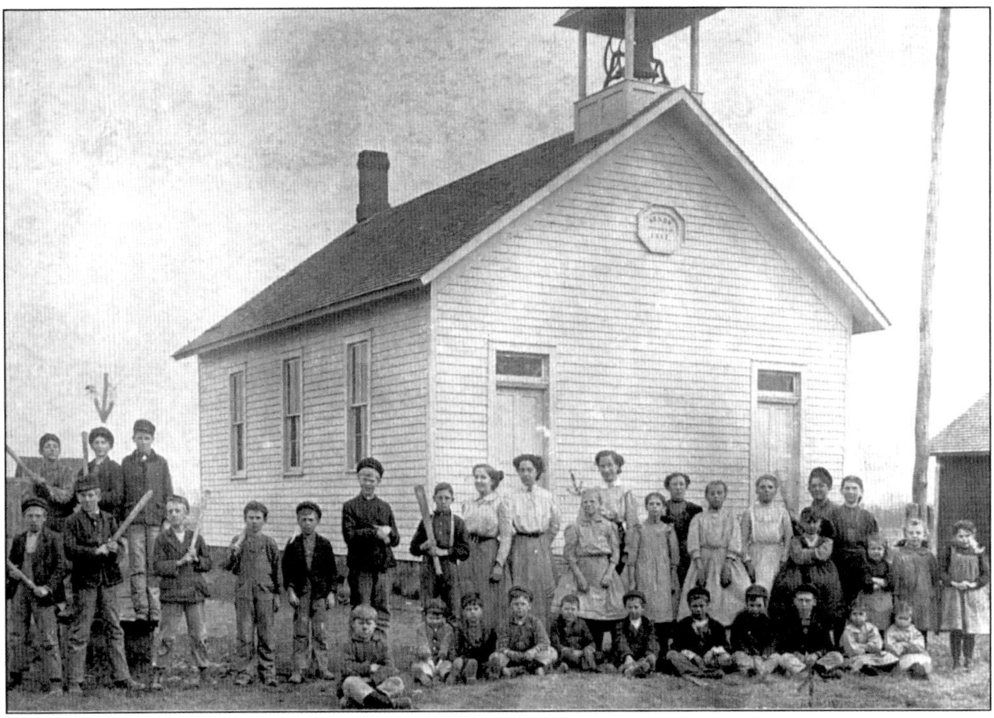

This photo of Brady Township District No. 10 schoolhouse was taken in 1897. The school has two front doors. The students and their teachers have gathered in front of the school before starting their ball game. Brady schoolteachers were paid $79.25 total wages for four months during the school year.

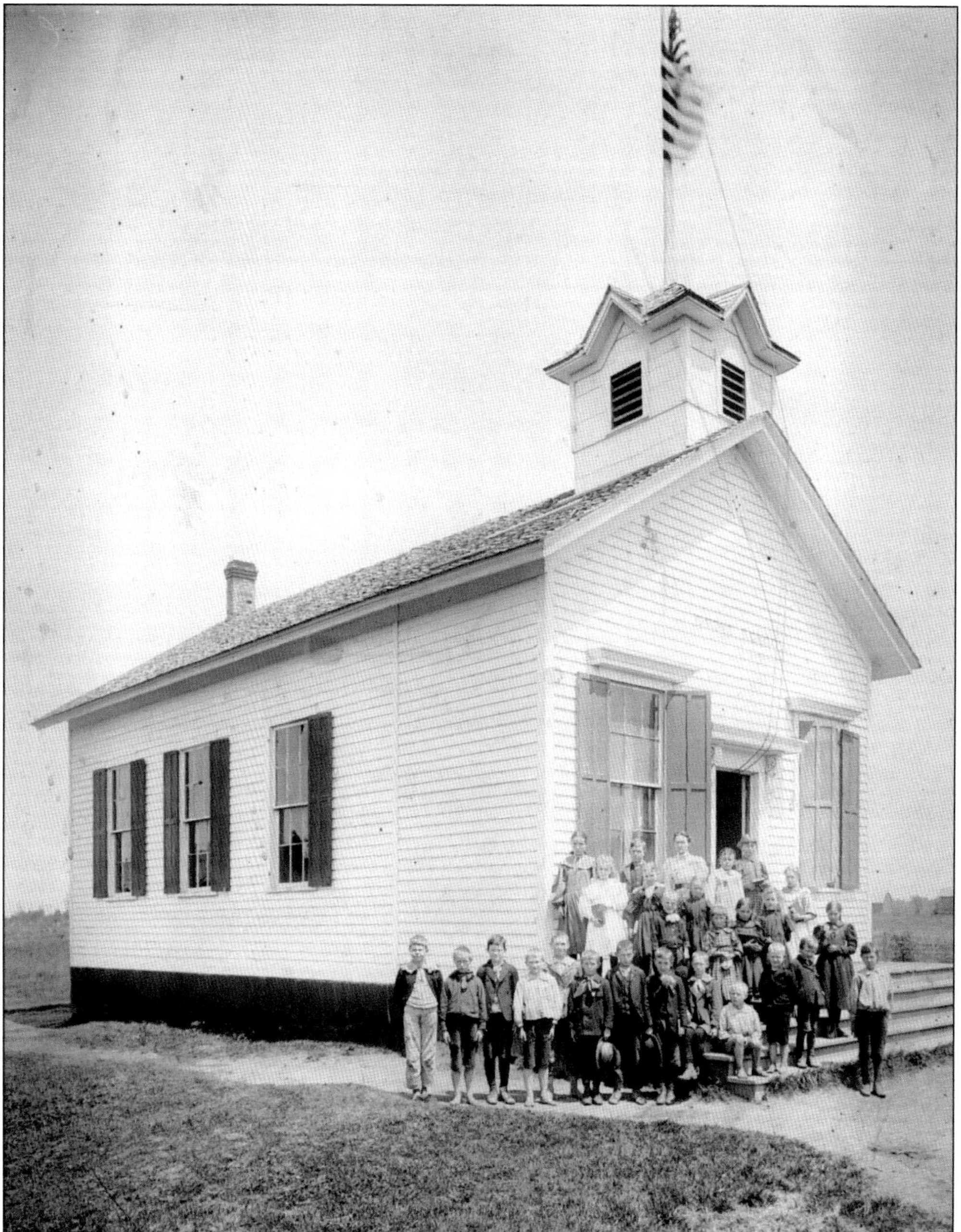

Grove School No. 4 was one of six Thomastown Township schools when it was built in 1873 in a grove of oak, maple, and birch trees on Gratiot Road where Meijer's store is today. This one-room schoolhouse was typical of many Saginaw County schoolhouses. The Methodist Circuit Rider held church services in this school building, in Hemlock City, and in Swan Creek until Methodist churches were built. The flagpole is on top of the enclosed bell tower in this 1890s photo. The school was later replaced with a brick schoolhouse.

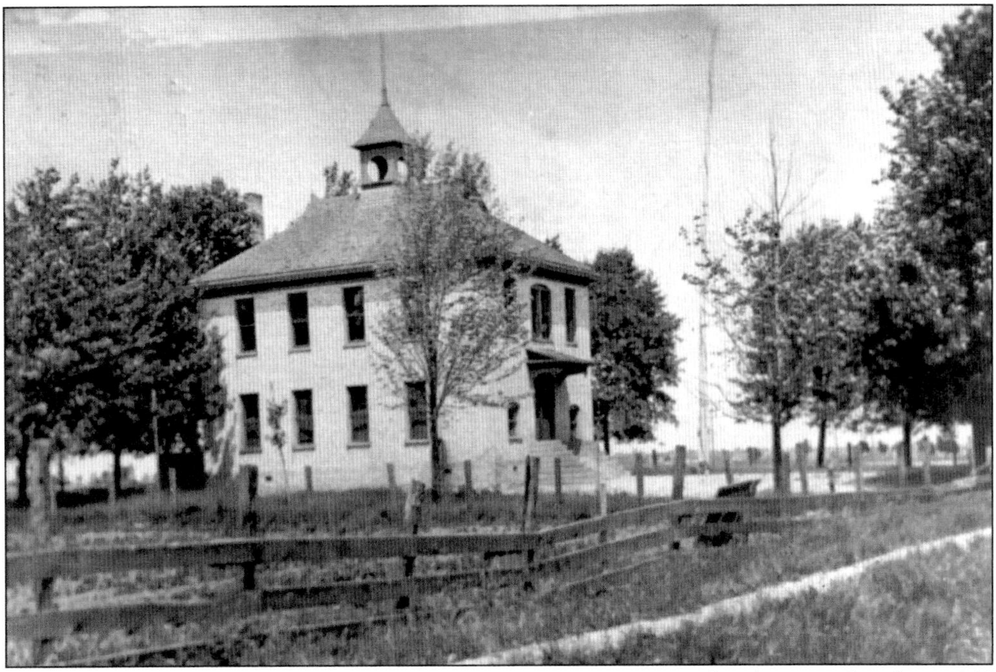

Organized in 1863, Hemlock School District No. 4's one-room school was replaced in 1869 with a two-room schoolhouse. Its third school for all eight grades was built in 1894 with the building shown above. A wood rail fence and a pine-planked sidewalk surround the school that was again replaced in 1914 by a brick school on North Elm Street.

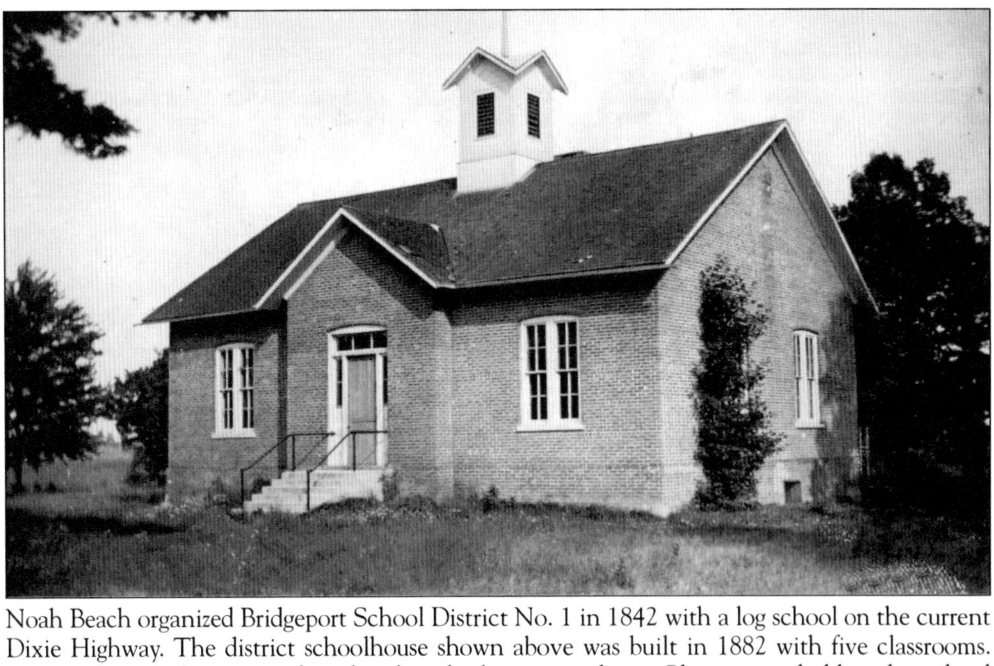

Noah Beach organized Bridgeport School District No. 1 in 1842 with a log school on the current Dixie Highway. The district schoolhouse shown above was built in 1882 with five classrooms. Misbehaving students were disciplined in the basement closet. Classes were held in this school until 1970 when it was converted to administrative offices for the Bridgeport-Spaulding Community School District.

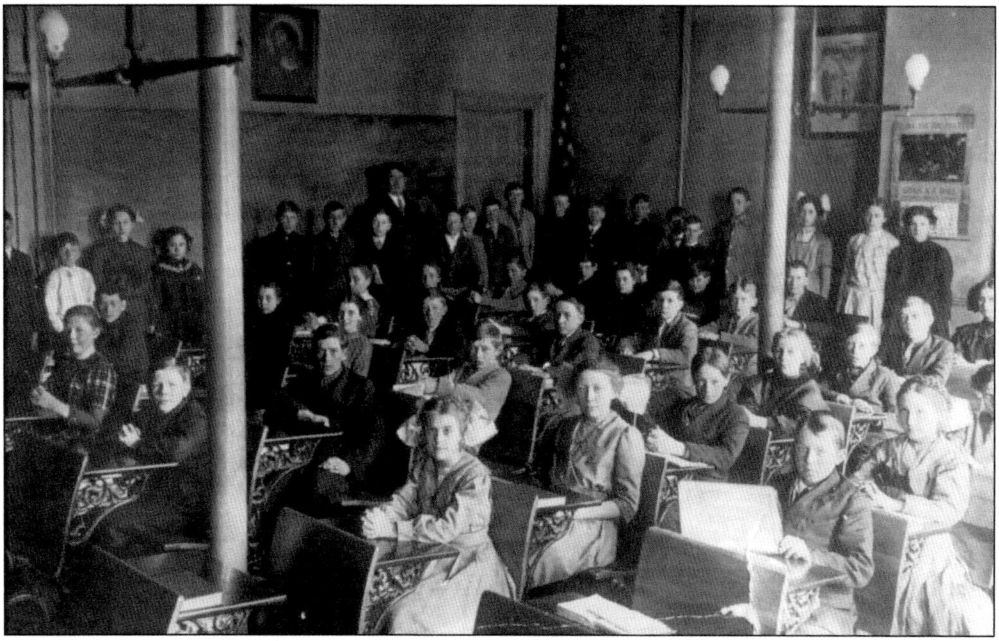

Saginaw City's Union School District was organized in 1865. Herig School built in 1907 was named after school board member Dr. E.A. Herig. This West Side brick school had eight classrooms, sanitary wardrobes, graded blackboards, and modern appliances. German was taught in all six grades. Herig School at 1905 Houghton Street is used today in the Saginaw Public School System.

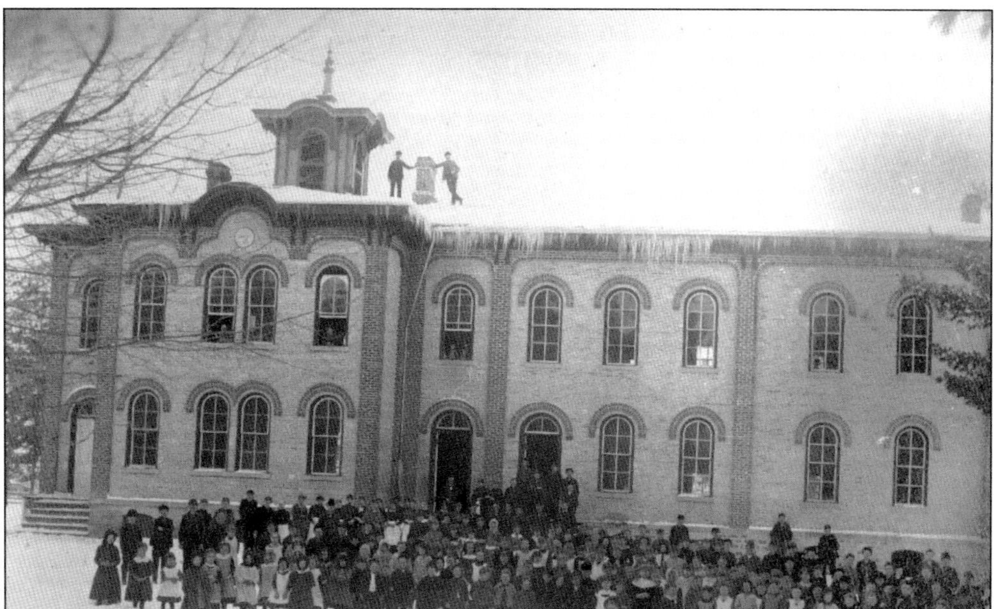

Chesaning incorporated as a village in 1869 and built this public school for $14,000. Primary, intermediate, and grammar classes were taught. It became a union school in 1870. Nine students were in the first graduating class in 1883. Town Hall meetings were also held in this school until the Annex was built in 1885.

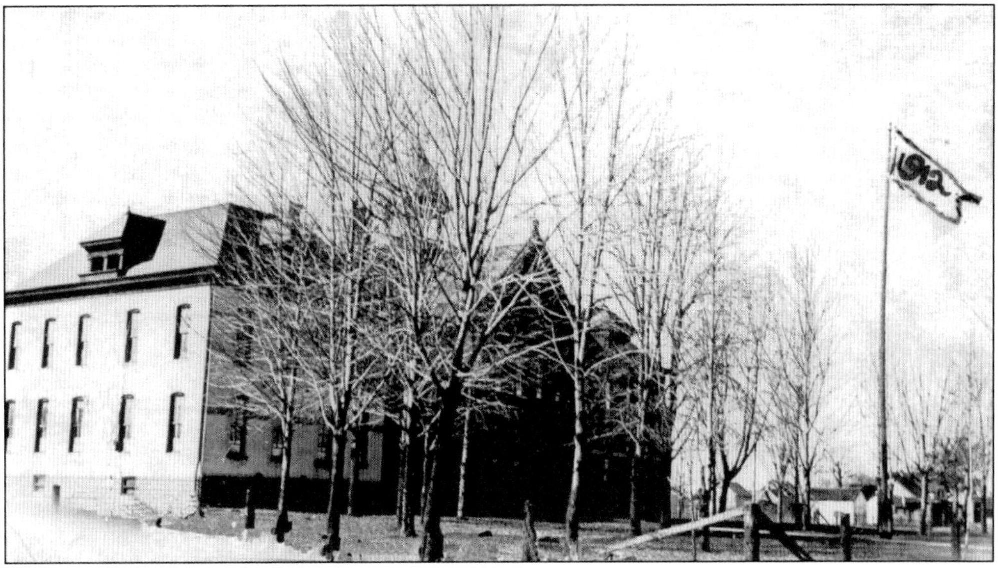

The first St. Charles log schoolhouse was opened in 1854 with Miss Joslin as the teacher. During a prosperous era, the school became a union school and the village built its high school. All grades, including high school, were taught at the school. The St. Charles Public School District has expanded drastically since this high school was built.

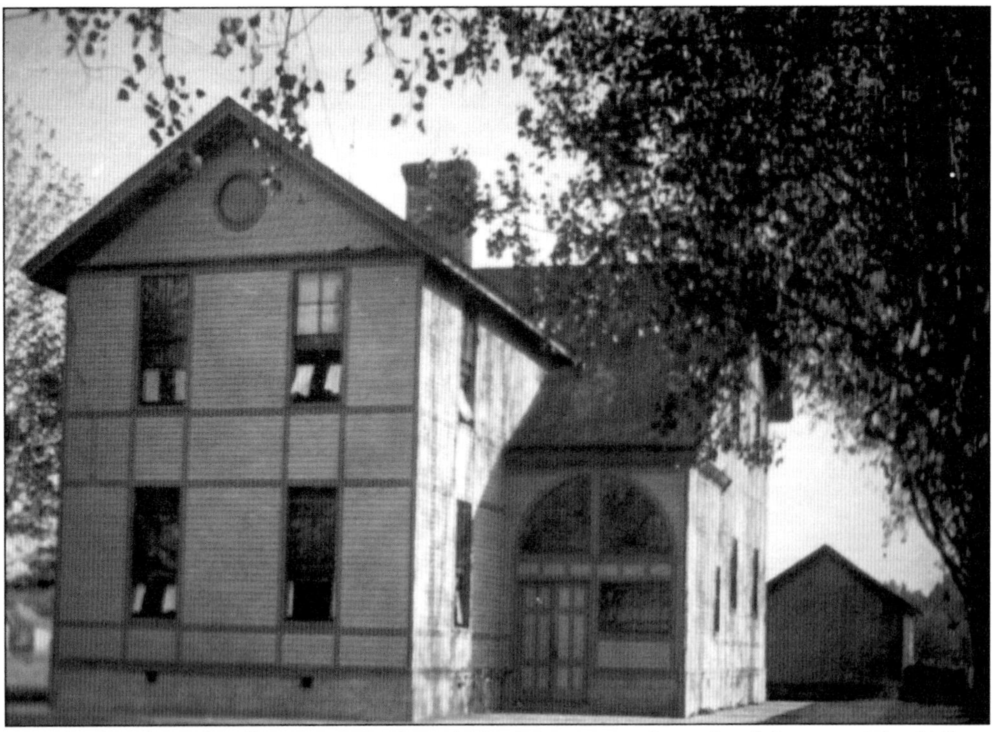

Merrill's first log schoolhouse was built in 1872. There were five school districts. The Village of Merrill outgrew its schoolhouse in 1887, so this four-room, two-story school was built. Ten grades were taught in this school until 1919 when all twelve grades were taught. In 1937, a new school was built under the WPA Program. This school remained until 1958.

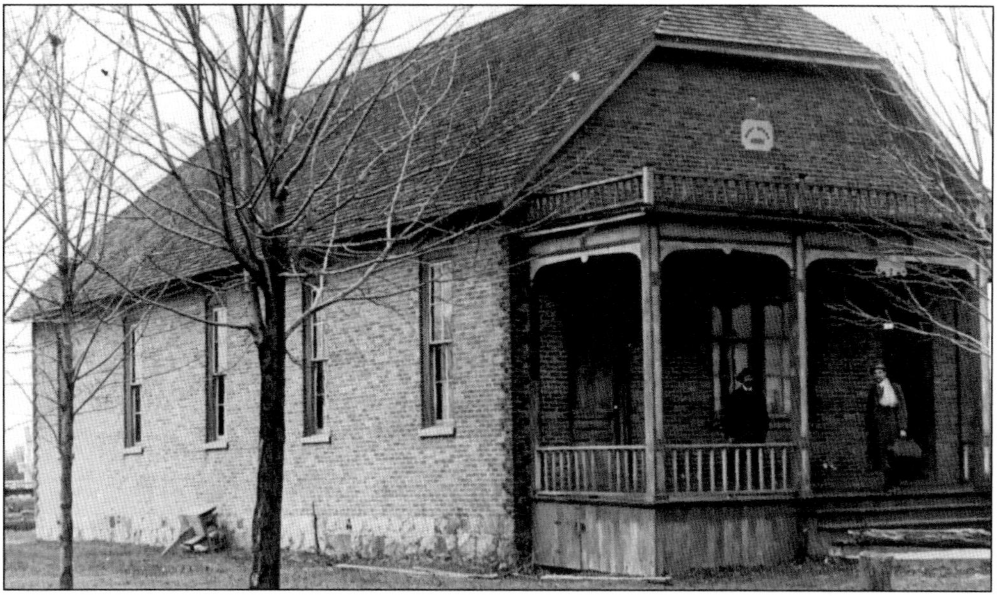

During an 1890 political rally in Burt, Wellington R. Burt gave the town $1,000 to build a community center with donated bricks. The Burt Opera House Association, organized in 1890, included representatives from Albee and Montrose Townships. Since 1891, many concerts, dances, weddings, and community events have been held at the Burt Opera House.

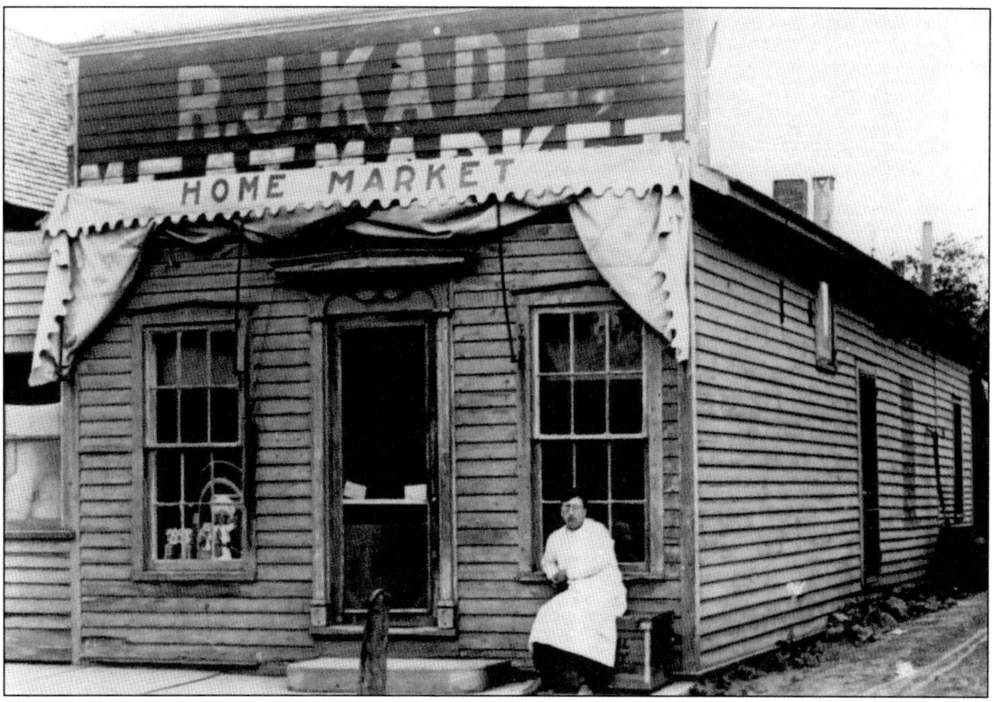

This Hemlock Main Street business was built as a pool hall in the 1800s. Then for some time it was used as the Hemlock Opera House for concerts and vaudeville shows. Kade Meat Market occupied it later, followed by Bottcher Meat Market. After being used as a movie theater and a dentist office, the Hemlock Cleaners is now operating there.

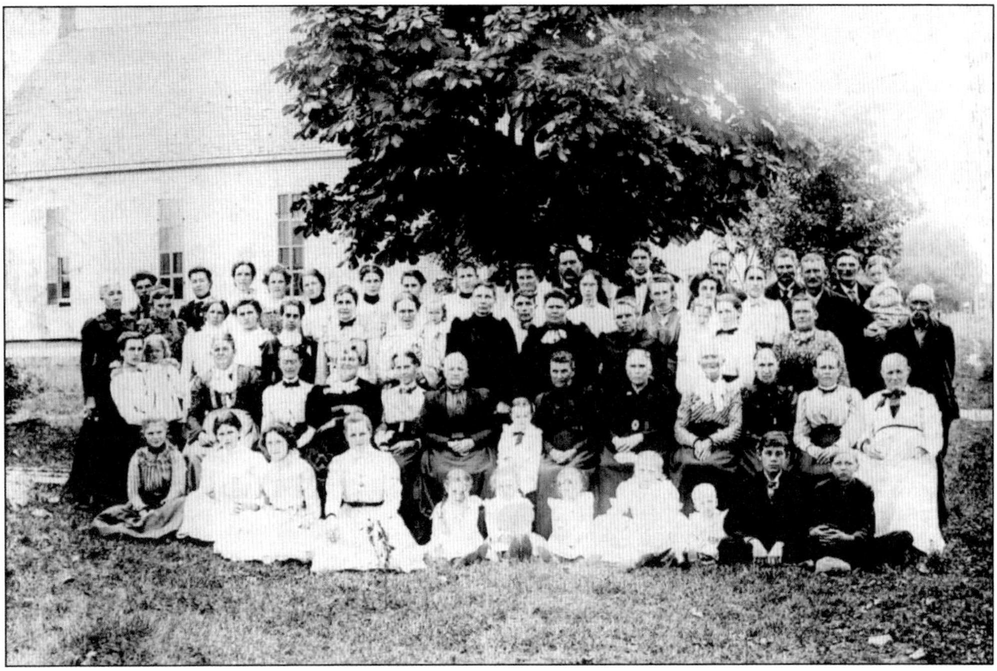

Birch Run's Methodist Protestant Church was organized in 1880. In 1896, the Church joined the Elva Mission in Arbella Township with its Olive Branch Church. This Birch Run circuit had its parsonage in Birch Run. The Methodist Aid Societies from both churches are attending a meeting at the Birch Run Parsonage in 1900. Reverend A.E. Miller is in the center back by the tree.

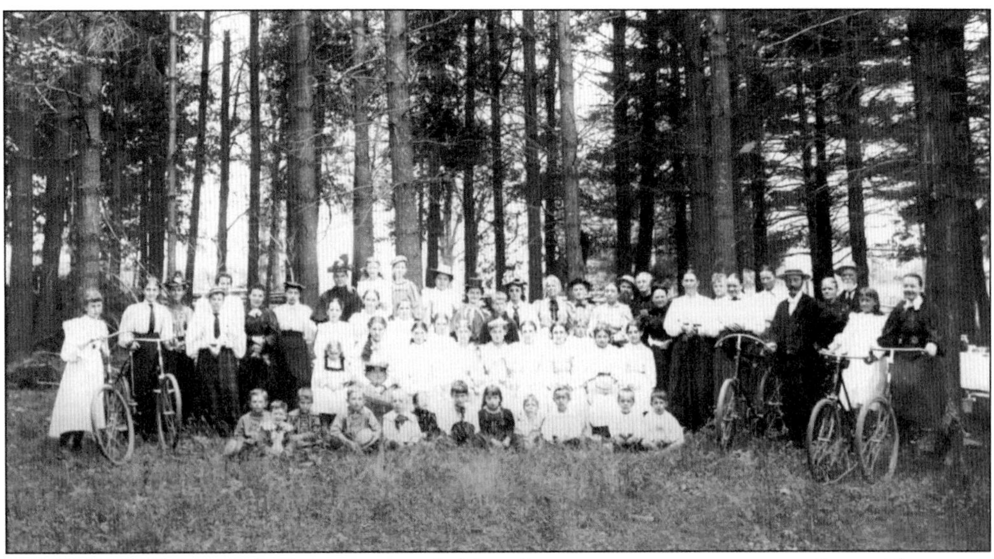

Members of Chesaning's Congregational Church are enjoying a picnic at Ponts Flats near the Shiawassee River in the 1890s. Some of the young people have traveled on their bicycles to the picnic grove. The Congregational Church had been in Chesaning only a short time before disbanding and selling their church to the St. John's Episcopal group, which also has since disbanded.

Six

Enjoying Life's Activities

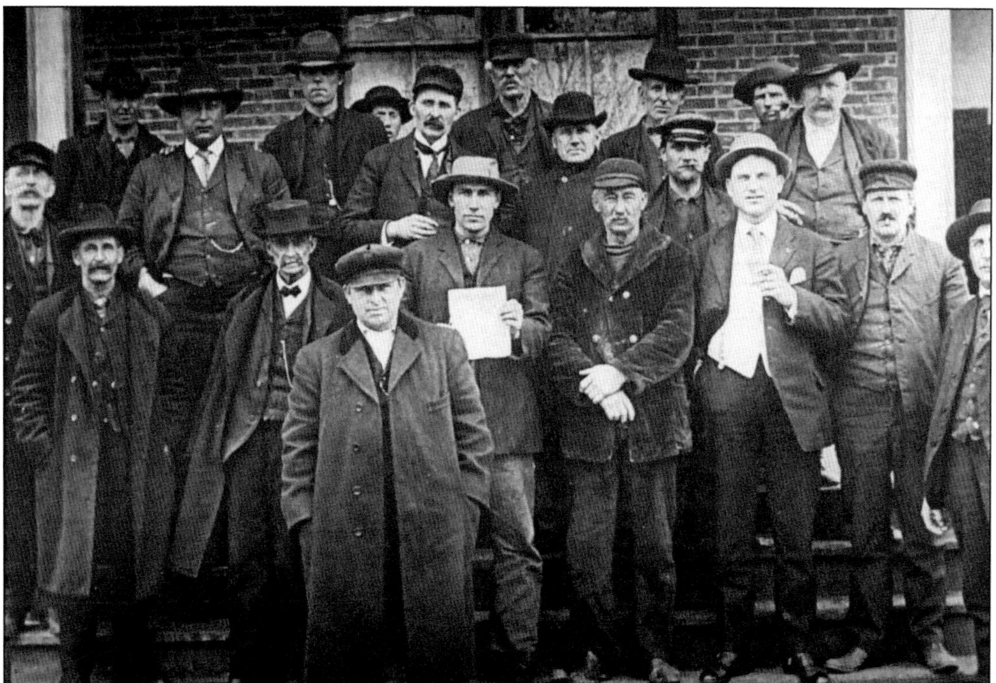

This 1900 Taymouth Township Board met regularly in Burt. In the front are Thomas O'Keefe and Manley Gibson. From left to right are the following: (on the first step) Wells Barrett, Herbert Barrett, Henry J. Fawcett, Charles McDonald, Andrew Leach, and David D. Ross; (second row) David McNally, George Baker, D.M. Hunter, Perley Becker, Steve Gagnon, and Frank McNally; and (back row) William Fitch, Henry McDonagh, John McMullen, Joseph Phillips, James Bell, and Andrew Logan.

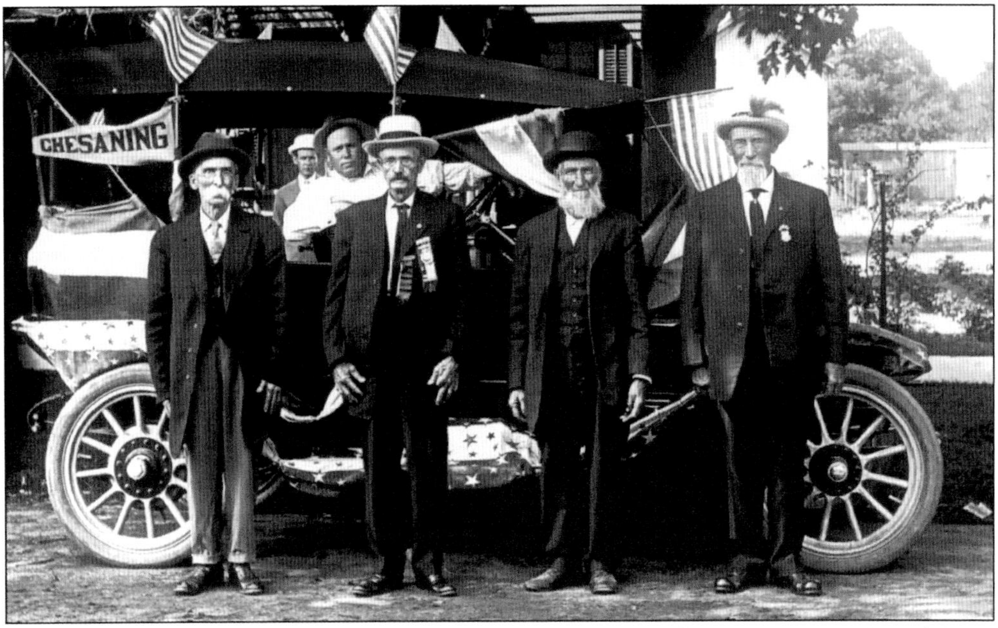

These four surviving Chesaning Civil War veterans from PAP Thomas Post 122, Grand Army of the Republic, are on their way to an encampment in this 1915 scene. Between April 1861 and April 1865, 2,039 Saginaw County men served in the Union Army. The returning veterans held annual reunions, reenacted battles, and participated in all patriotic parades.

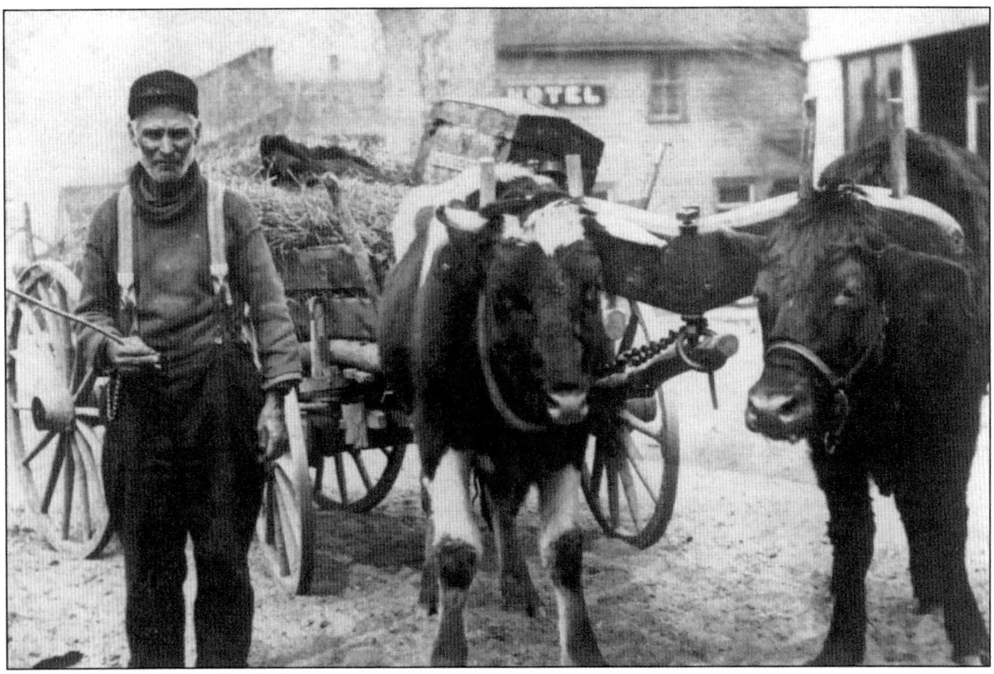

The Taymouth Township Fair was held yearly over the county line in Genesee County from 1863 to 1933. Local residents displayed their crops, livestock, flowers, canned goods, and handiwork. They enjoyed many pleasurable activities with their neighbors. Mr. Vincent is leading Buck and Bright through Burt's Main Street on their way to the fair.

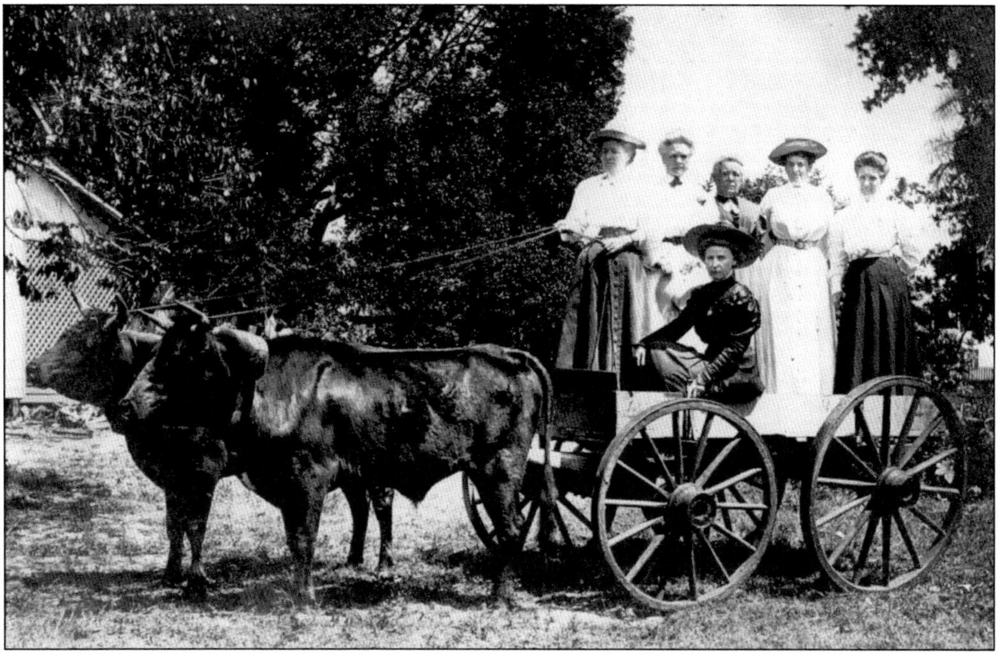

These young ladies have hitched up their ox cart and are traveling through Bridgeport to visit their friends and enjoy a pleasant Sunday afternoon. After working hard all week, local residents enjoyed themselves dressing in their Sunday best, attending church, visiting friends, picnicking, or attending social functions.

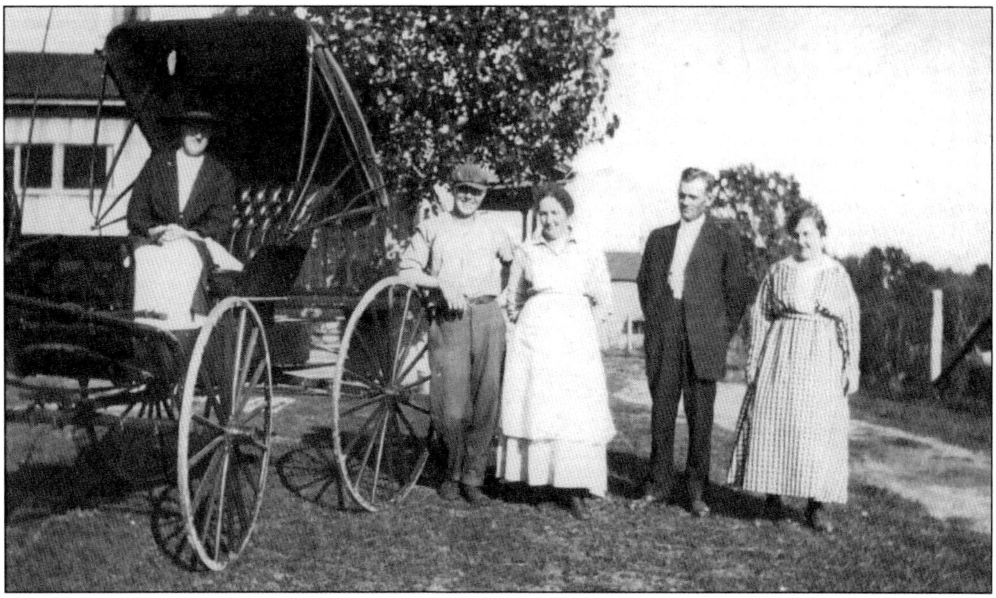

Newlywed Christine Ederer Wegner, in the buggy, is visiting the folks back home in Thomastown Township. She traveled by horse and buggy from James Township, three miles away, on this Sunday in 1913. Standing from left to right are her brother Edward Ederer, mother Mrs. Joseph Ederer, family friend Ferdinand Sparks, and sister Ella Ederer Zoellner.

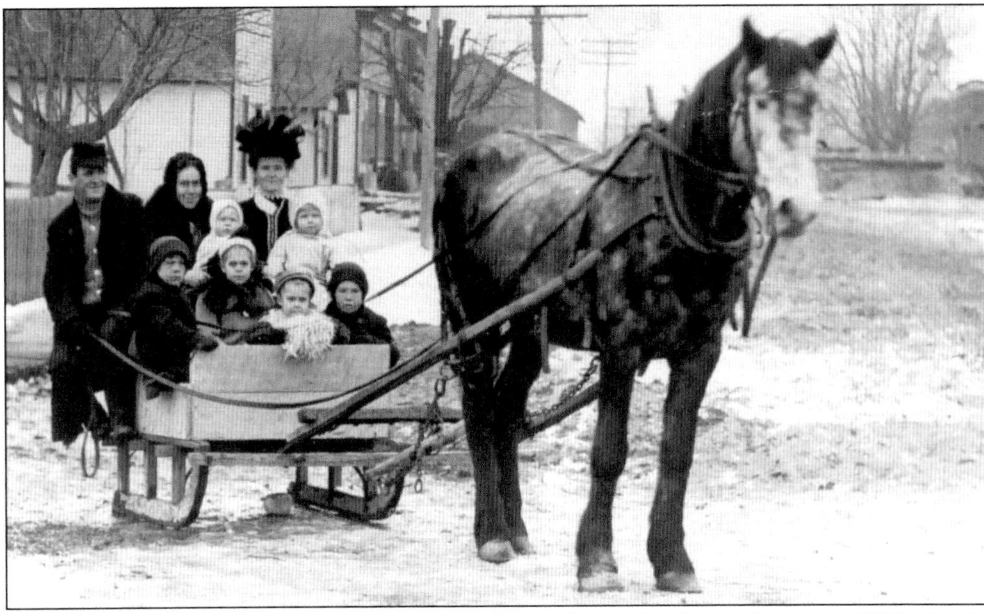

This family is enjoying a winter sleigh ride down Hemlock's Main Street in 1907. In the distance, on the right, is St. Mary's Catholic Church. On the left side are a drug store, Pahl's General Store, and Stroebel House. From left to right in the sleigh are Gustave and Bertha Laurenz, his sister Bertha Kolschmidt, and their young children.

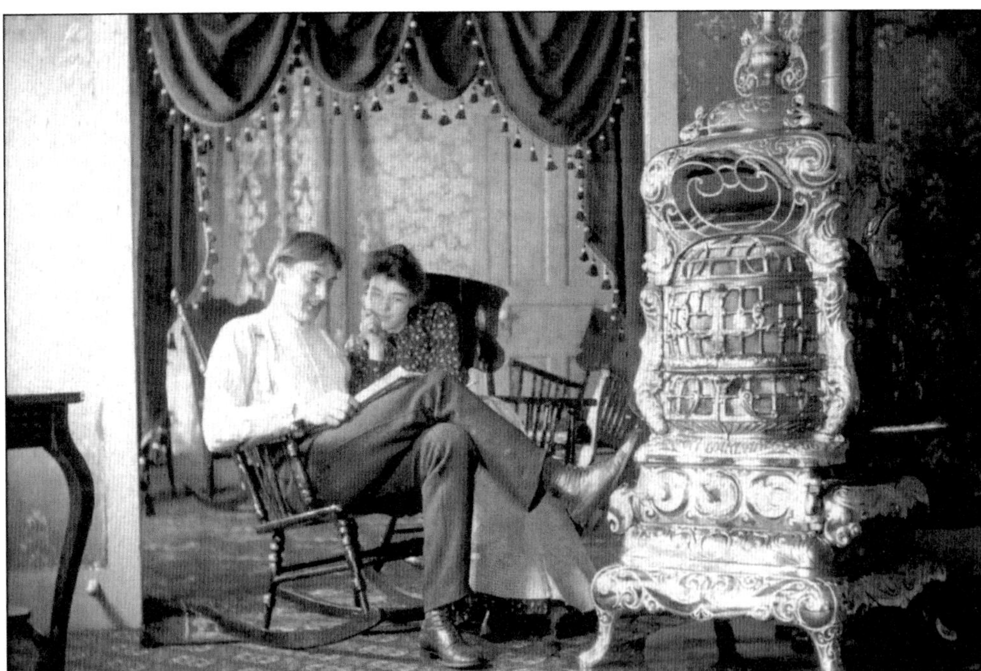

This young St. Charles couple is spending an enjoyable evening reading by the fireside while the blizzard roars outside on this cold winter day in the late 1890s. The potbellied stove has been stoked and keeps the house cozy and warm. The drapes have been closed to keep the heat in their sitting room.

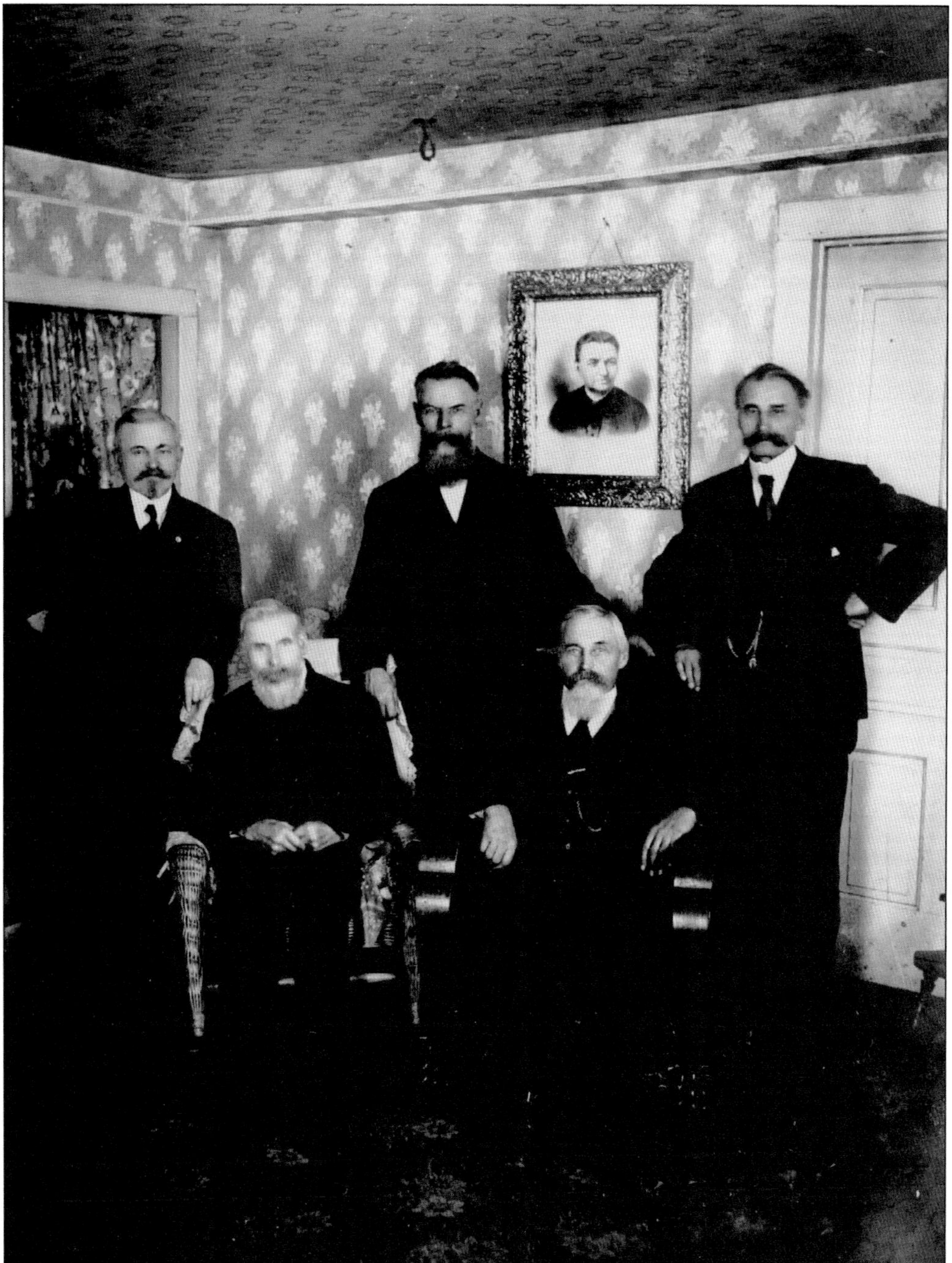

Immigrating from Franken, Germany, in 1850, August M. and Johanna Vasold and their children settled in Tittabawassee Township. All were Freeland farmers, businessmen, and politicians. Saginaw's Goodridge Bros. Photographers took this family photo of the Vasold brothers at Henry's North River Road Vasold homestead on January 23, 1910, which was August Jr.'s 77th birthday. He died on February 1, 1910. From left to right are the following: (sitting) Henry and August Jr.; and (standing) Herman, Hugo, and Otto. The wall picture is of their sister, Therese Vasold Roeser, who died in 1893.

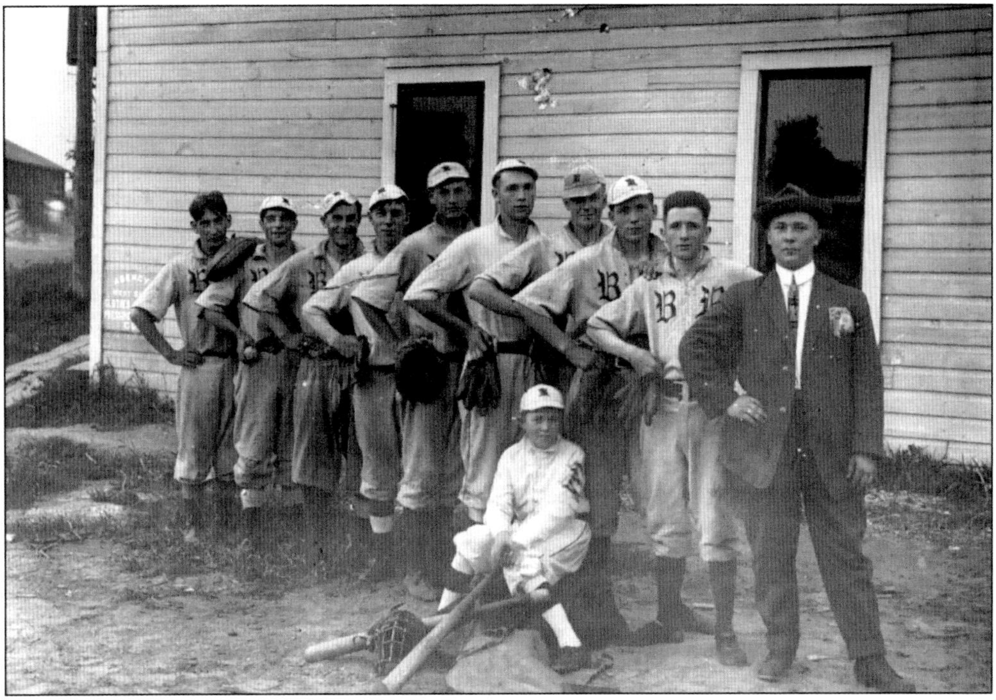

After the Civil War, small towns in America developed a passion for baseball. Every small town had its own organized baseball team and played against teams from neighboring towns. The newspapers reported about the games for eager readers. Birch Run's team, pictured with their coach, is waiting to play that winning game against their neighboring town.

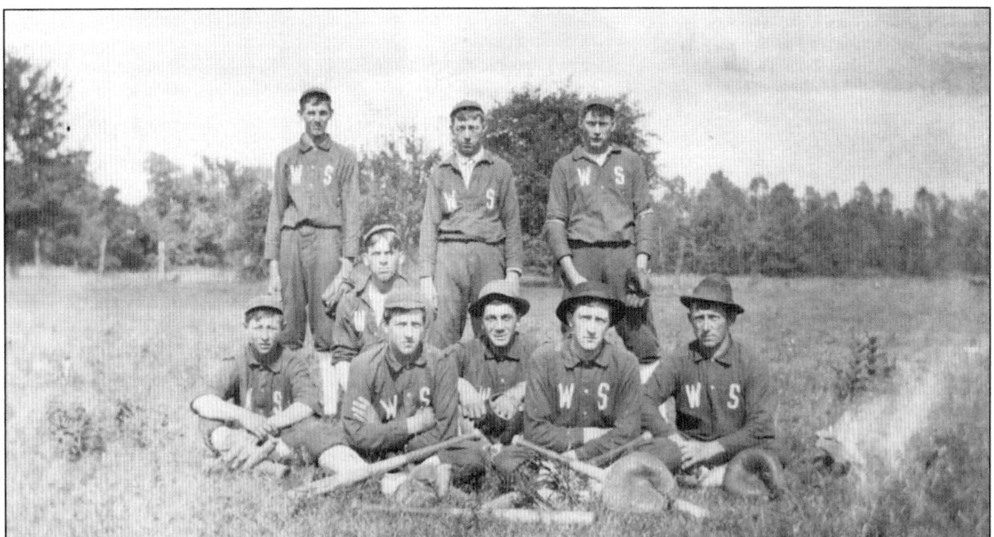

Larger cities such as Saginaw had many baseball teams from several neighborhoods. Teams within the city often played against each other. This is the Liskow White Sox Baseball Team in 1910. Elmer Steele is standing in the back middle. Sitting from left to right are Frank Madler, unidentified, Louis Summerfeldt, William Ederer, and George Ederer. Other are unidentified. The team got together several times each week to practice their skills.

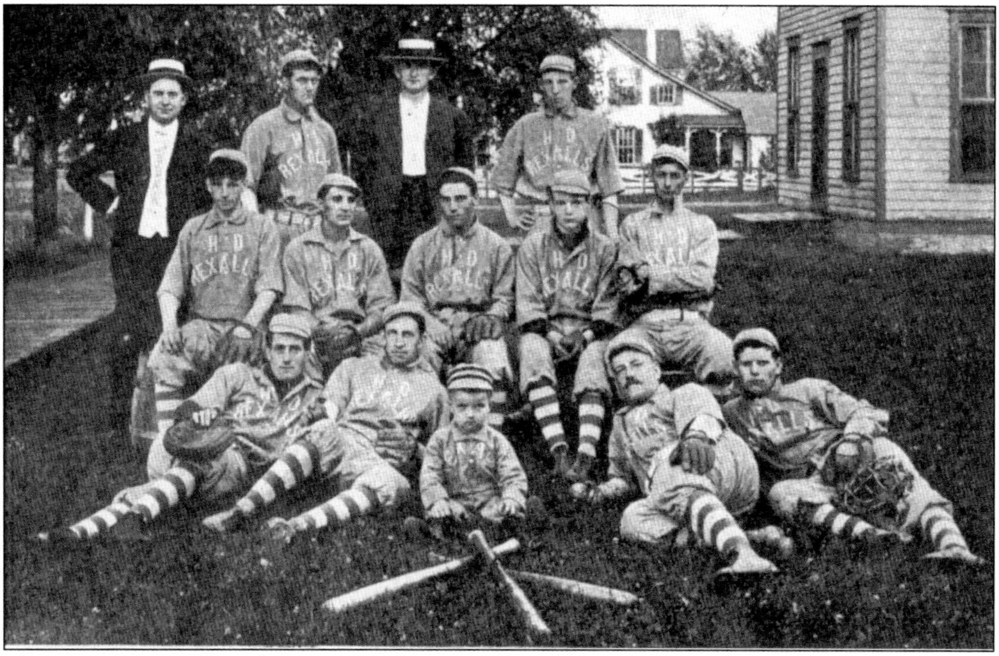

Communities were proud of their home team and rallied around them, whether they won or lost games. Local newspapers helped to defend the losing team or boost the community's pride for a winning team. Dolson's Rexall Baseball Team brought a unified community spirit to St. Charles in all the games they played with neighboring towns.

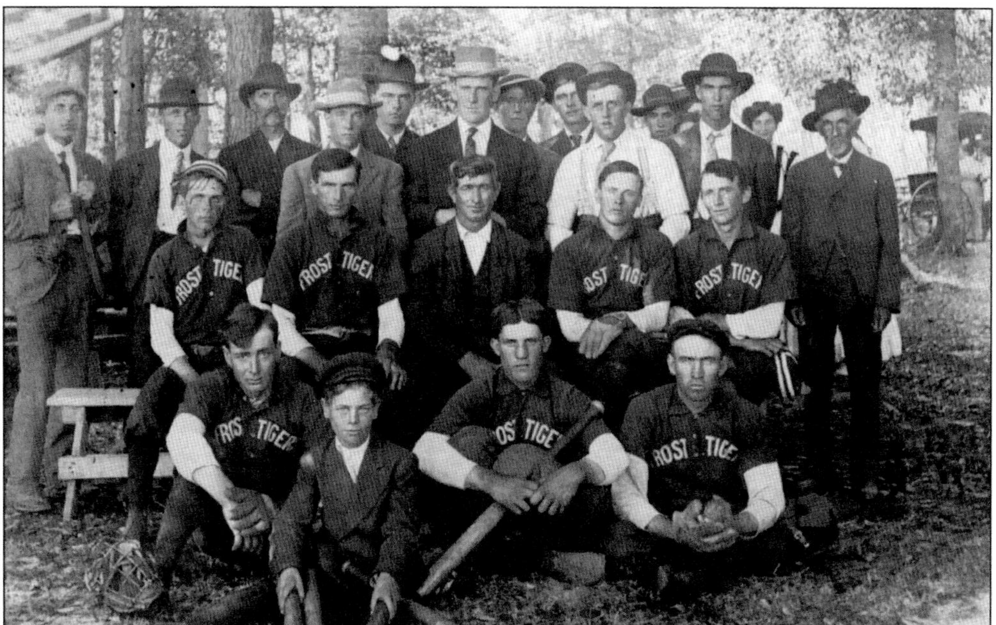

Freeland's Frost Tigers are about ready to play a baseball game while their friends watch on the sidelines. The spectators standing in this photo are dressed in their Sunday best. The baseball team is seated. Ed Wurtzel is second from the right in the front row. A community was always proud of its amateur baseball team and never missed a game.

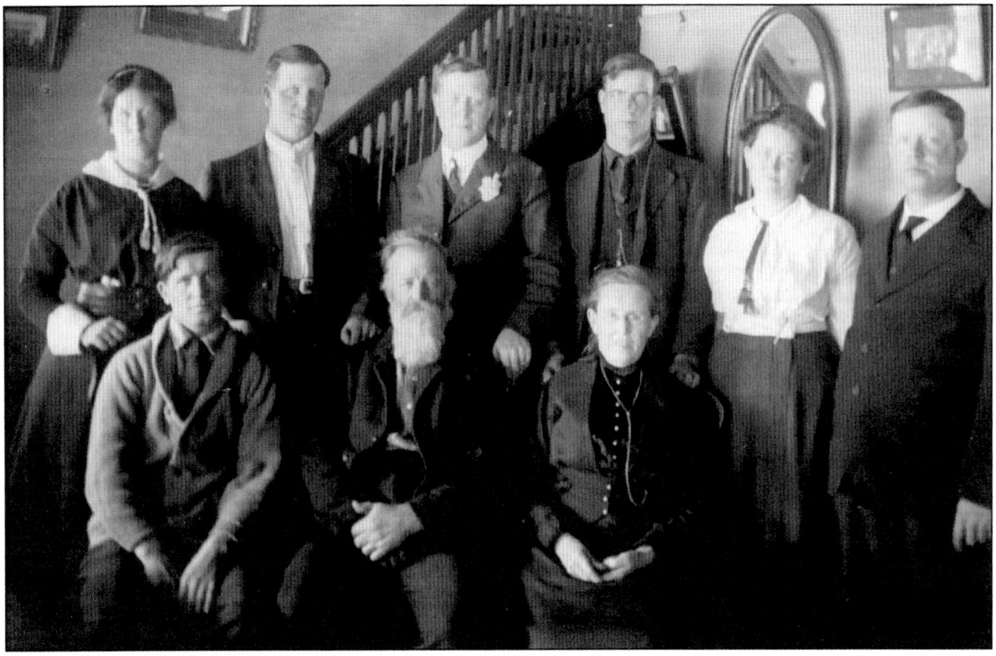

Soon after their 1872 marriage in Ohio, John A. and Kate Hill came to Oakley, where their children were born and became lifelong residents. John Hill was a railroad foreman. The Hills are enjoying a family get-together in their parents' well-kept Oakley home. Pictured from left to right are (seated) Arthur, John A., and Kate Hill; (standing) Belle Hill Jones, Samuel, Frank, Emmett, Sebra Hill Towne, and Henry Hill.

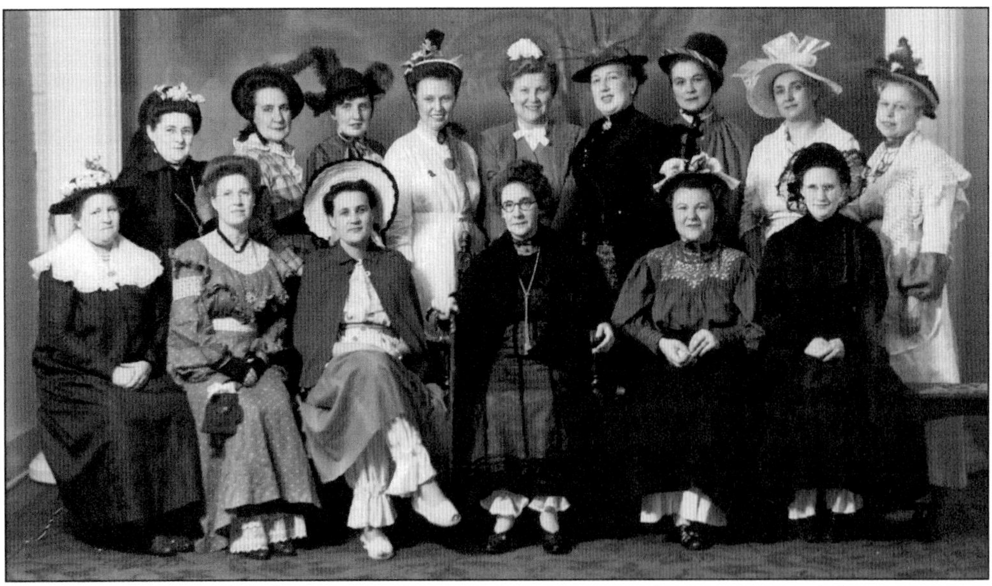

The Oakley Ladies' Club dressed up in bygone era costumes and gave an annual free community performance at Oakley Hall. These ladies performed a play wearing costumes in this 1929 photo. Pictured from left to right are the following: (seated) Ada Smith, Alma Fickies, Stephina Bila, Eva Welch, Kate Sovis, and Doris Brenner; and (standing) Helen Jordan, Gladys Coss, Arlyle Brainard, Bertha Kuchar, Mary Glaska, Helen Kogne, Rose Dorn, Alliene Morman, and Daisy Clark.

These young Birch Run ladies are sampling the wedding cake during a break at a wedding celebration. Alama Clinter is on the left. The other two ladies are unidentified; the happy bride appears in the middle. Weddings were joyous occasions in small towns, and they were some of the towns' most important social events.

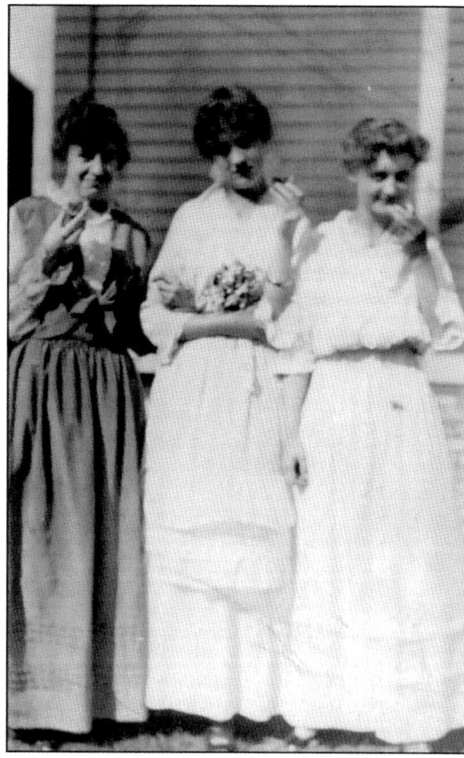

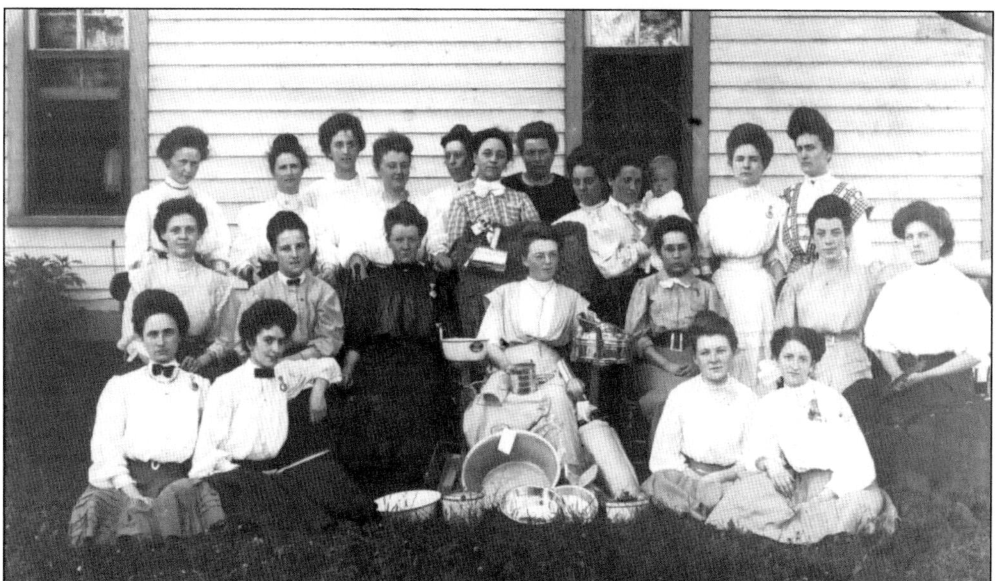

These Freeland ladies are attending a bridal shower for Ethel Kitchen, seated with the gifts. Sitting on the left front are Edith Munger and Florence Baird. Seated on the right are Sadie Kitchen and Zoa Munger. In the next row, from left to right, are the following: unidentified, Dora Kitchen, Jessie Frasier, Ethel Kitchen, unidentified, Rilla Sanford, and Florence Roachie; and in the back row, beginning fourth from left, are Nellie Frasier, Gertie Munger, Miss Smith, Pearl Houd, Lottie Baubarin, two unidentified, and Mrs. Albert Munger.

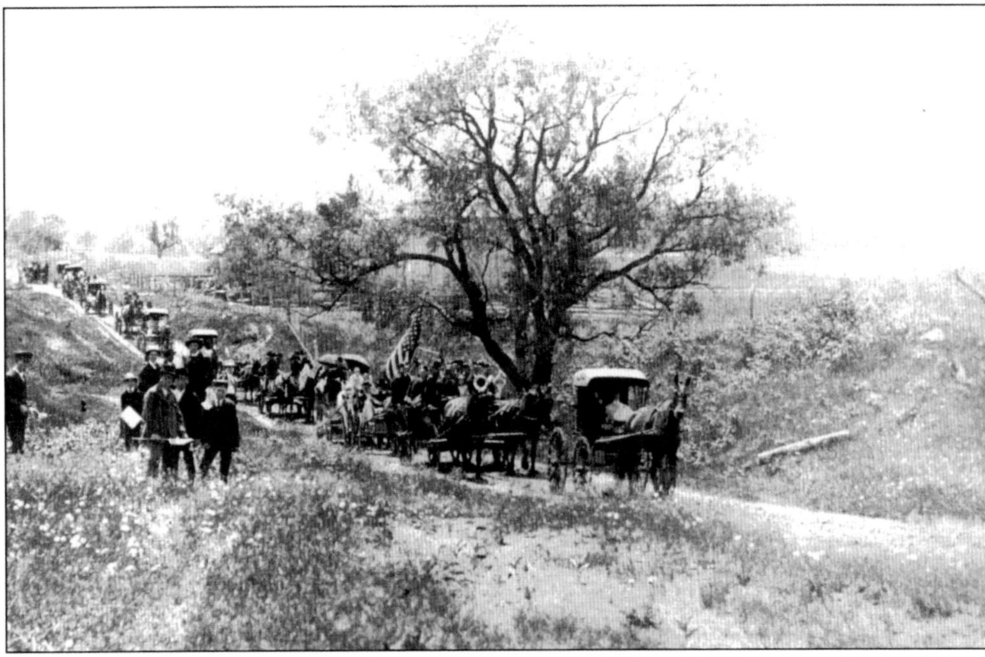

The Freeland Band leads this grand Decoration Day parade from Main Street in Freeland down Midland Road to the Pine Grove Cemetery. A patriotic ceremony with music, speeches, and prayers honors those local Civil War heroes who gave their lives during the War. Civil War veterans participate in the ceremony.

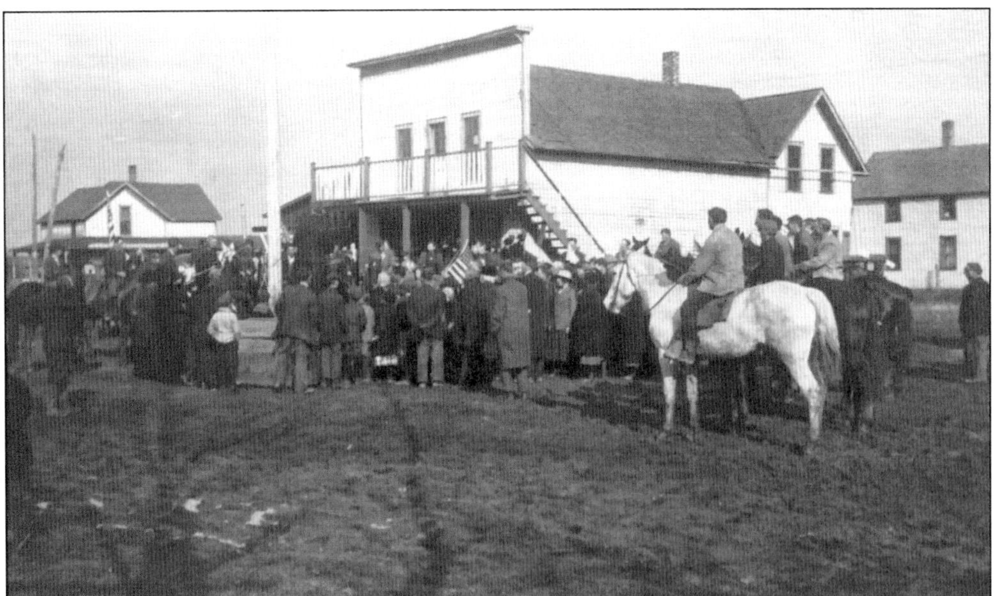

Local residents from miles away have gathered at a store in Nelson Corners in Fremont Township on Armistice Day, November 11, 1918, to hear the good news about the end of World War I. Some people have come by horseback. Some are holding flags. It was a joyous occasion celebrating the war's end and the soldiers' homecoming. The store is no longer there.

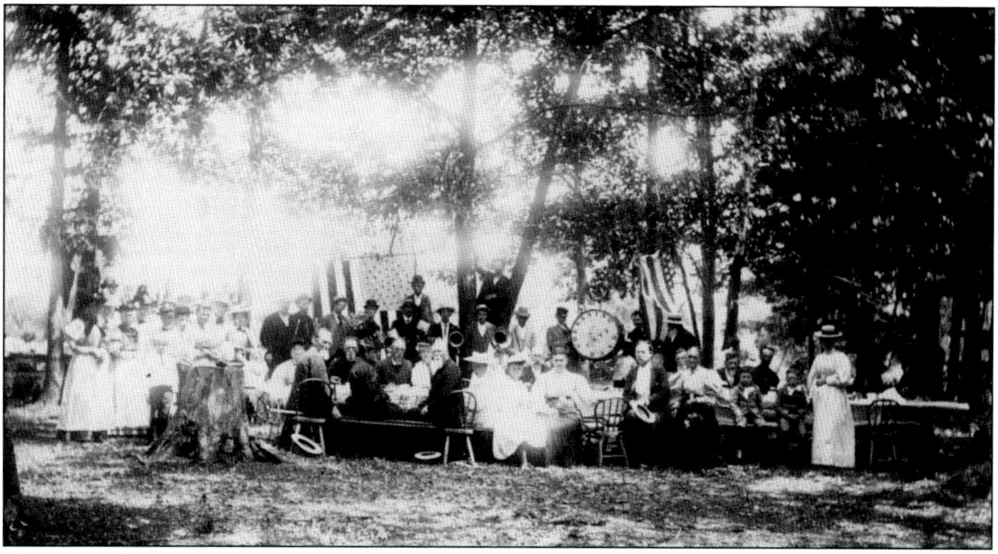

Chesaning had its City Band from 1855 through the end of World War II. This band played in many community activities, parades, concerts, and the Friday evening concerts on Broad Street. In this 1890s photo, the City Band is entertaining in a public park during a Fourth of July celebration. After World War II, the high school band participated in community events.

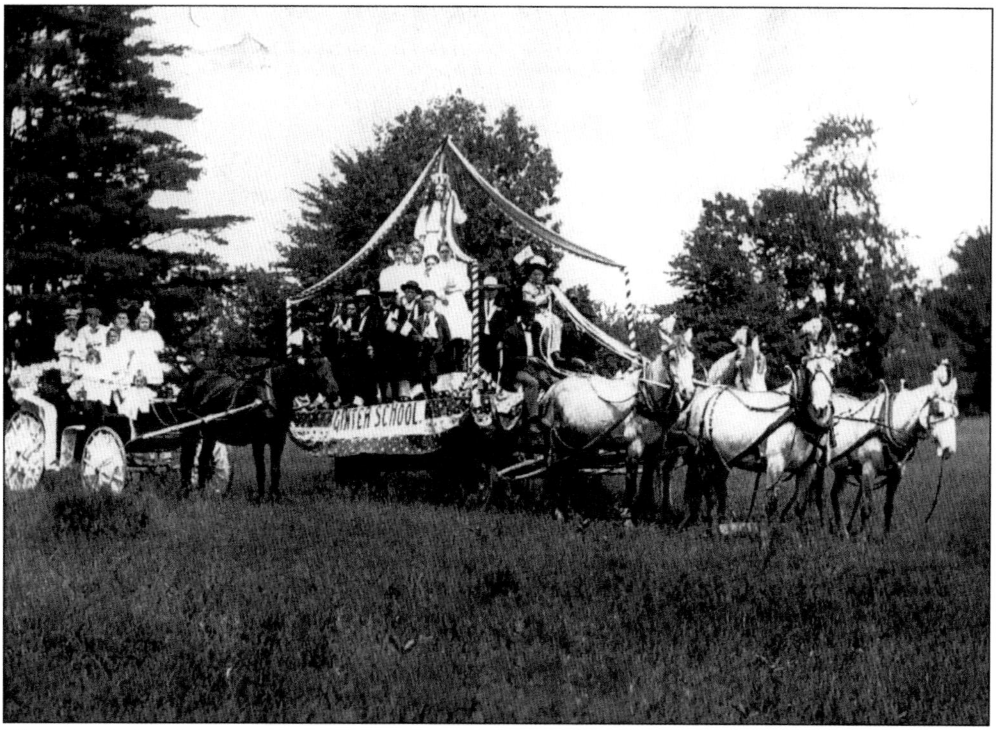

With the help of their parents, the children from rural Ginter School on Volkmer Road have decorated a wagon and a buggy and are on their way to a Chesaning Decoration Day parade in the 1800s. An adult man is driving the four-horse team, pulling the patriotically decorated hay wagon. Children dressed in their Sunday best are riding on the wagon and in the buggy.

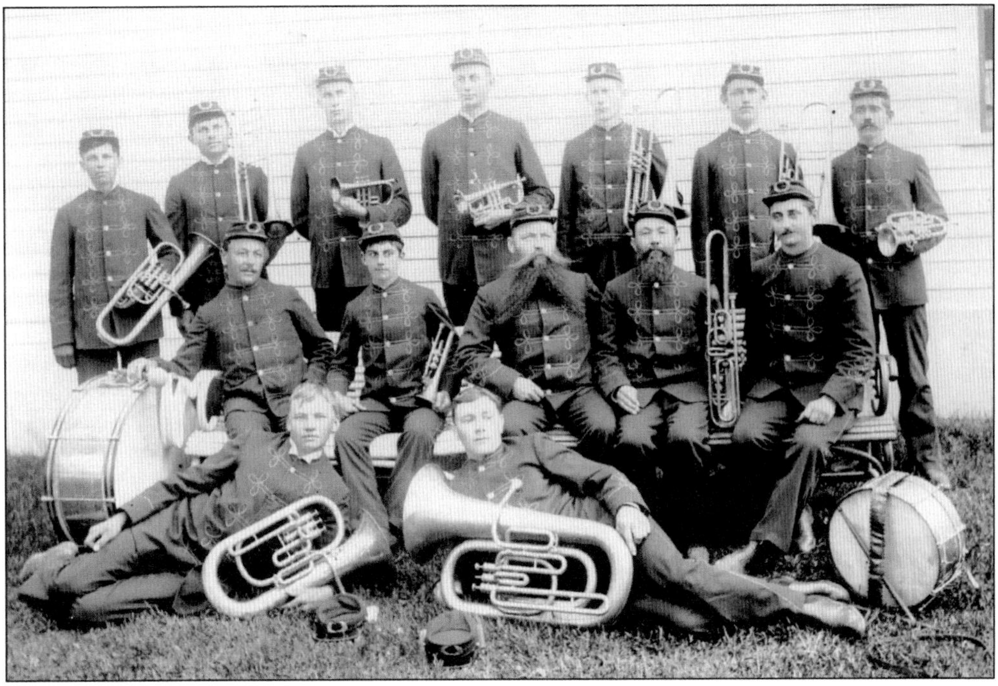

Frankenmuth Band members dressed in their braid-trimmed uniforms and hats pose prior their performance in this 1902 photo. Identified band members, from left to right, are the following: (back) Herman Hubinger, unidentified, Mr. Kern, Herman Kern, Rick Kern, George Rummel; and (middle) John Zehnder, Leon Rummel, Ernst Strieter, Fred Zehnder, and Jacob Rummel. German music was the band's specialty.

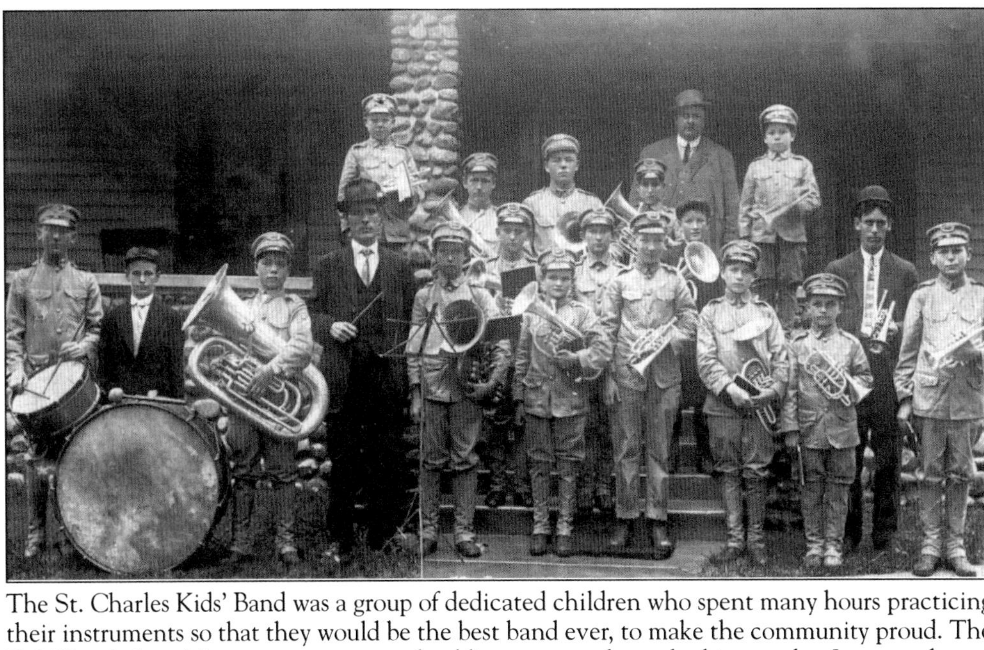

The St. Charles Kids' Band was a group of dedicated children who spent many hours practicing their instruments so that they would be the best band ever, to make the community proud. The Kids' Band played for many concerts and public events and marched in parades. It was an honor to be selected as a member of the Kids' Band.

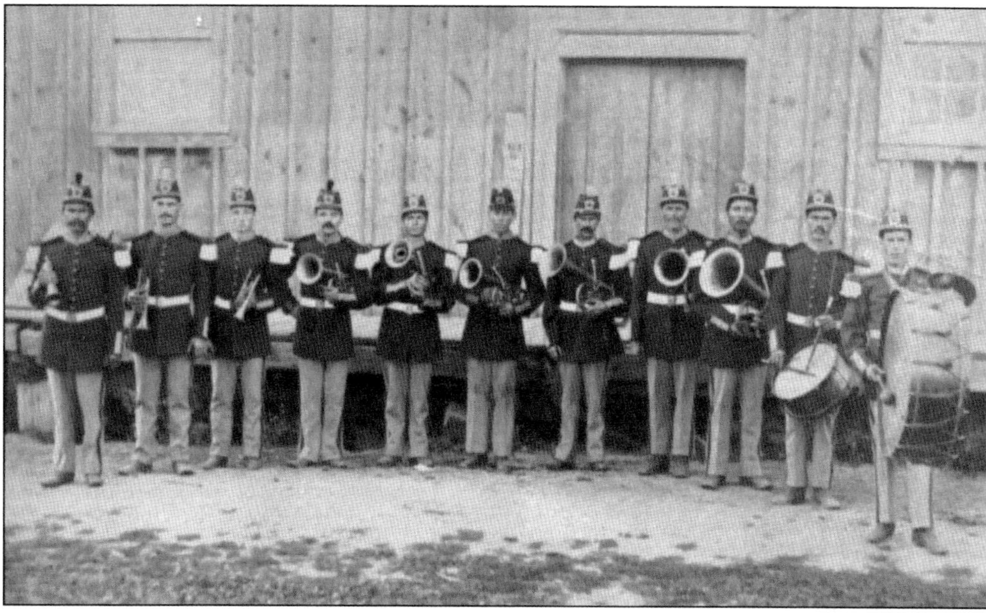

The handsome Taymouth Brass Band poses in front of the cheese factory in Burt before marching in the town's parade. The band was always ready to participate in any community event, concert, or parade for Taymouth Township.

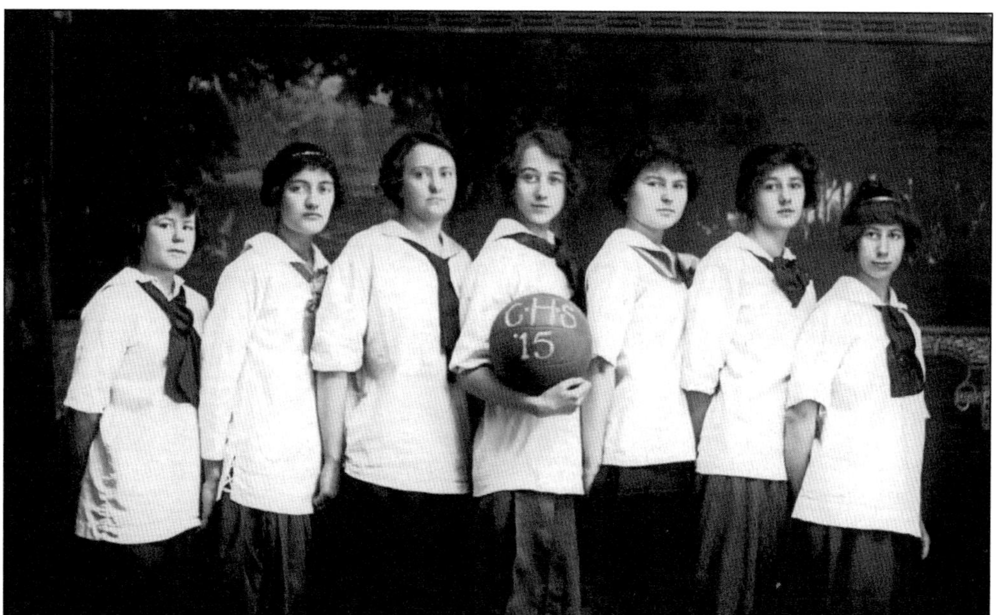

The 1915 Chesaning High School girls' basketball team was the team to make the town proud. Dressed in their uniforms, from left to right are Margaret Sackrider Dankert, unidentified, Ethel DeBarr, Mebba Shortridge Kressbach, Reva Smith Goodenaw, Ruth McKenzie, and Ferne Johnson Walser.

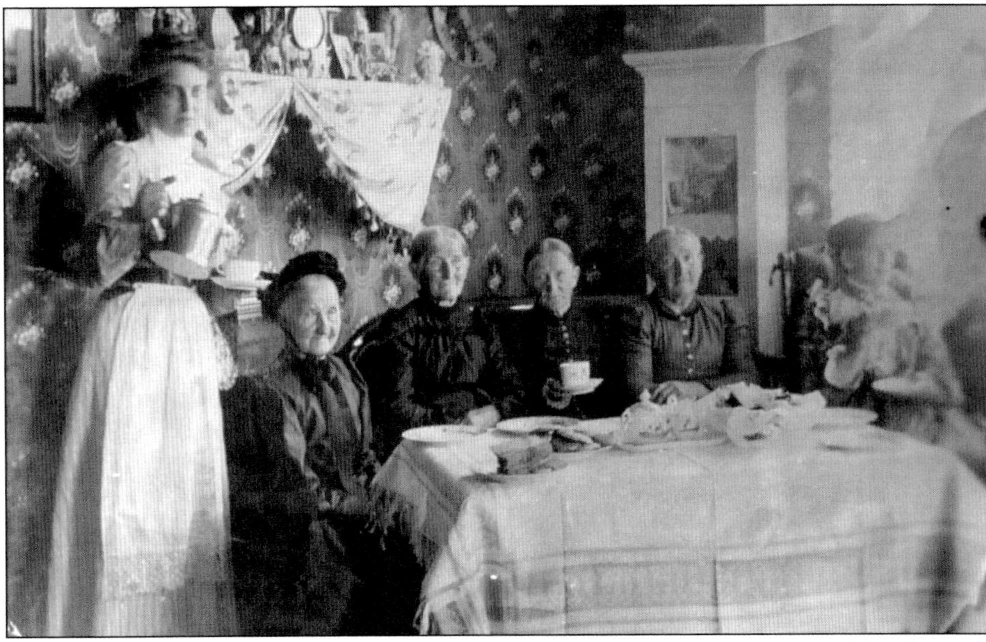

Five Frankenmuth ladies dressed in their Sunday best are having an enjoyable afternoon visiting, while Mrs. Lillie Voss Hubinger is serving them dessert and coffee. Grandmother Hubinger is one of the ladies. The room is attractively decorated in early 1900s décor with flowered wallpaper, a draped whatnot shelf, mantel clock, and wall pictures.

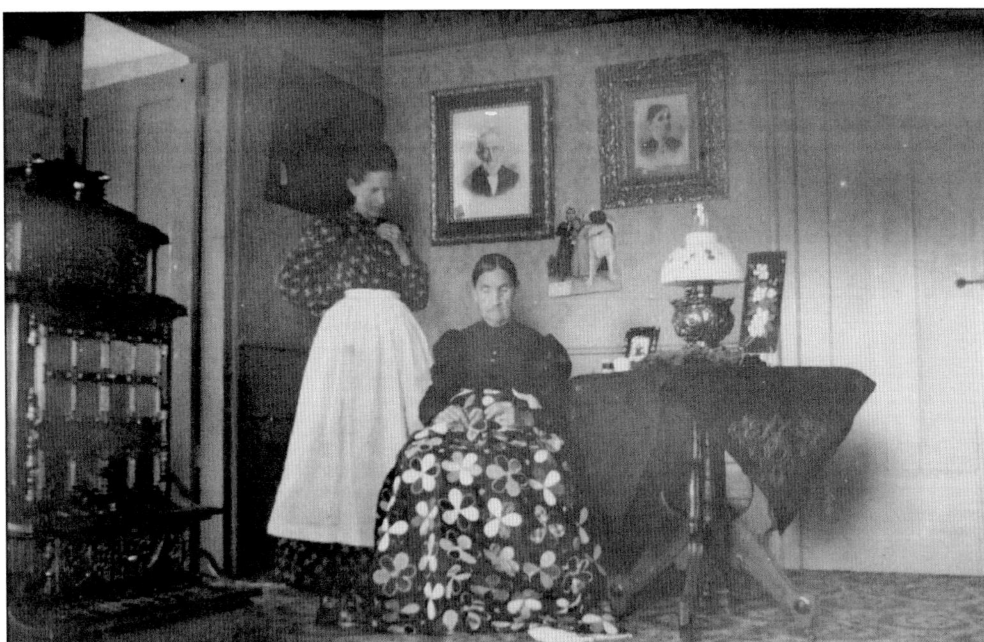

Mrs. Andrew Crofoot and her daughter, Lomalina, had been using a corner of their living room for several weeks to make a quilt. The completed quilt is spread over Lomalina's lap in this picture. Their home was on the northwest corner of Broad and Main Streets in Chesaning. Photographs of their early ancestors hang on the wall behind them.

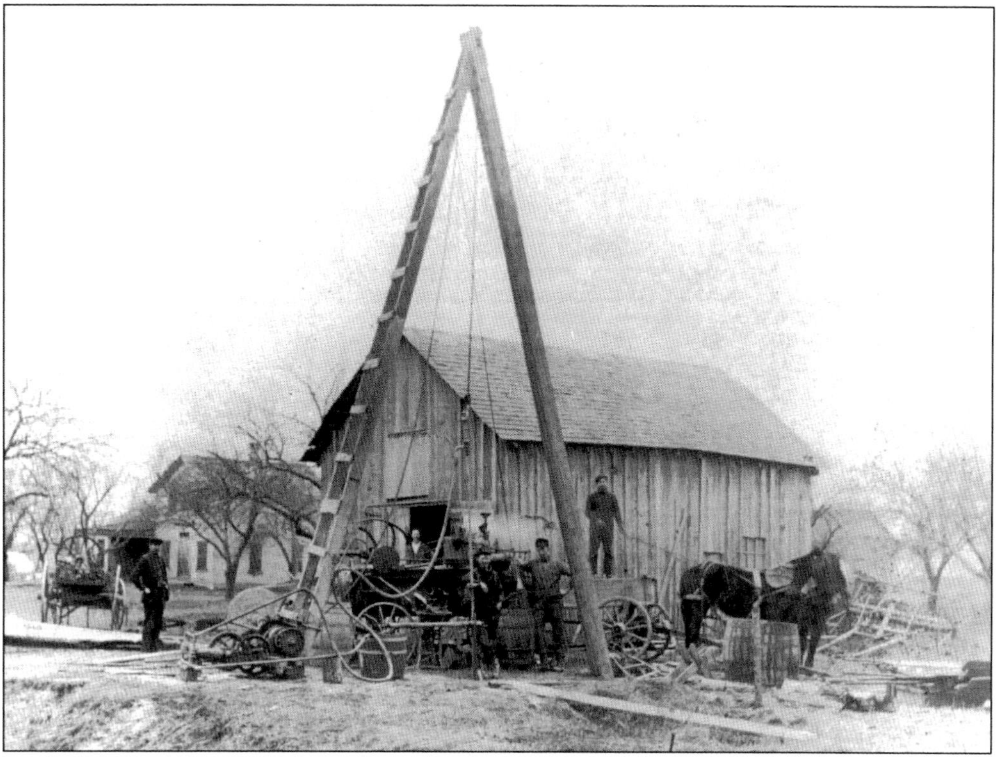

This was a scene repeated many times throughout Saginaw County in the 1800s and early 1900s. The men are digging a deep water well for Dennis McCarty in Freeland. All work was done manually and with teams of horses. Every rural residence needed a well because this often was the only source of drinking water available.

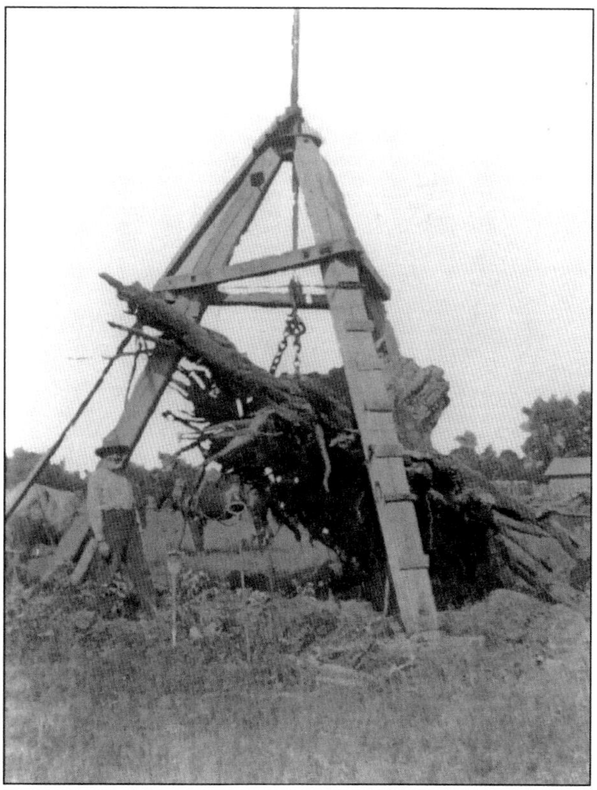

A huge tree stump is being removed in Burt in this 1890s photo. The county's earliest settlers had to clear their land of its trees before they could farm. Tree stumps were either dynamited out or removed with this stump puller. All work was done manually with the help of horses or oxen. Such activities were conducted many times, year after year, in Saginaw County.

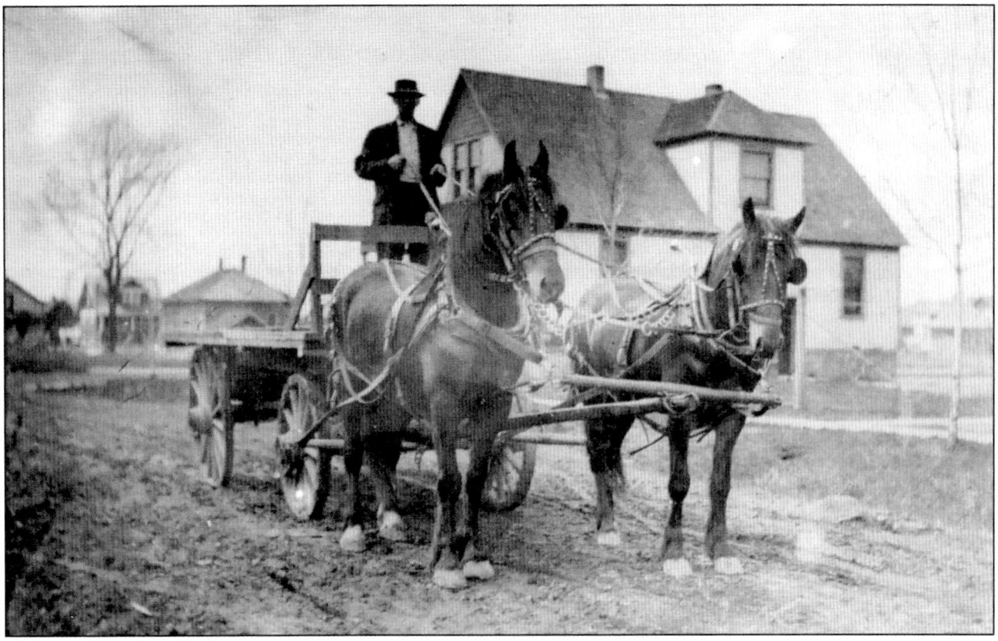

In this picture, James Van Wormer has hitched up his perfectly matched two-horse team and hay wagon and is ready to begin work in the fields or go for a ride into town on a sunny day in 1910. His farm is on Portsmouth Road in Bridgeport Township.

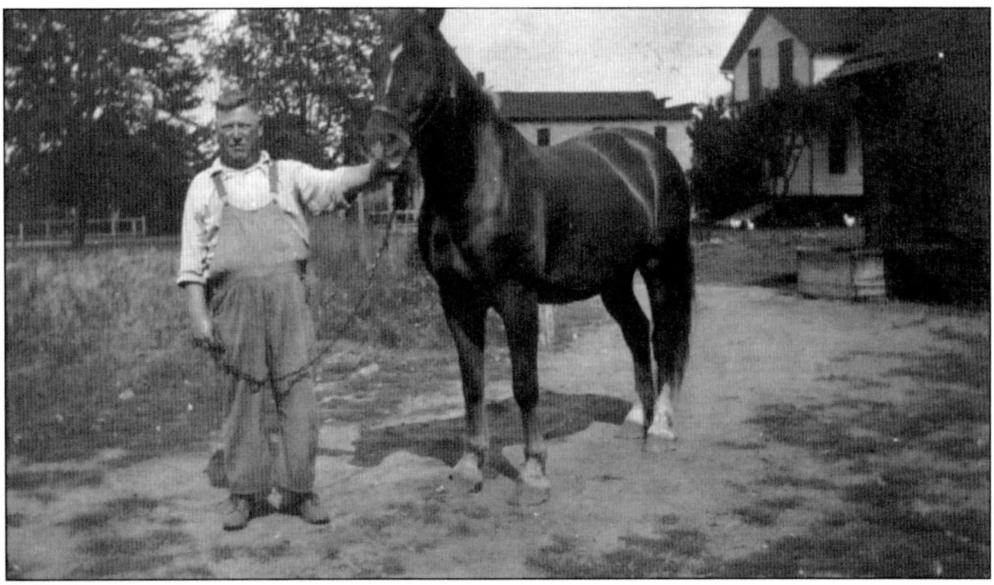

John Frost was proud of his fine three-year-old horse, which he had raised since its birth. His farm was on Frost Road in Thomastown Township. Horses were needed for transportation and for working in the farm fields. After World War II, horses were replaced with tractors and gasoline-powered machinery, and then were used mainly for recreational purposes.

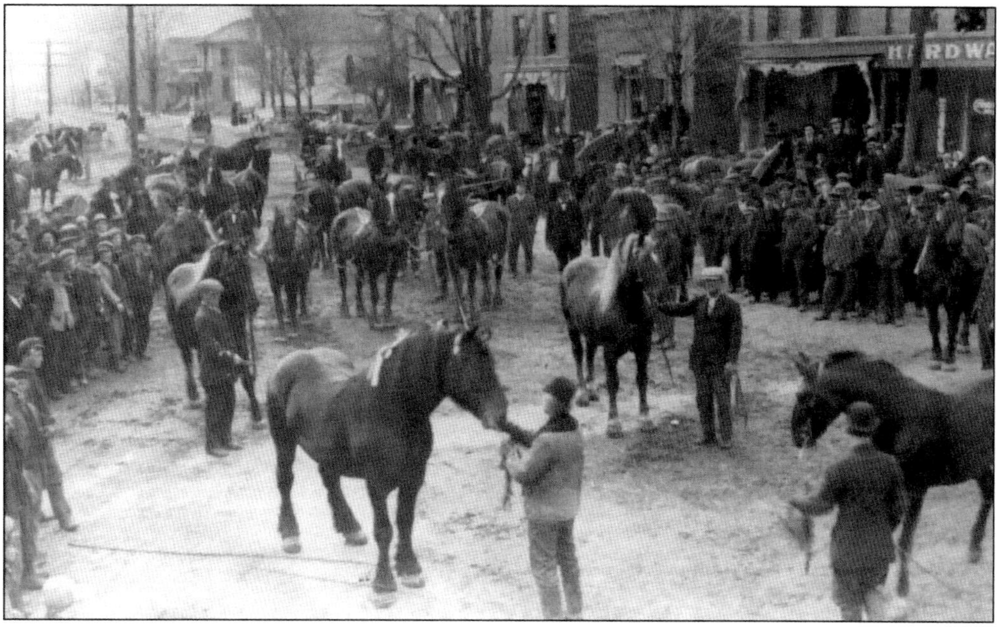

This horse auction is taking place in the middle of Saginaw Street, or M-46, in Hemlock. On the right are the Hardware Store, IOOF Hall, and Hemlock Bank; St. Mary's Church is in the distance. People came to the horse auctions to buy or sell their horses. In the late 1800s, all local traffic stopped during the auction because this main street was used as a community park.

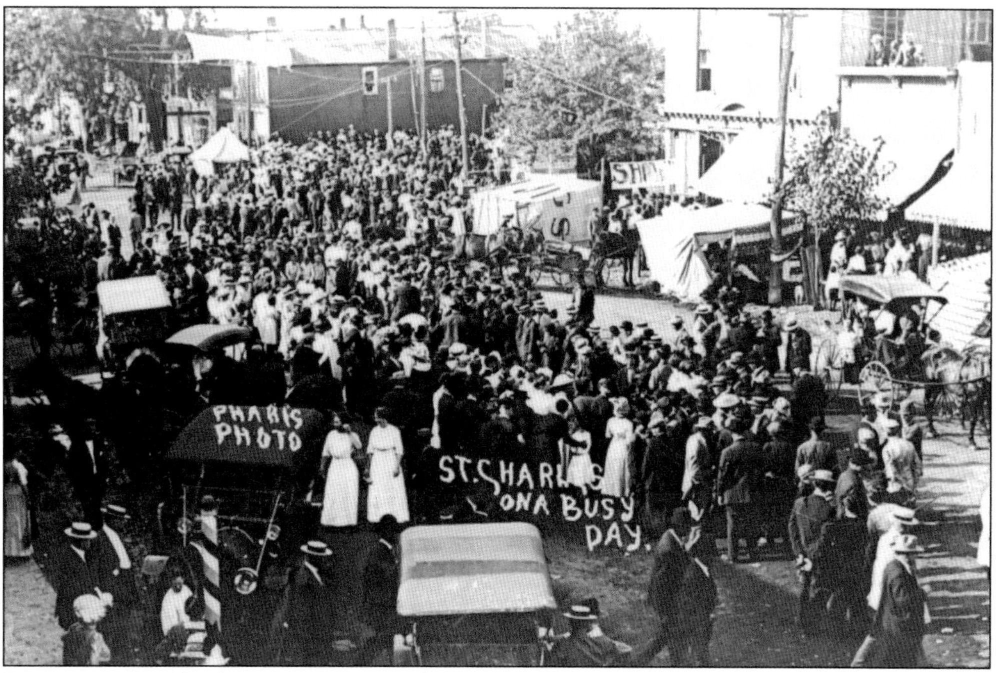

Downtown St. Charles streets are crowded with farmers and local residents at the intersection of Belle and Saginaw Streets in the 1920s. It became a ritual for local residents to intermingle and socialize with each other on the streets every Friday night. The outlying township farmers came on Saturday night. That was the time for isolated farmers to visit their neighbors.

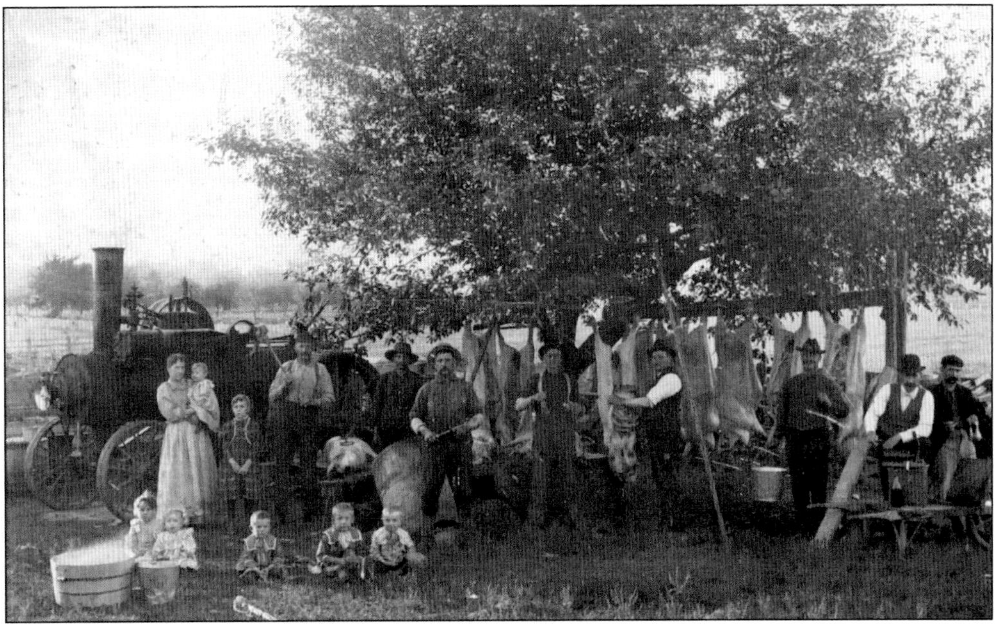

This annual butchering fest brought the Kern family together on their Frankenmuth Frank Road farm. With their children seated, Anna holds a baby and Mike stands near a child. Standing in the back from left to right are Martin Eischer, William Kern, and George Kern. Lorenz Kern is in the white shirt in the middle. Since 1949, Kern's Sausages has made and sold traditional German sausages.

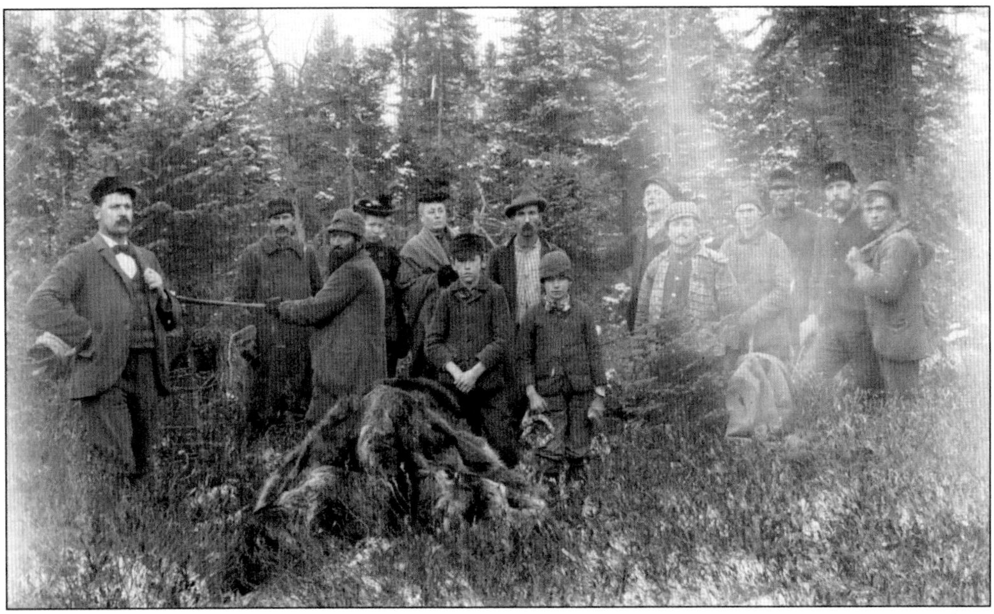

In this picture, G.J. Hubinger and his men have just returned from their four-day Grayling trip with two bob sleighs loaded with Christmas trees to sell on Frankenmuth's Tuscola Street woodlot. One tree is for St. Lorenz Church. The horsehides cover beer kegs. G.J. Gugel is on the far left. Some of the men are Fred Heine, Richard Hubinger, Leon Heine, Christ Hubinger, and Ludwig Honold. The woodlot owner and his family are also present.

Seven

ESTABLISHING FAMILY ROOTS

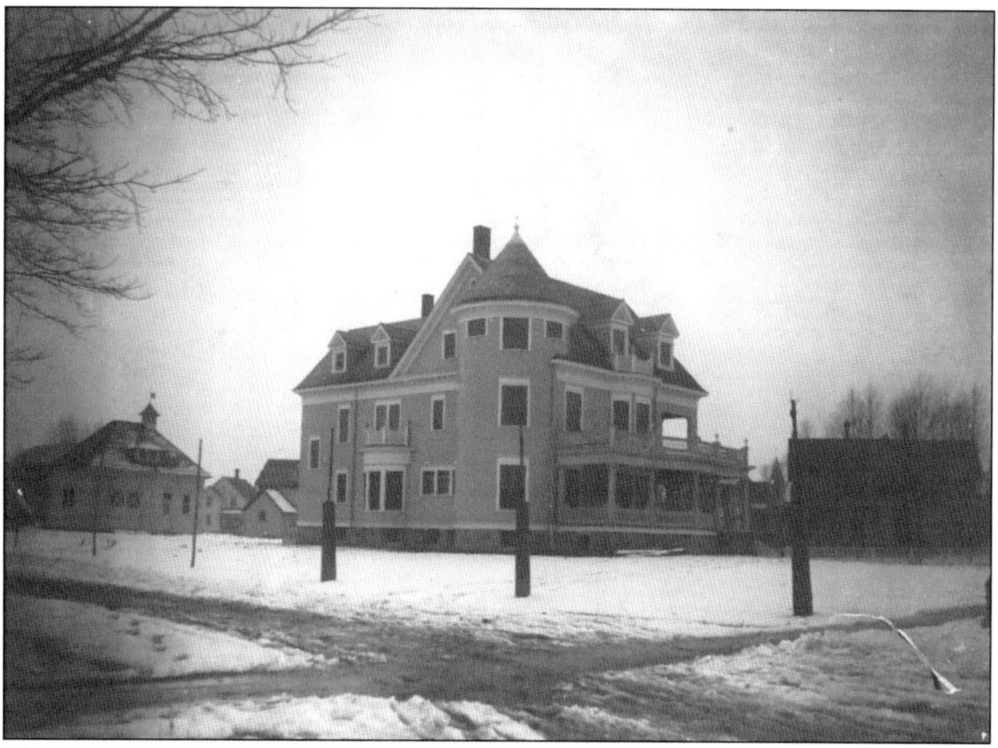

Chesaning's Broad Street was an attractive boulevard with stately mansions built for the local lumbermen. Bryan J. and Emma Coryell's house on West Broad Street is shown above. B.J. Coryell's private bank began in 1881 and merged with the stockholder-owned Chesaning State Bank in 1901. Coryell remained president. Coryell's house was moved from its site in 1900. An IGA store and gas station later occupied the site.

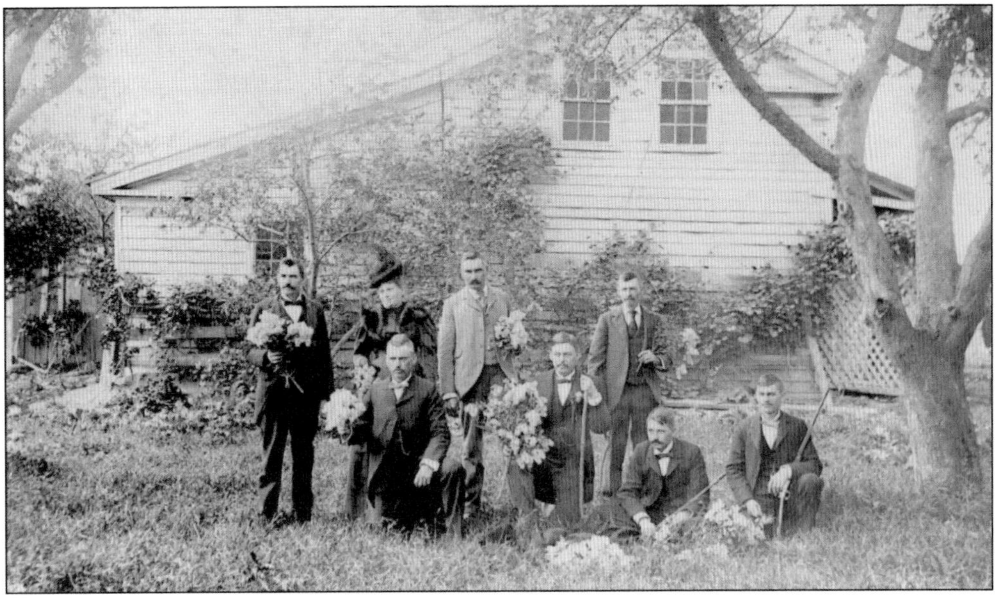

After leaving Germany in 1850, Wilhelm Roeser settled in Tittabawassee Township, helped organize the township, platted Freeland Village, was postmaster, opened the first general store in 1855, and then opened a farm implement store in Saginaw City. The above photo, taken May 25, 1898, upon Wilhelm's death, shows his eight children holding flowers and shotguns at the family home. The home site at Freeland's Memorial Park is a Michigan Historic Site. The family poses below. Sitting from left to right are (front row) Albert, Wilhelm, wife Therese Vasold Roeser, and Frederick; (back row) Charles, Frances, Oscar, Clara, Herman, and William.

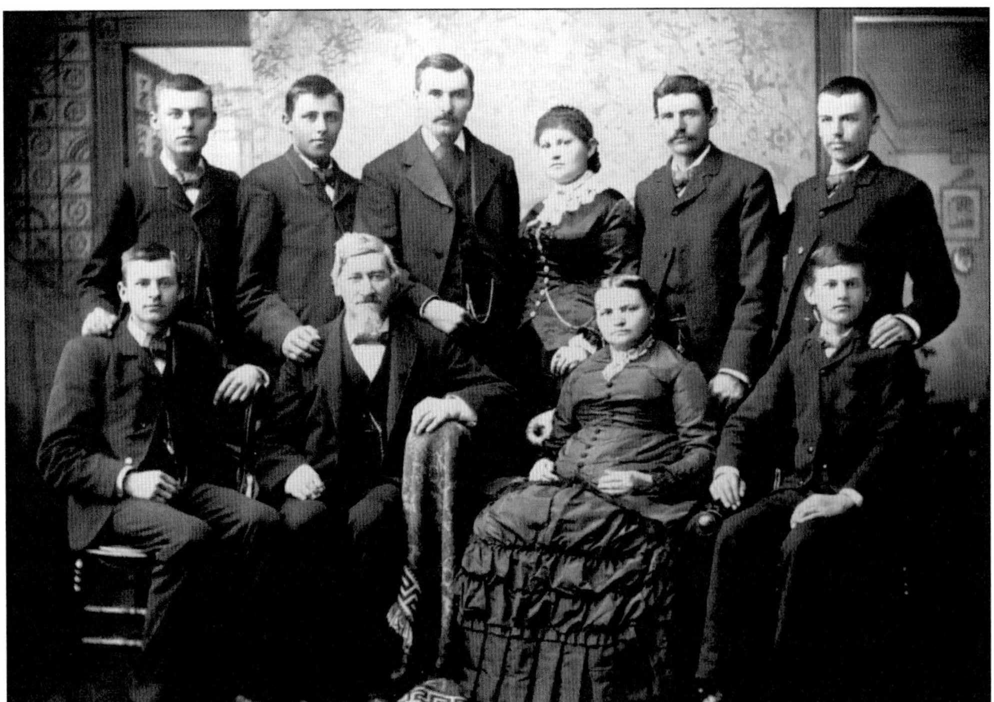

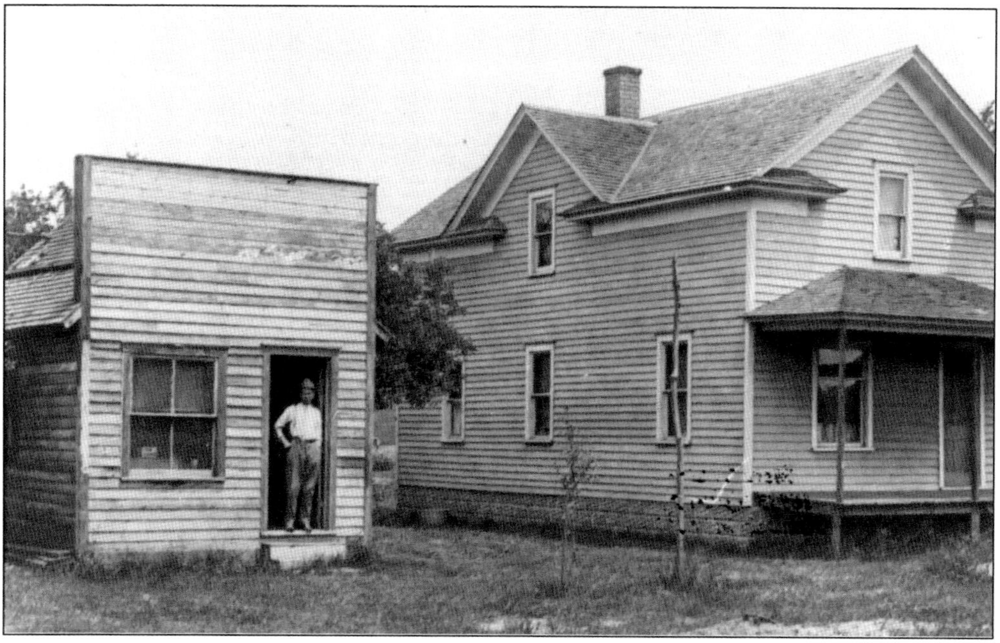

Albert Pretzer stands in the doorway of his cigar factory on Thomas and Elm Streets in Hemlock in 1910. For several years he made cigars at the Hemlock Cigar Factory. He and his mother lived next door. The cigar factory moved, but the house remained in the family until it was sold in 1986.

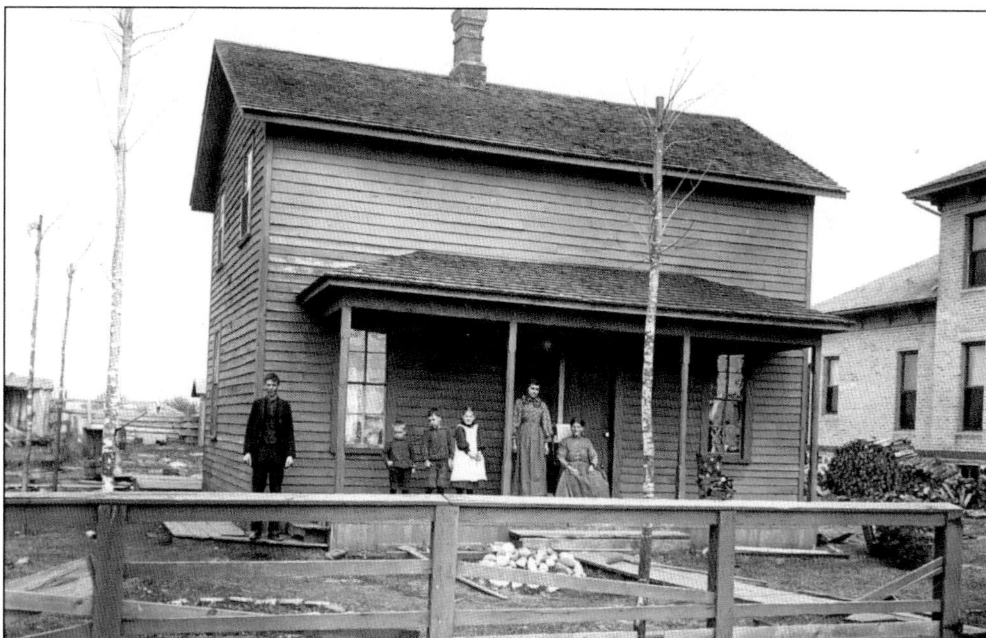

This Hemlock home was located on Main Street next to the St. Mary's Catholic Church parsonage. An unidentified family stands on the porch of their frame house. Stacked woodpiles are to the right. Pine planks line the walkway, and a rail fence encloses the yard. This was a typical village house and yard in the late 1800s.

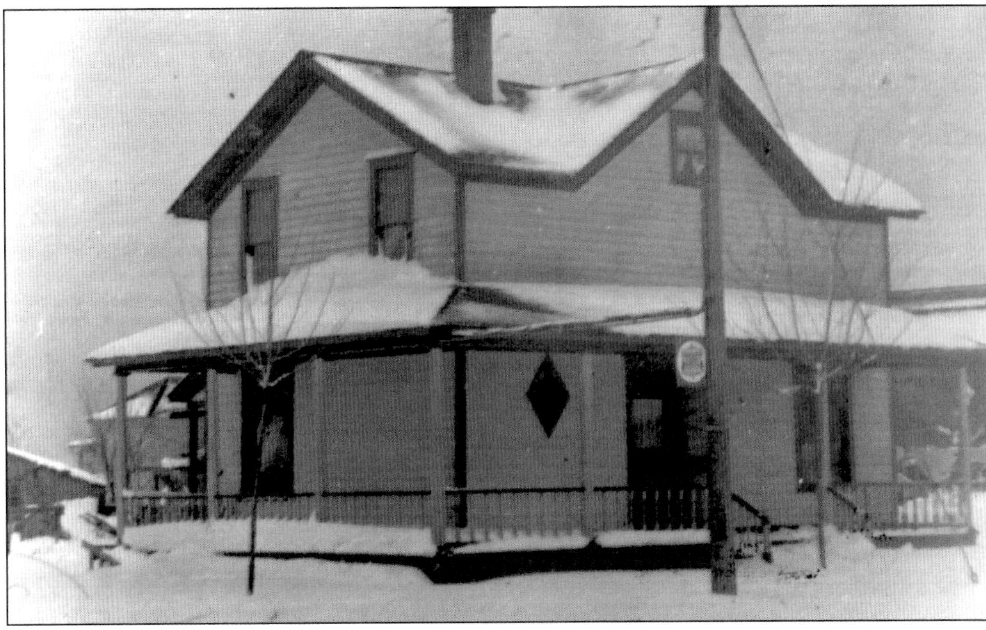

The Archibald McCullagh house on Washington Street near Hemlock's Town Hall provided the first telephone service in the area. For 37 years the telephone equipment was kept in the home, as seen in 1909 photo above. Mrs. McCullagh, with the help of Ada Wehner, ran the switchboard 24 hours a day, as shown below. Every call went through this switchboard. People eavesdropped and gossiped. The phone equipment was moved to the upstairs IOOF Hall when Mrs. McCullagh retired.

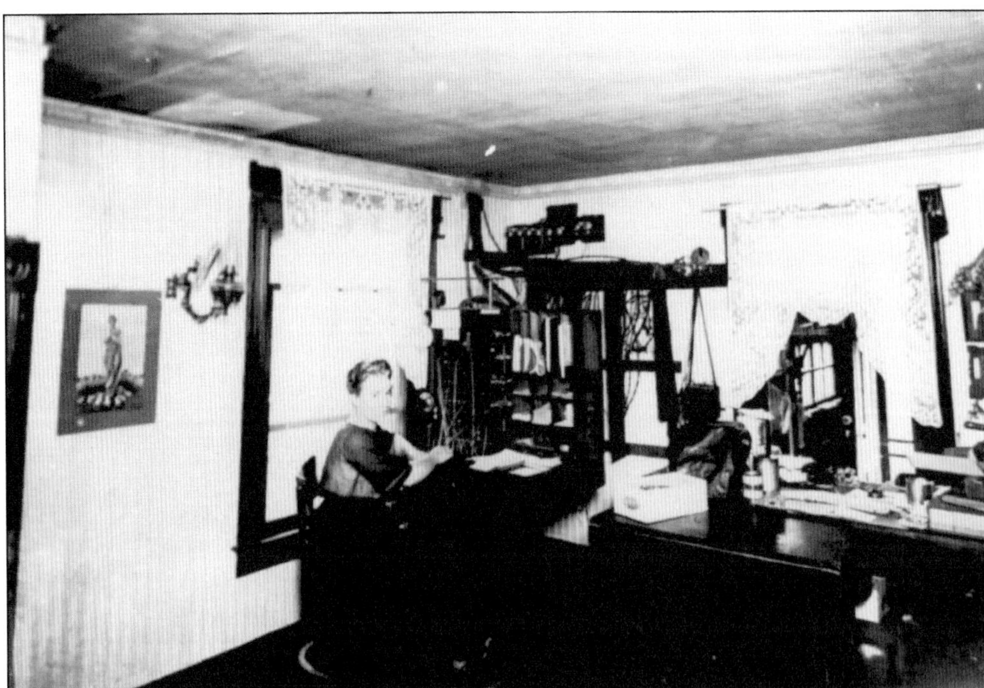

George Baker's home on the southwest corner of East Burt and Nichols Roads in Burt is shown here. George Baker, a lifelong resident, had operated many businesses. Among them were a blacksmith, mason, general store, gas station, and saloon. Standing from left to right are Mrs. Elizabeth (Mike) Baker, unidentified, George Baker, and Lew Al Green.

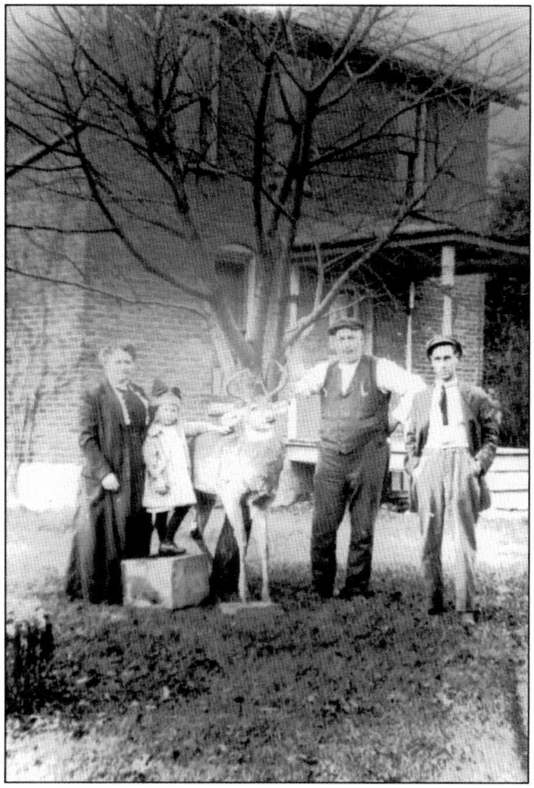

The brick home of Mr. T.L. Greene on South Saginaw Street in Chesaning is shown in this 1887 photograph. Mark L. Ireland is the child standing at the gate. A white picket fence surrounds the yard. After Chesaning incorporated as a village in 1869, several homes were built in the village.

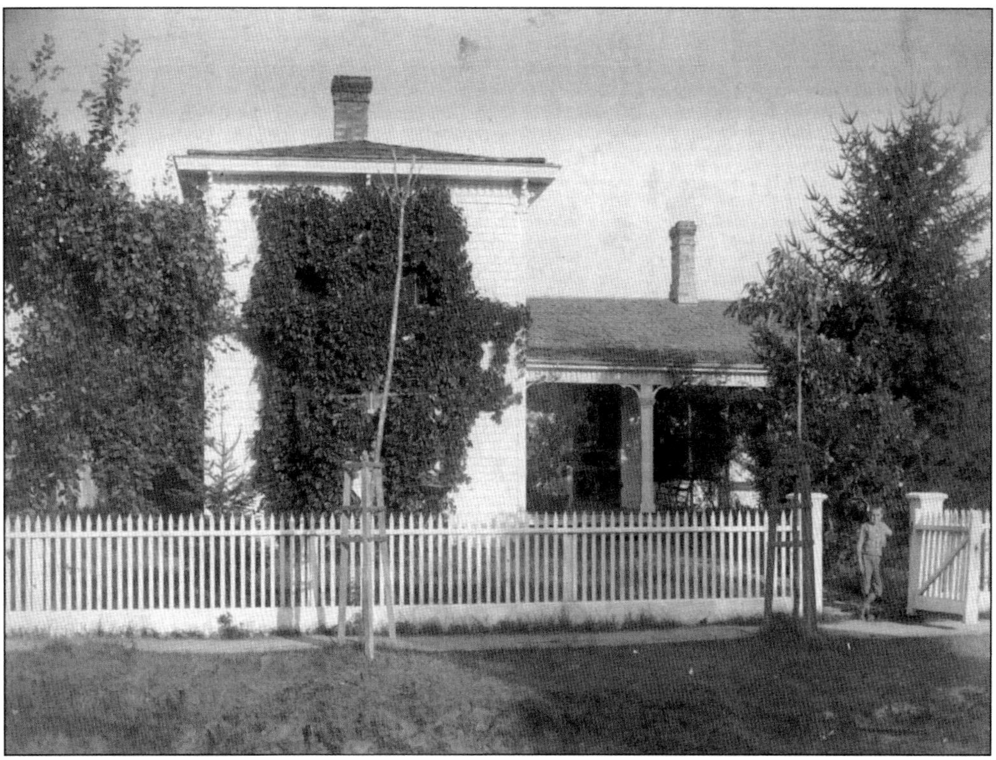

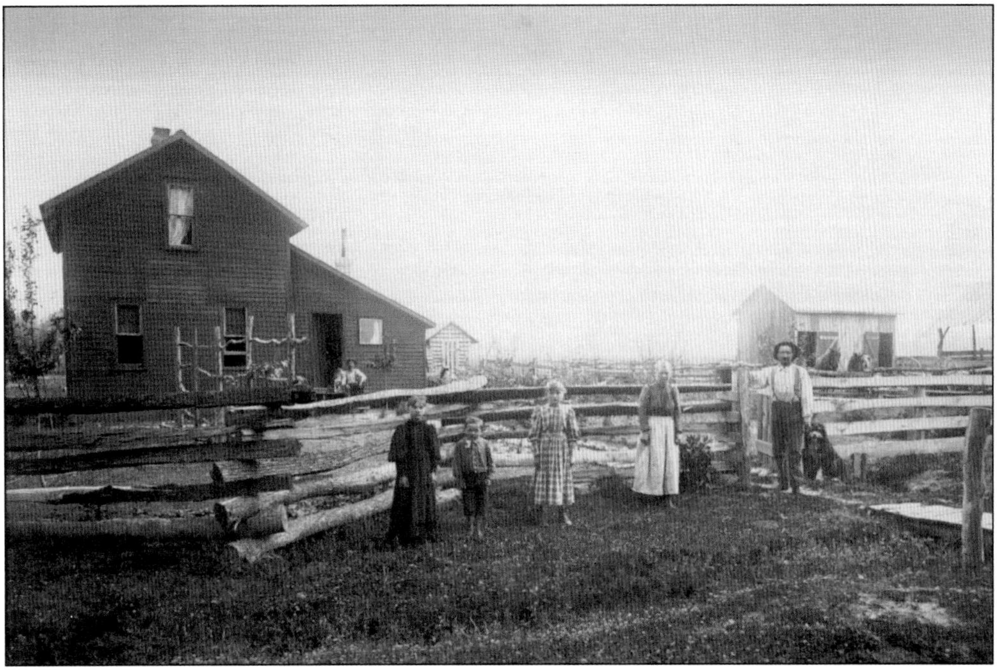

The Wardin home in rural Hemlock kept the entire family busy on the farm. Son August sits by the house. Standing from left to right are daughter Anna, son Carl, unidentified, wife Anna Hinskey Wardin, and husband August Wardin, with the family dog. The log rail fence kept the livestock in the yard. A plank walkway leads to the house.

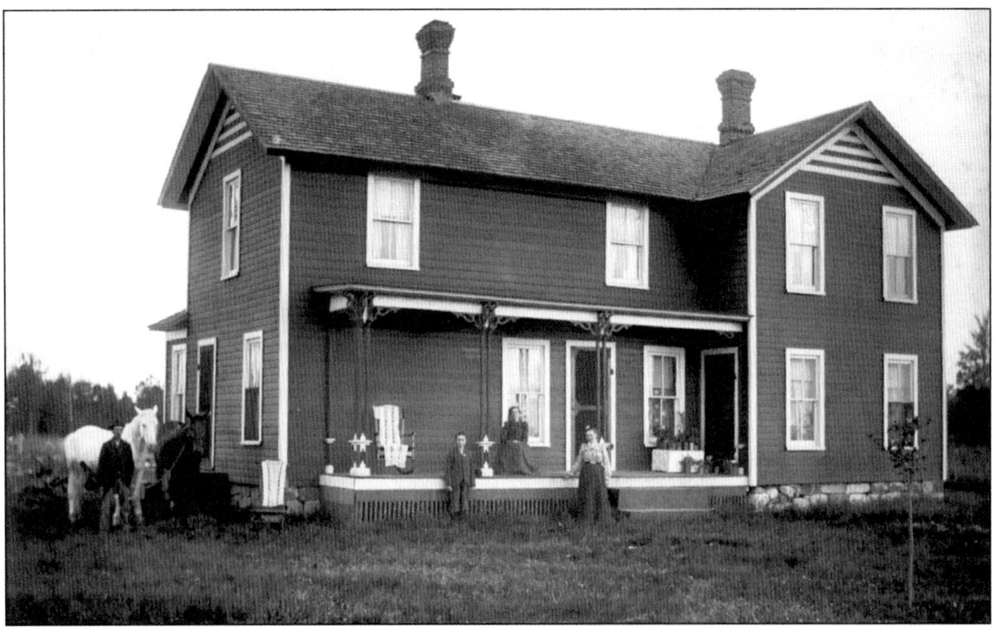

This family is relaxing at their freshly-painted rural Chesaning home. The house was built on a solid stone foundation. A planter box, plants, and rocking chairs on the porch give the house a cozy appearance. The father leads his horse team by the side of the house. The house is typical of an 1800s rural home built for a large family.

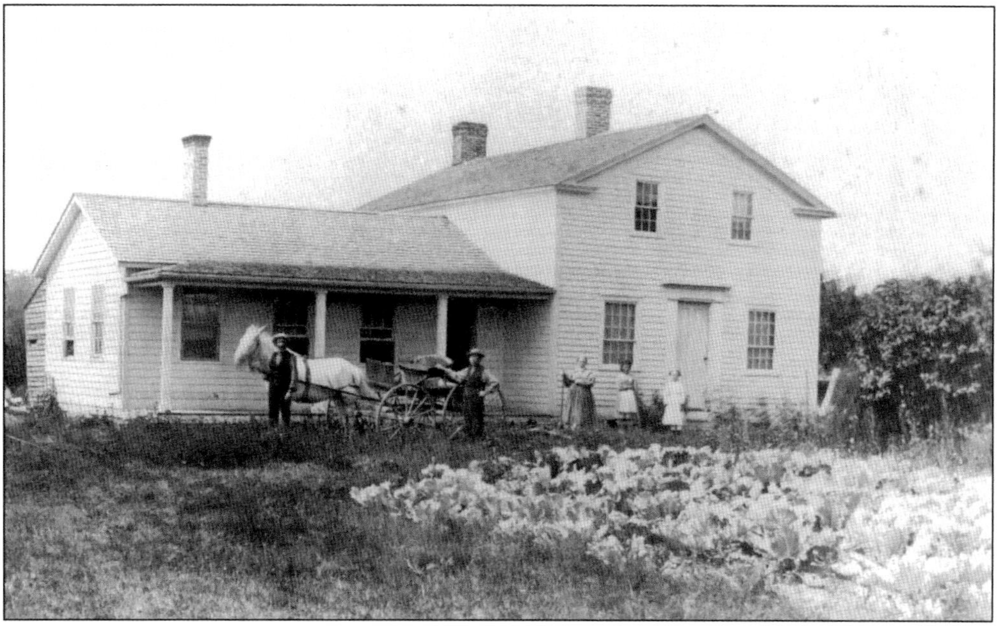

John and Jane Thomson settled in Tittabawassee Township with their nine children in 1837. Shown in this 1879 photo are William D. Cole near the horse, John Thomson near the buggy, and Jane Thomson. A cabbage patch grows in the front yard. The house at 5825 Midland Road, built in 1845, is the oldest remaining house in Freeland today.

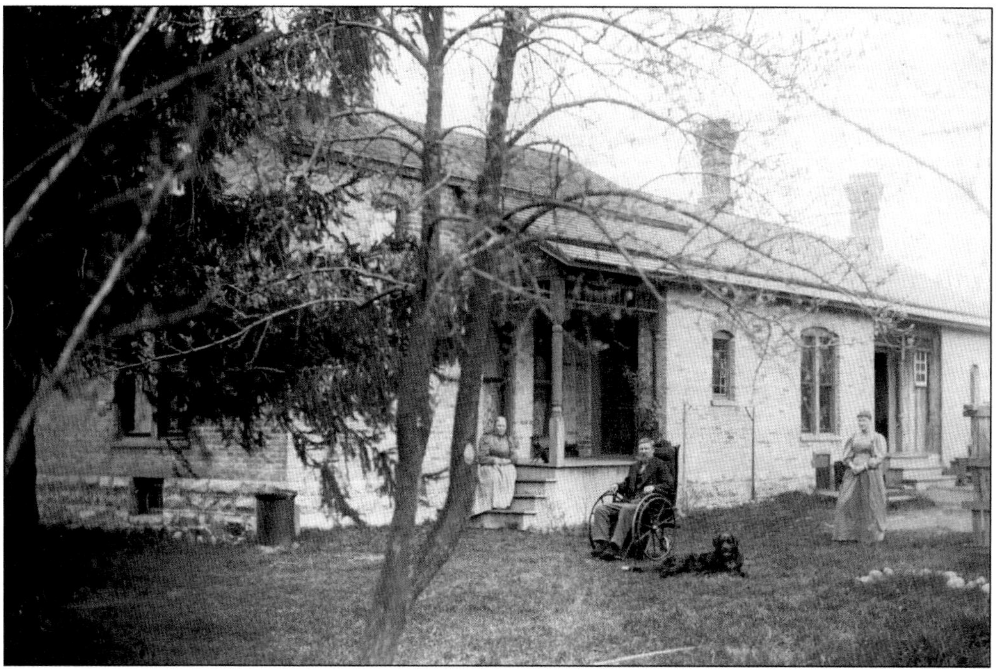

Shown at their King Road farmhouse in 1884 are wife Alfretta King, William King (in the wheelchair), and daughter Mabel King. After a bull injured William, he was confined to a wheelchair but he hired farm hands and ran his farm from the window. The house has three chimneys and three fireplaces. The house still stands in Bridgeport Township today.

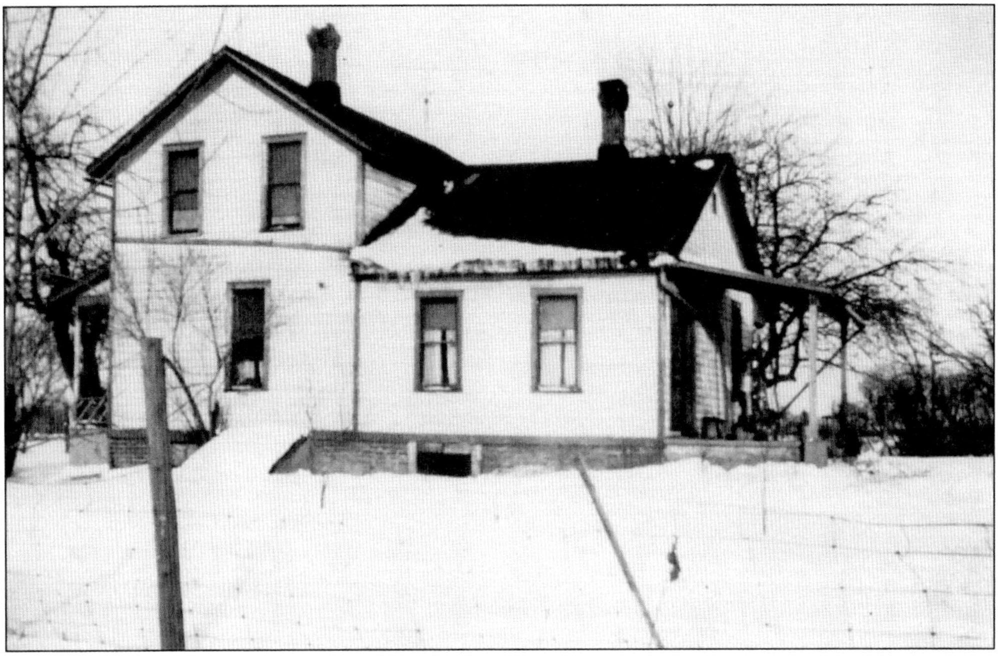

Widow Lucinda Frost and children, Louisa, Climena, Samuel, and John, came from Ohio, settling in Thomastown Township in 1854. John built a log cabin on the corner of Frost and Lone Roads. After the front two-story house (shown above) was built, the kitchen remained a separate building until it was added to the back portion. Nine-year-old Ethel Frost Brugge plays with her chickens below. Frost Corners, across the road, had two stores, a post office, and Meade's Hall. The Frost family often traded their eggs and farm produce at the stores for supplies. The farm is a centennial farm owned by the same family today.

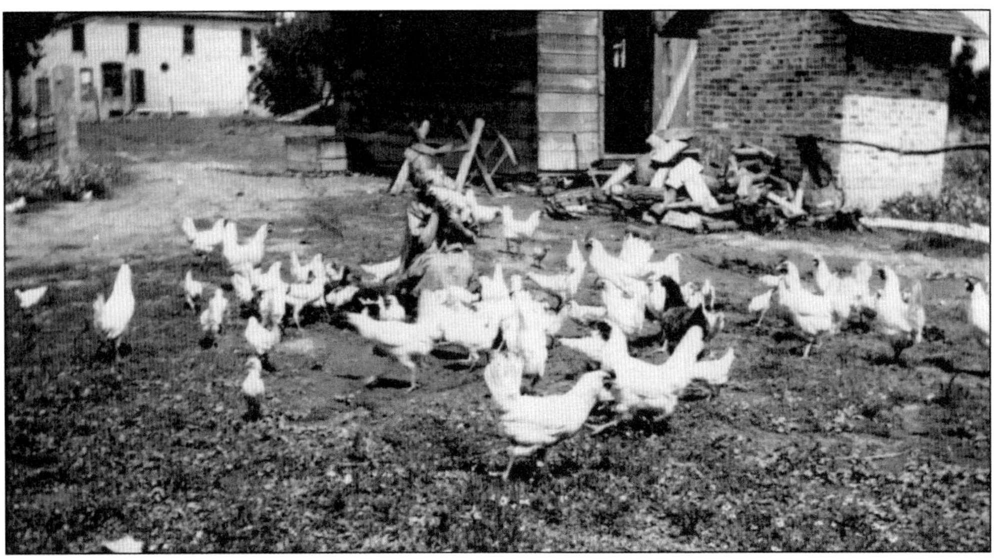

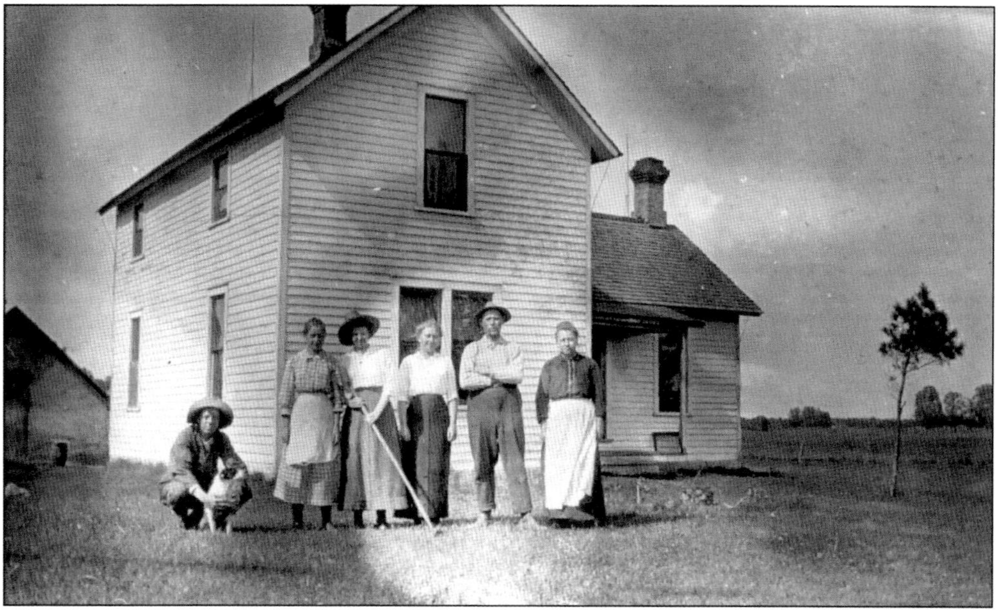

The Schmidt family poses at their Summerfeldt Road farm in Thomastown Township in the 1910s. Shown above from left to right are son Henry Schmidt, daughter Ella Schmidt, two unidentified, husband Albert Schmidt, and wife Mary Summerfeldt Schmidt. In the photo below, Herman Summerfeldt and Louis Summerfeldt are planting a garden behind the house and outhouse. Henry Schmidt is carrying the pails.

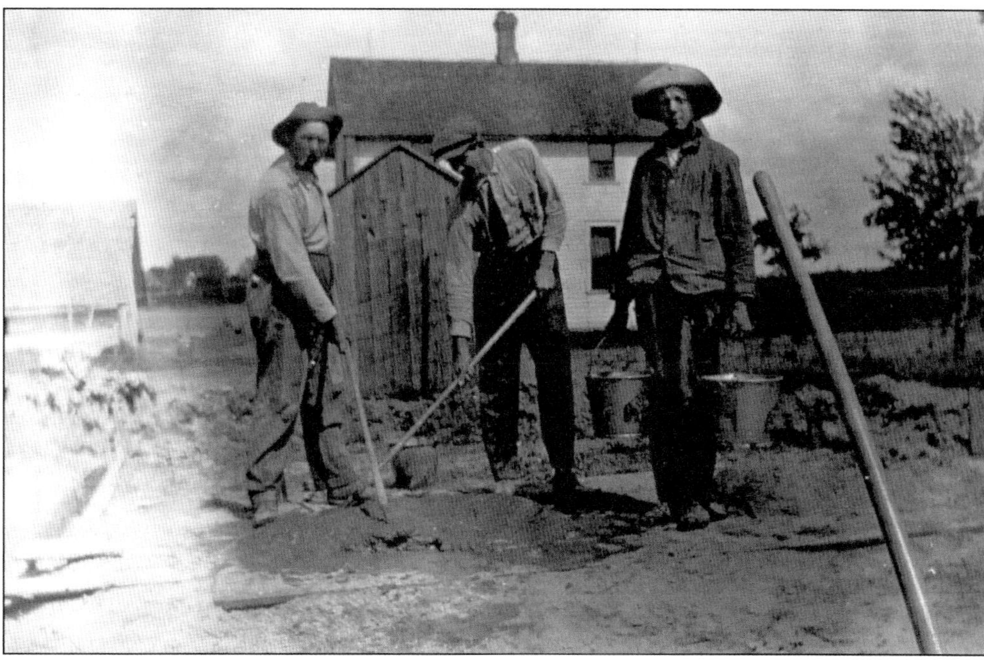

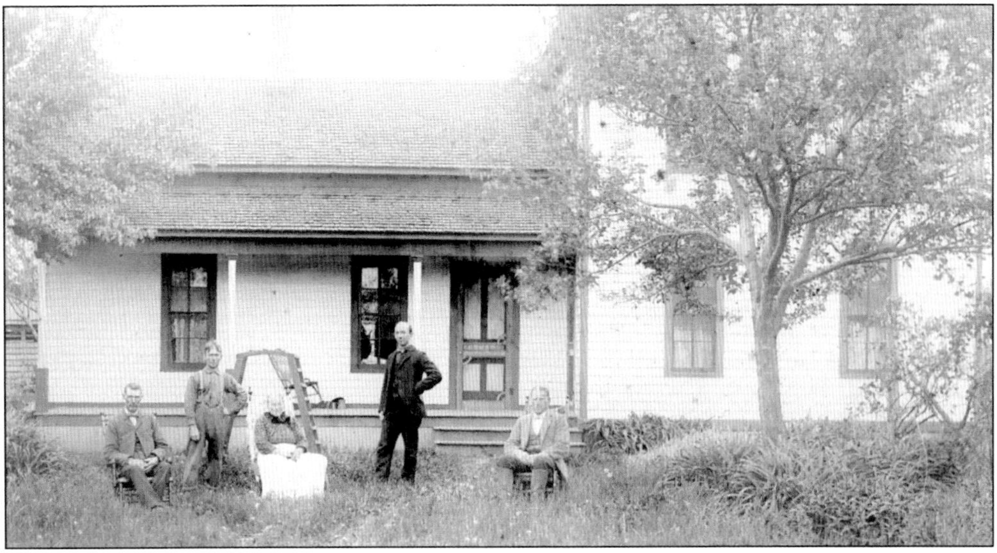

Arriving from Germany in 1855, Wolfgang and Mary Ederer lived in Saginaw City until buying their James Township farm in 1866. Shown at their new Ederer Road home in the 1880s are, from left, Wolfgang, son Joseph, Mary, unidentified, and son John Ederer. Carpenters Wolfgang and Joseph built houses and barns. County Road Commissioner John built roads. Rural yards were uncut. The farm is a centennial farm today.

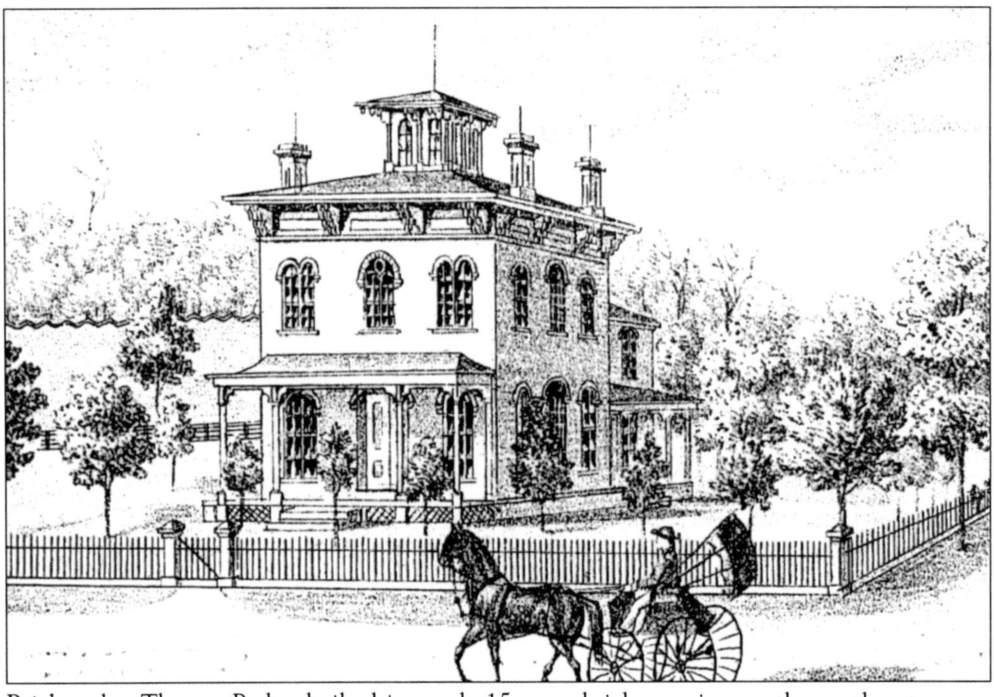

Brick maker Thomas Parker built this stately 15-room brick mansion on the southeast corner of Midland and State Roads in Saginaw Township in 1865. His brickyard, kiln, and clay pit were on the east side of the house. Mules hauled the bricks to Saginaw. He and Thomas Day manufactured clay bricks on South River Road in James Township. The House of Oak furniture store occupies the house today.

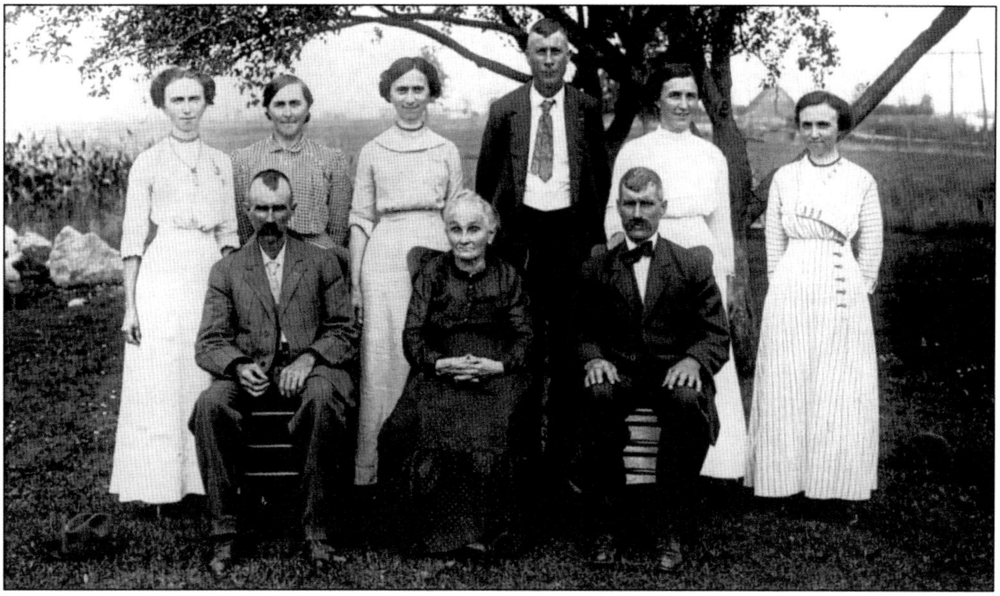

Arriving from Germany in the mid-1800s, Frank and Ella Fickies settled in rural Chesaning Township. The family has gathered about the front porch for the photo below. Their grown children have reunited for a family get-together at Maud Byam's home on Baldwin Road in Chesaning (shown above). Pictured from left to right are: (seated) Jacob Fickies, and Ella and Frank Fickies; and (standing) Maude Byam, Alice Hartman, Emma Fickies, Hank Fickies, Martha Beebe, and Lane Fickies.

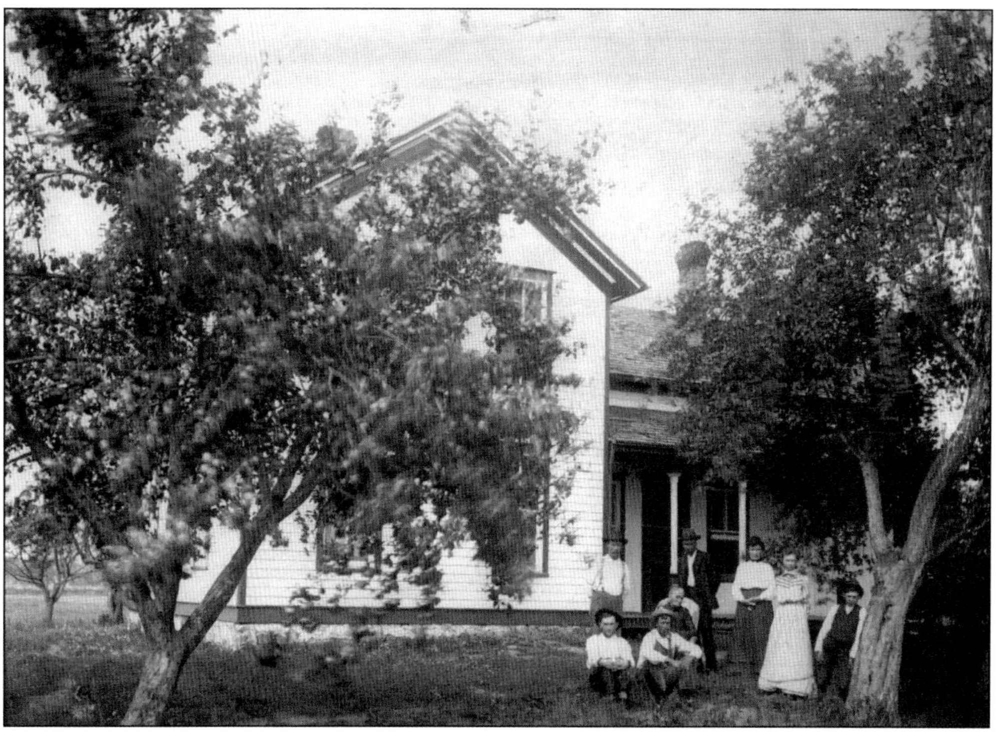

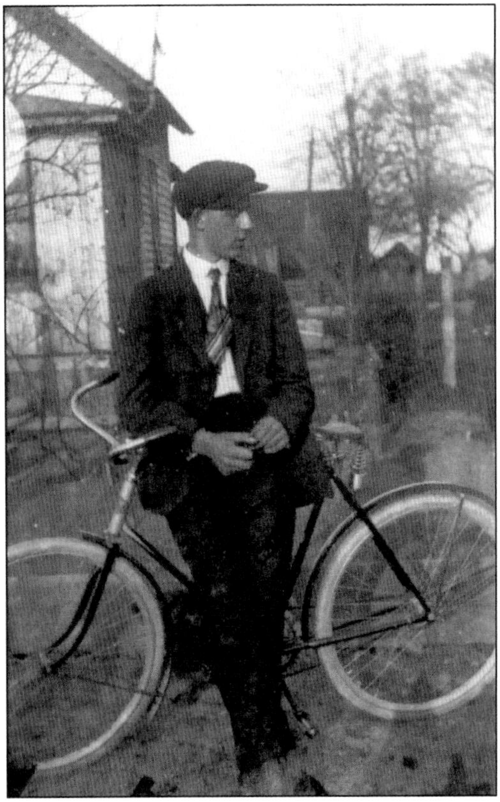

The Rachow family home at Bay and Genesee Streets in Saginaw was within the city limits in the early 1900s photo below; a barn and several fruit trees are on the right. On the porch are children Ervin and Elda, wife Sophie, husband Herman, and son Alfred Rachow. In the photo at left, Walter Rachow poses in the backyard with his bike in 1917. There are still a number of barns or sheds on the city lot.

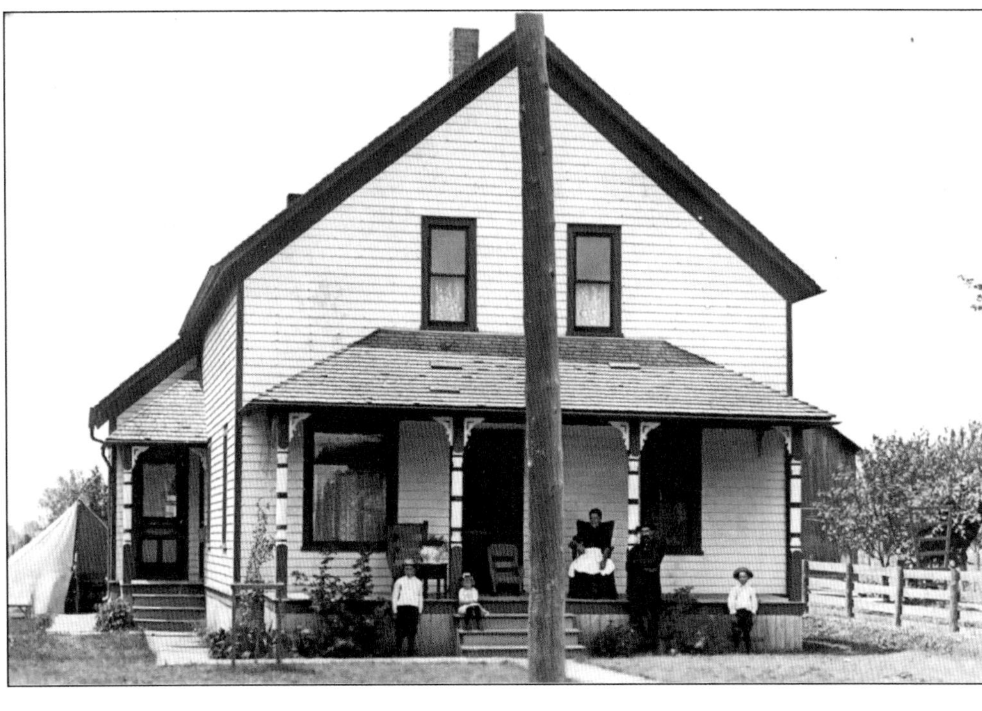

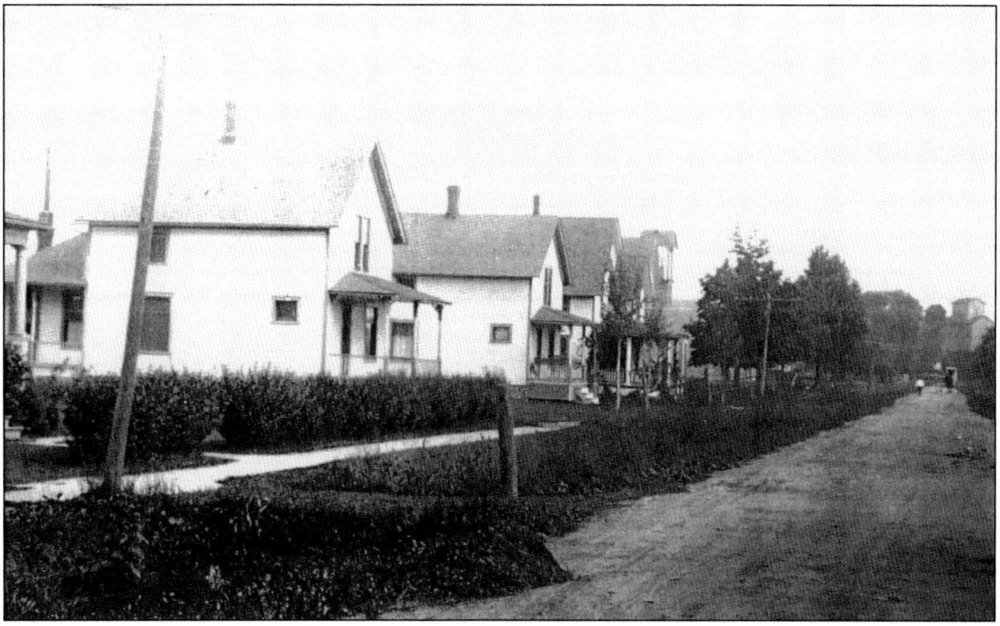

The Pine Plank Road and the railroad brought new settlers and travelers into Birch Run. By the late 1800s, the village had several stores, an IOOF Hall, a post office, a blacksmith shop, a cheese factory, churches, and hotels. Many local residents were employed at the Charles Wolohan Elevator, Birch Run's largest business. In the top photo, the elevator is at the end of the street. The well-kept similar homes were built around the same time. In both *c.* 1909 photos, the street is still unpaved. The sidewalks are pine planks. Hitching posts line the street. The bottom photo shows houses and businesses on Main Street.

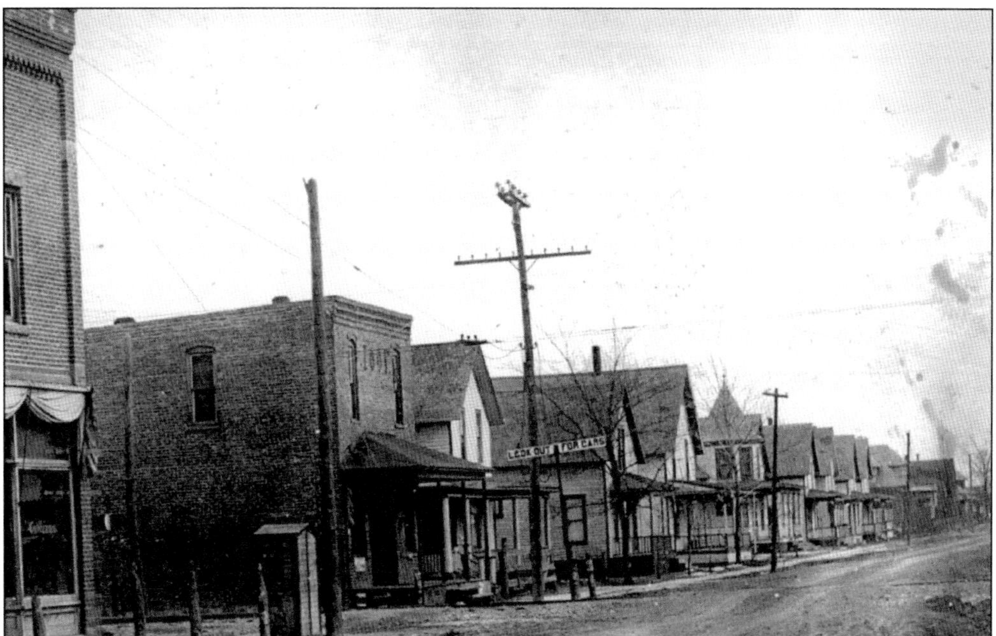

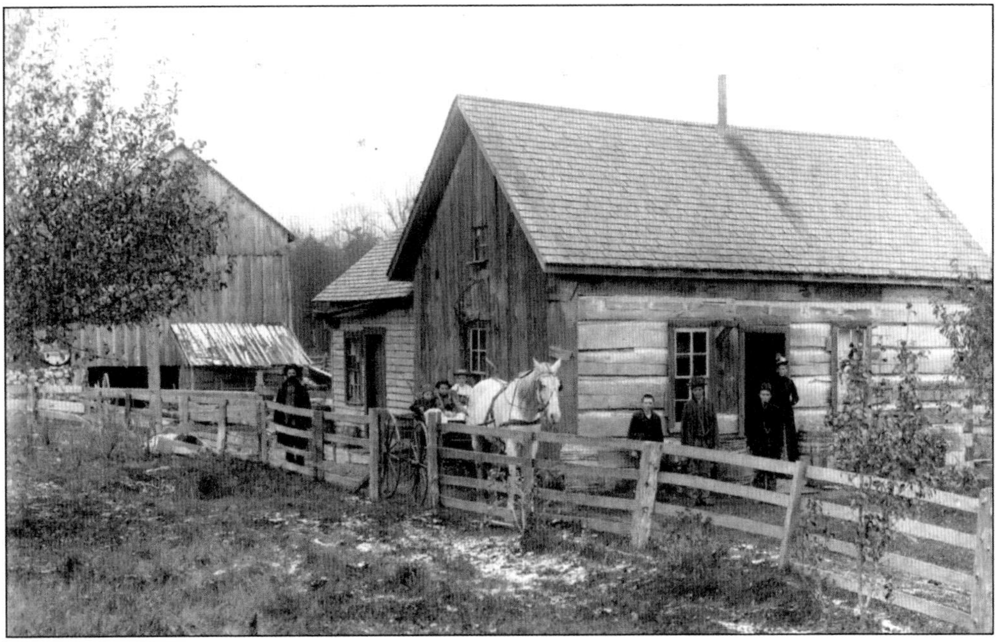

Edward Goslow, his wife, and six children are preparing to take a horse and buggy ride into town. This photograph was taken on November 2, 1891. Their square-cut log house with clapboard siding and wooden shingles on Bell Road in Bridgeport Township was typical of many early settlers whose first house was made of logs. The abundant timber was used for houses, barns, fences, walkways, and roads.

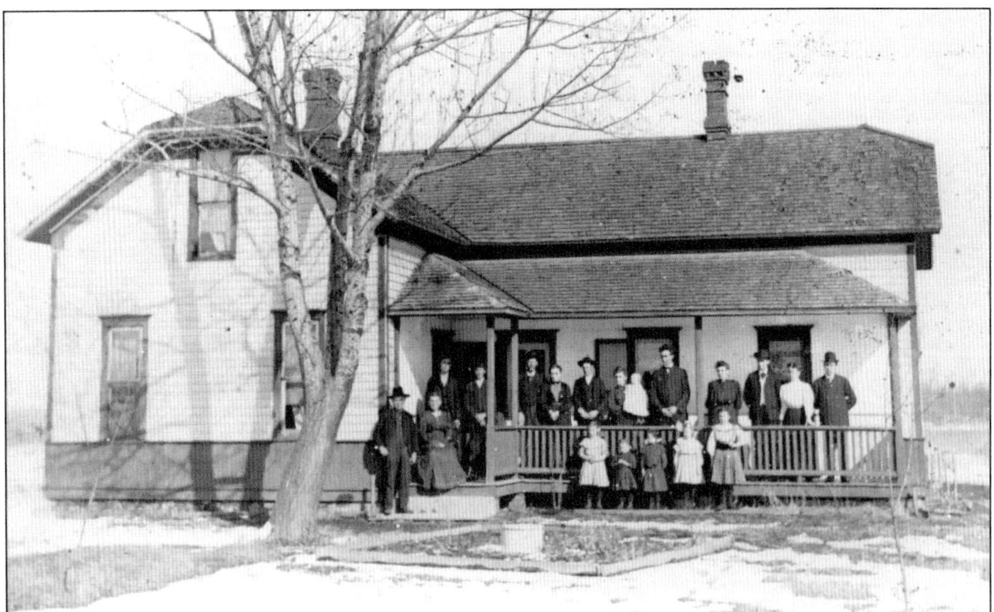

This rural house was northeast of Chesaning on Stuart Road. The unidentified family members have gathered on the front porch to pay their final respects to the two infants who are buried in the front yard by the tree. Many families had their own private cemeteries on their farms. When babies died at birth, home burials were easier than traveling to a public cemetery.

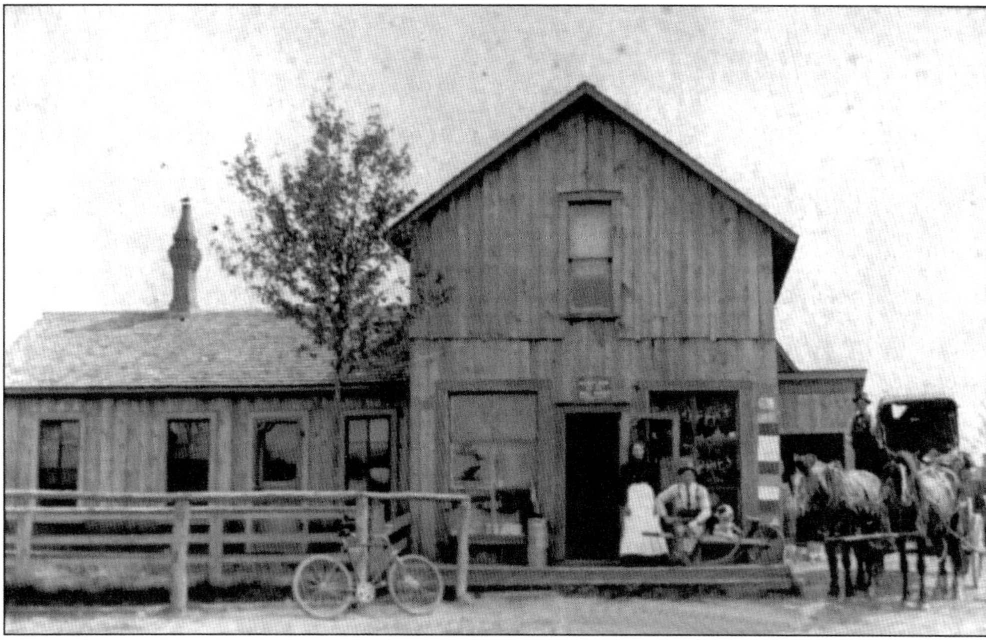

When a post office was added to the Richland Township general store on Dice and Iva Roads ,shown above in this 1895 photo, the corner became Iva. Albert and Lena Fiting, shown in the above photo, lived at the store on the left. They also ran a millinery shop in the general store, which faced Dice Road. A blacksmith was across the road. When the Herman Feusse family took over the store, shown in the bottom photo, an addition changed the front of the store to face Iva Road. The original store is shown on the left and became the living quarters. Iva remains today.

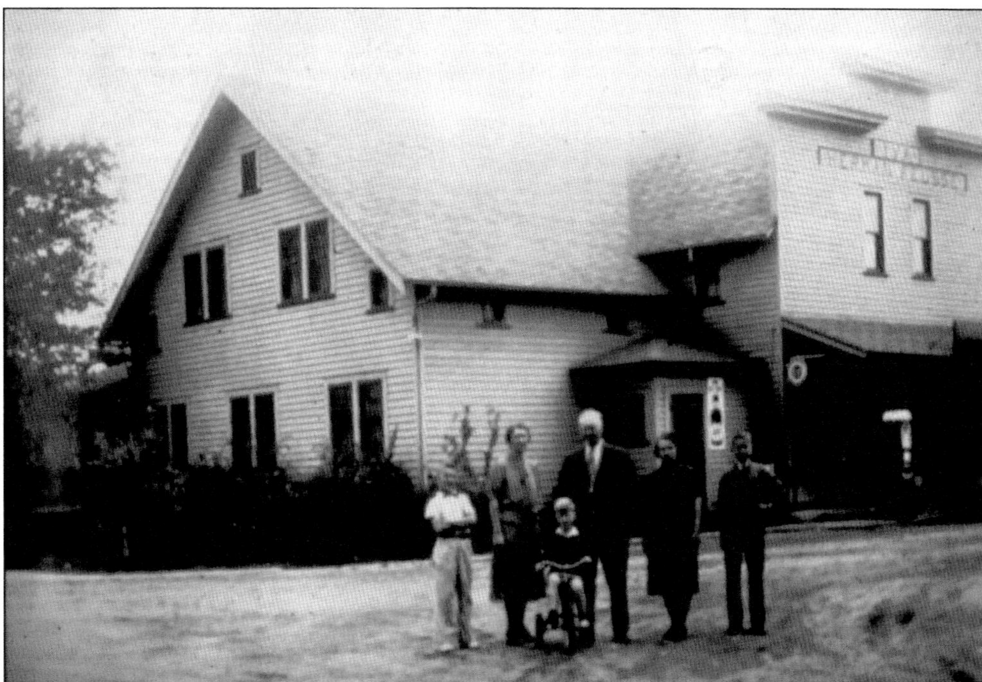

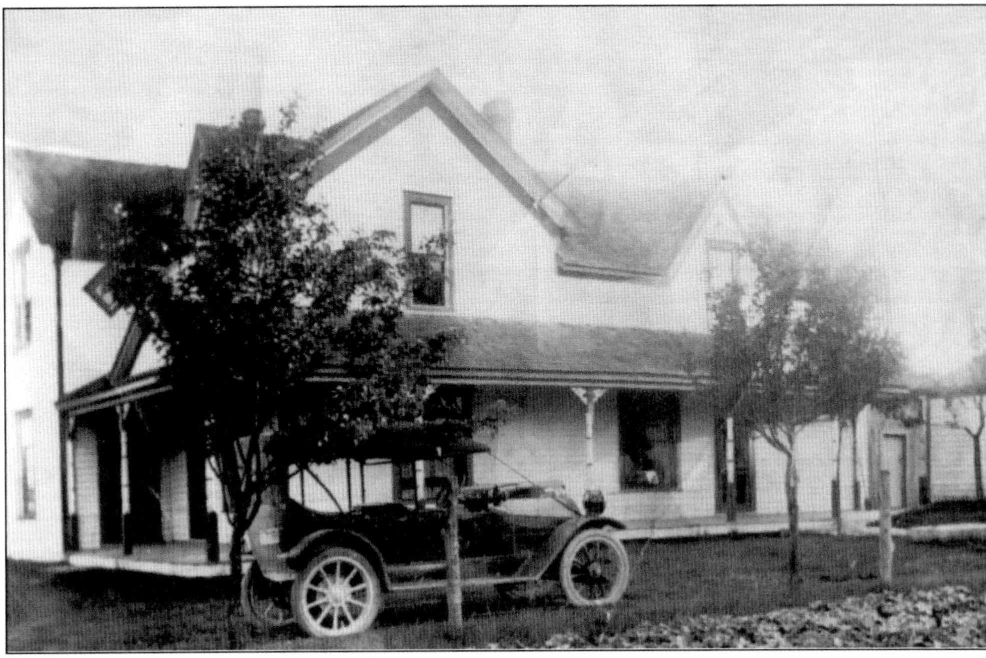

Dr. Thomas McEwan's home was built in 1891 on Elm Street right next to the Hemlock Town Hall. He lived in this home for most of the 26 years that he practiced medicine in Hemlock. Dr. McEwan had a driver to take him on house calls throughout the township area. The house has since been converted into apartments and is used yet today.

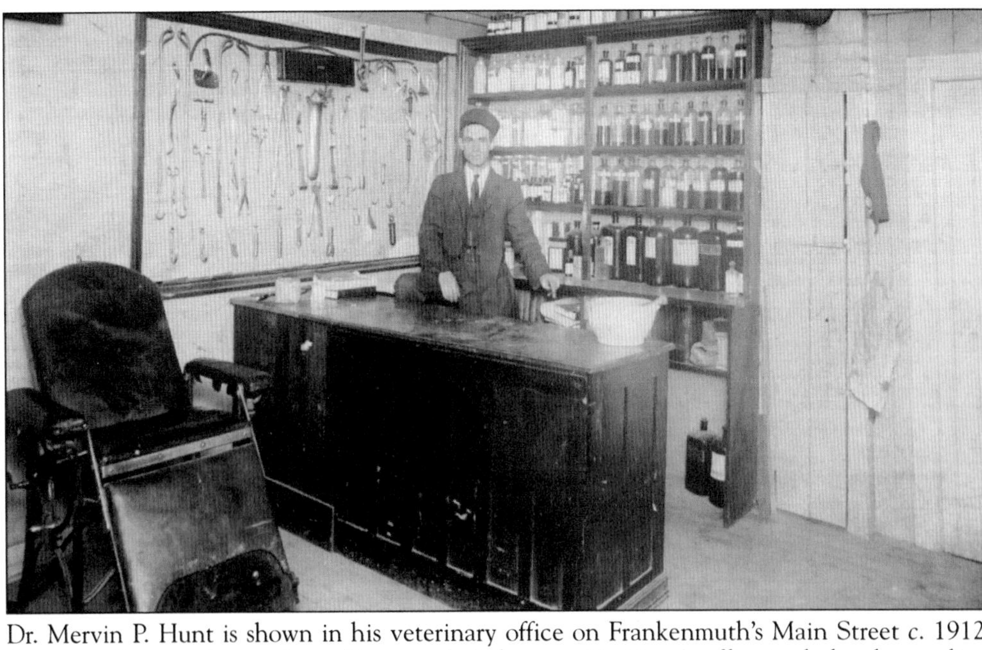

Dr. Mervin P. Hunt is shown in his veterinary office on Frankenmuth's Main Street c. 1912. Some small town doctors had offices in their homes. Dr. Hunt's office includes the medical equipment of the day: examining chair, counter with mortar and pestle, medical tools on the wall, medical books, and medicine bottles on the shelves. He undoubtedly made many house calls to township farms.

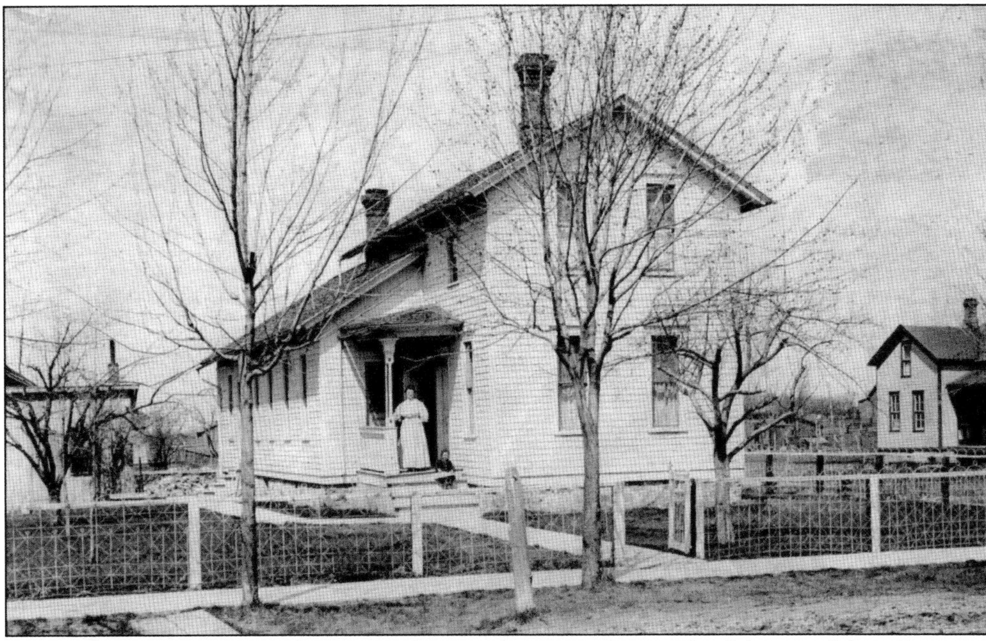

Mrs. J. Adam List and her daughter Edna are shown on the porch of their well-kept home on the southwest corner of School and Main Streets in Frankenmuth in 1904. The yard is fenced with an attractive wire fence. Wooden planks line the walkway and the sidewalk. The horse barn and woodpile are in the back. Colorful flowerbeds will decorate the yard in the spring.

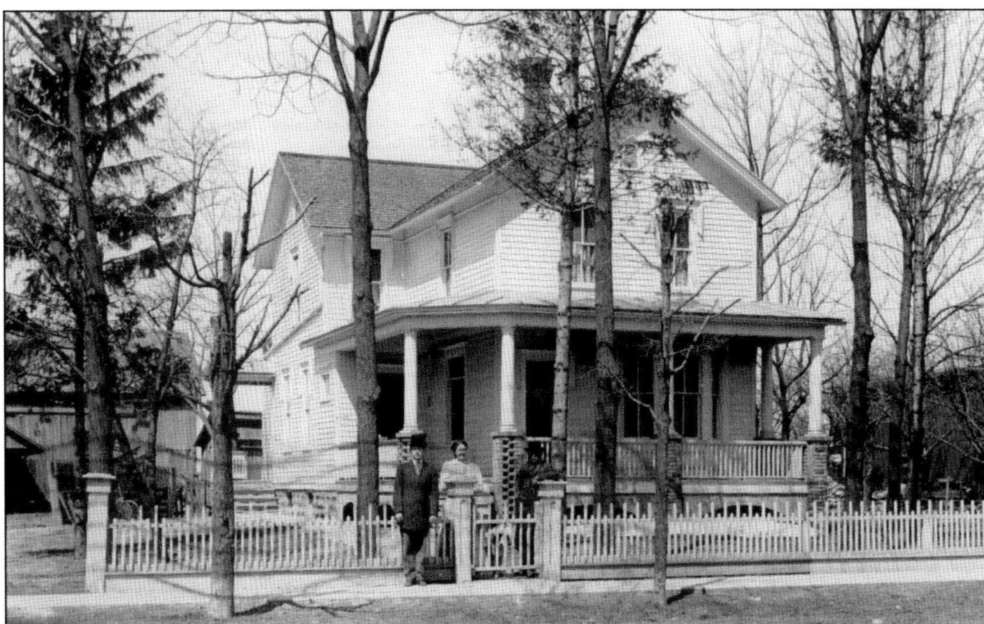

Augusta List and her dog stand by the white picket fence surrounding her home on Main Street in Frankenmuth in this 1910 photo. Her comfortable two-story home had a wrap-around porch, a back porch, and arched brick foundation. The horse barn was in the back. Her house was removed in the 1960s when the house on the right became the Black Forest parking lot.

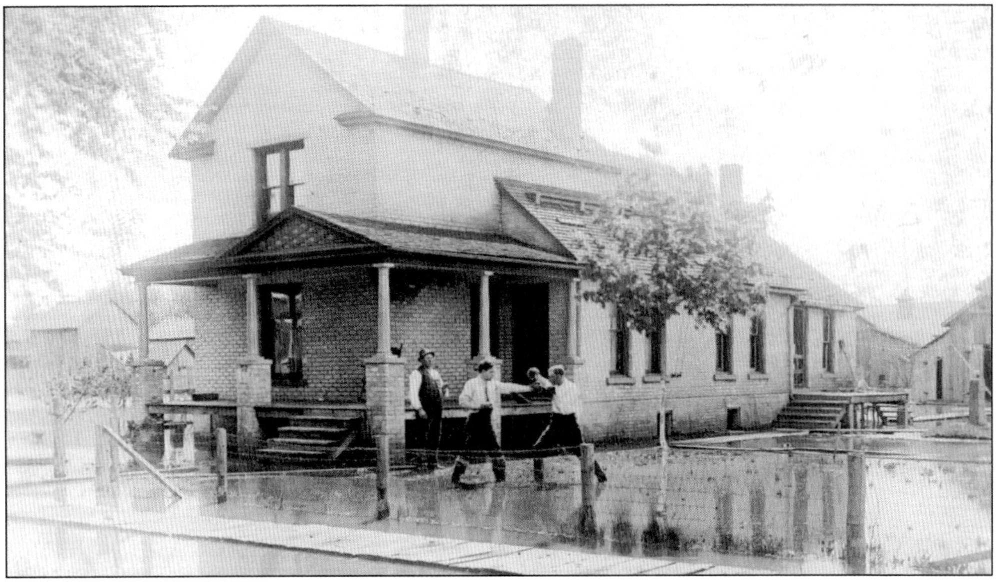

With its marshy land bordering both sides of the Saginaw River, Zilwaukee has always experienced flooding. Zilwaukee Township organized in 1854. The village emerged with and survived after the lumber industry. This brick house built in the 1800s stands in water during the 1912 flood. Norman Burke stands by the Daman house on Franklin Street. Plank sidewalks float on the water.

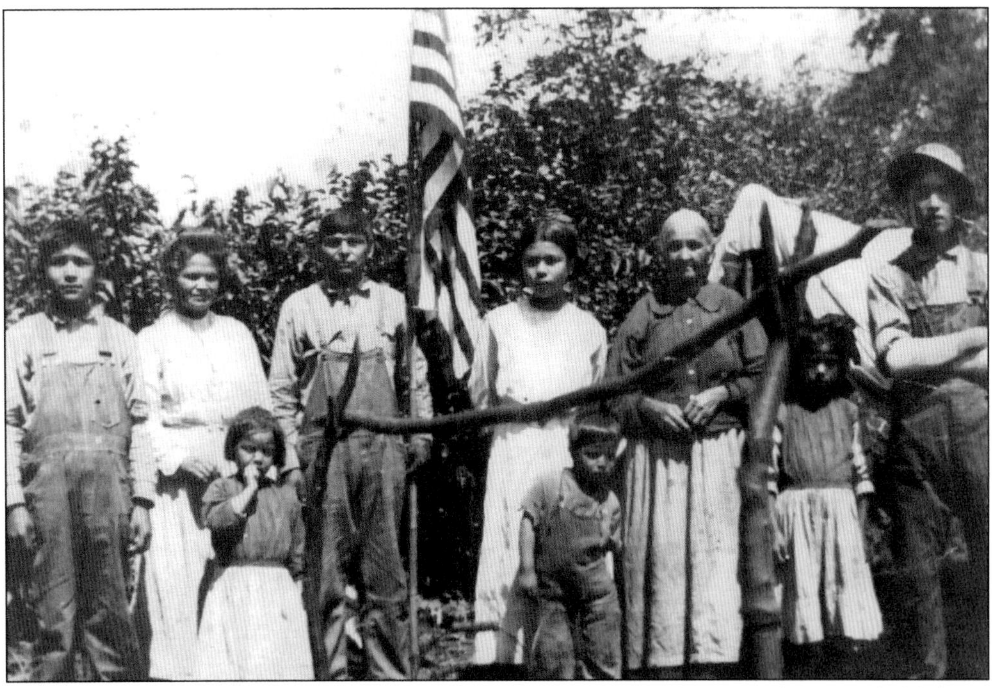

The Sauk and Chippewa Indians built their birch wigwams near the rivers that provided fishing, hunting, and travel. Many county sites today retain those Indian names. The Flint River's Pewonogowink Indian Village in Taymouth Township existed before the settlers. Although they have assimilated the American culture, these Daniel Wheaton Indian descendants continue their Native American customs.